PRAISE FOR VISION

"Bravo to the authors of this book dedicated to John Roeuche, a man who has dedicated his life to 'paying it forward.' With a commitment to students, he is exemplary in creating an outstanding talent pool of community college leaders. Among the many testimonials to his passion and contribution, I stand proud to call him a friend. John is tireless in his efforts to change people's lives through access to higher education, with a heartfelt celebration of the importance of equity. The authors are among thousands who have left their mark on community colleges, in many ways due to John. This book is inspiring reading for anyone interested in higher education and the impact of strong leadership." —**Barbara Gellman-Danley**, PhD, president, Higher Learning Commission

"John Roueche is an icon and has greatly influenced the shaping of the community college landscape. This is a must read for professors, teachers, researchers and leaders in higher education. The stories within this book reflect his remarkable vision, his consistent and constant dedication to students, teaching and learning, while highlighting his focus and commitment to building leadership excellence. Read this book and learn from the best. He will have a profound impact on your life as an educator and a leader!"— **Sheree Utash**, president, WSU Tech

"All of us engaged in community college reform—especially in the realm of developing transformational leaders—owe much to the foundational work of John Roueche. By helping readers understand the origins and motivations behind his tireless efforts, this volume illuminates the incredible contributions Roueche has made to community colleges and the diverse students they serve"—**Josh Wyner**, founder and executive director, Aspen Institute's College Excellence Program

"Without reservation or hyperbole, John E. Roueche is among the most influential leaders in the history of the community college movement. This volume documents the many ways in which JER has nudged, cajoled, called-out, and loved the institutions about which he wrote, and with whom he fellowshipped. For those who have heard of him but have never met him, or those who are just learning of him, this volume will let you learn about John the scholar, the leader, and the man. I was privileged to be at his side on some of the events documented here. Most importantly, I have been the generous recipient of his counsel and friendship. I say this as someone who came from outside the Roueche family described in this work, but who was nonetheless welcomed as a family member. That in a nutshell is JER. I invite you to read and get to know this incredible individual. Then I invite you to join the family and join in our ever-present task to improve our institutions for the students we serve." —**Rey Garcia**, collegiate professor and program chair, doctor of Management in Community College Policy and Administration, University of Maryland University College

"This timely book details how John E. Roueche's commitment to students and mentorship of community college leaders throughout his tireless career has made community colleges what they are today. The significance of this book on the life and influence of John E. Roueche as an important contribution to the community college literature cannot be emphasized enough."—**Stefani Gray Hicswa**, PhD, president, Northwest College

"There is no discrete or concrete recipe for making a profound and powerful difference with your life and leaving a loving and lasting legacy. There are, however, models of lives well lived from which we can draw insight and inspiration. This book is an inside look at one the most important and meaningful models in the world of community college education and beyond: Dr. John E. Roueche. The family, friends, and colleagues that tell his story in the pages that follow—all of whom are models themselves, and all of whom count John as family, friend, mentor, teacher, and catalyst—help the reader see how the award-winning, game-changing, and often deeply personal impact of Dr. Roueche's professional and personal life has rippled out to mean so much to so many."—**Mark David Milliron**, PhD, co-founder and chief learning officer, Civitas Learning

"In my career, which has taken me to more than 500 community colleges in 44 states, no one has been more interested in connecting his work to practitioners than has John Rouche. He has had his critics—myself at times included—and his career has not been without controversy. But, as this book shows, the sheer scope of the issues he has tackled, and the longevity of his efforts demand that attention be paid to the philosophy that has motivated this driven, committed man. Non-Texans and Texans alike will benefit from learning more about what John Rouche set out to do, why, and how he accomplished his objectives."—**Stephen G. Katsinas**, PhD, director, Education Policy Center and Professor of Higher Education and Political Science, The University of Alabama

"The mission of community colleges has never been more relevant or more complex. As open-access institutions that serve more than one third of all students in American higher education, community colleges have the tall order of staying in-step with the changing needs of the country—meeting both current and future workforce needs and serving as an engine to bachelor degree completion. This book highlights the impact of Dr. John Roueche, who has artfully navigated the evolving landscape of community colleges for many years, while also influencing of some of the nation's most notable community college leaders. In this book, Dr. Roueche's unwavering commitment to America's community colleges, their leaders, and students is evident—as is his tremendous impact. As a new leader in the field, this book provides me with a profound appreciation of his work and the broader context of how we work together as a community of community college leaders."—**Lynn Tincher-Ladner**, PhD, president, Phi Theta Kappa

"It is difficult to write a book about a legend and at the end feel like it truly captures the heart and soul of the legend. Dr. John Roueche is a legend in the community college world and this book truly does justice to the spirit of Dr. Roueche through the eyes of colleagues, friends, former students, and those of us who feel we must be related to the legend. His uncompromising and unwavering passion and commitment to student success, and his genuine caring spirit is well documented in this book. Those of us to be blessed by his friendship and mentorship over the years join me in saying, 'We love you, John.'"—**Richard M. Rhodes**, PhD, president/CEO, Austin Community College District

"Many of today's community college leaders, including myself, find few degrees of separation between those who helped influence who we are today and where our journeys began. For many of us, John Roueche is a significant presence in that intersection. His contributions to the community college movement are considerable, and are influenced by his belief in diversity. He understands that each individual is different and should be recognized for those differences and the distinctive contributions that stem from them. This book chronicles John's influence on the community college movement.

John's commitment to diversity led to his focus on the lack of it in community college leadership. As highlighted in this book, he has helped build inclusive programs that extend avenues for success to those who may not see themselves on leadership paths. He helped establish the Expanding Leadership Diversity (ELD) Program with Terry O'Banion and the League for Innovation in the Community College. I am a proud member of ELD's class of 1989–1990. This year-long program changed my life, giving me permission to believe that being a chancellor/CEO was a possibility. Many authors in the book share similar stories of how John's work has changed their lives." ELD continues as the league's longstanding Executive Leadership Institute (ELI), the cornerstone of its leadership initiative. John continues to support the program as a member of the ELI faculty, and I thank him for his commitment to community college leadership."—**Rufus Glasper**, president and CEO, League for Innovation in the Community College; chancellor emeritus, Maricopa Community College

"I can't think of a more befitting way than to share with the world these reflections recognizing one of the most visionary leaders of the community college movement, Dr. John Edward Roueche. Leaders from across the country captured stories of his bold and innovative strategies that positioned community colleges as extraordinary places of higher learning. This book is a must-read for all current and future community college leaders.
Privileged and *honored* are the best words to describe my association with Dr. Roueche because of his advocacy for my growth and development as a community college leader. As a Roueche Scholar and graduate of one of his CCLPs, I stand in awe of Dr. Roueche's spirit of care for the students in our cohort. He challenged each of us to transform our respective institutions and never forget to dream, imagine, and take risks to prove the worthiness of our dreams. Personally, his influence on leadership transcends the arena of higher education to the work that I currently do as an entrepreneur in workforce development. Thank you, Dr. Roueche, for instilling in me to be a transformational leader in all my pursuits. This book captures not only the influence of John on community colleges but also on individuals."—**Linda D. Woodard**, EdD, president, LDW Group LLC

Vision for Opportunity

Vision for Opportunity

John Roueche and the Community College Movement

Edited by Martha M. Ellis

AACC AMERICAN
ASSOCIATION OF
COMMUNITY
COLLEGES

ROWMAN & LITTLEFIELD
Lanham • Boulder • New York • London

Published by Rowman & Littlefield
An imprint of The Rowman & Littlefield Publishing Group, Inc.
4501 Forbes Boulevard, Suite 200, Lanham, Maryland 20706
www.rowman.com

6 Tinworth Street, London SE11 5AL

British Library Cataloguing in Publication Information Available

Library of Congress Cataloging-in-Publication Data

Names: Ellis, Martha M., 1952– editor.
Title: Vision for opportunity : John Roueche and the community college movement / Martha M. Ellis [editor]
Description: Lanham : Rowman & Littlefield, [2020] | Includes bibliographical references. | Summary: "John Edward Roueche is the most productive and the most recognized community college leader in the history of the community college movement. This book explores the influence of John on individual lives and community colleges across the United States through stories and research of his years in the community college vineyards"—Provided by publisher.
Identifiers: LCCN 2019046889 (print) | LCCN 2019046890 (ebook) | ISBN 9781475846423 (cloth) | ISBN 9781475846430 (paperback) | ISBN 9781475846447 (epub)
Subjects: LCSH: Roueche, John E. | Roueche, John E.—Influence. | University of Texas at Austin. Community College Leadership Program. | College department heads—United States—Biography. | Community colleges—Administration—Study and teaching. | Community colleges—United States—History.
Classification: LCC LD5332.8.R68 2020 (print) | LCC LD5332.8.R68 2020 (ebook) | DDC 378.1/5430973—dc23
LC record available at https://lccn.loc.gov/2019046889
LC ebook record available at https://lccn.loc.gov/2019046890

♾ ™ The paper used in this publication meets the minimum requirements of American National Standard for Information Sciences Permanence of Paper for Printed Library Materials, ANSI/NISO Z39.48-1992.

This book is dedicated to:

The past, present, and future community college educators and leaders who commit each and every day to improving the lives of individuals and communities.

The millions of students who come to community colleges with hopes and dreams of a bright future for themselves and their families. We are continually inspired by your perseverance and determination to learn, succeed, and achieve that dream in the face of incredible challenges.

The contributing authors of this book who shared their time, talents, personal experiences, and a part of their heart and soul in telling the story of a remarkable leader.

My husband, Steve, who continually provides his love and support. He is one of the aforementioned community college leaders who devoted his career to helping students attain their goals and dreams.

Contents

Foreword

Karen A. Stout

Leaders who transform institutions into versions of their better selves are true artists. Not only must leaders have a clear vision of what their institutions can and should become, they must be able to see it within the confines of what already exists—they must be also be able to see 'what is not'—to look beyond the obvious, beyond what is known, beyond the reality of the present to the potential of the future.—John and Suanne Roueche, *The Art of Visionary Leadership: Painting a Face on the Future*, NISOD, "Celebrations," September 1, 2008

I am sure most of today's community college leaders have a favorite John Roueche quote. This quote has anchored my leadership aspirations. I use it often to begin my presentations on the role of leadership in institutional transformation around student success. In fact, I carry a copy of the NISOD article that includes the quote in my leadership files.

I am not a graduate of the University of Texas Community College Leadership Program (CCLP). But, I grew up and through community college leadership knowing about the renowned and heralded program. My doctorate is in Educational Leadership from the University of Delaware, a choice I do not regret, but a choice that I knew could limit my career options as, for several decades, the primary path to the presidency was through CCLP and Dr. Roueche. Dr. Roueche was and is a legend—the master architect of today's community college. Like thousands of us in community colleges, I have admired his work from afar, sharing and quoting his articles, reading his books (most of mine are filled with highlighting and scribbles in the margins and they line the bookshelf in my home office) and listening to him speak in many venues over the years. I am one of Dr. Roueche's students moving through the curriculum of the program as I absorbed the lessons in his writings.

This new book illustrates how central the work of Dr. Roueche and the CCLP program and its offshoots—the Center for Community College Student Engagement, Student Success Initiatives (SSI), and the National Institute for Staff and Organizational Development (NISOD)—have been and still are in shaping and leading the community college movement. This is the perfect book at the perfect time. We are, again, addressing leadership pipeline challenges to carry our sector through another period of redesign that calls for the type of leadership and scholarship that John Roueche embodies. This book is an important personal and poignant account of Dr. Roueche's extraordinary contributions to preparing, enriching, mentoring, and expanding opportunities for an important generation of transformational community college leaders. Dr. Roueche's story is told through the eyes of his students, colleagues, and friends who have carried on his legacy. You will know their names and their work in the field—Terry O'Banion, Byron McClenney, Kay McClenney, George Boggs, Belle Whelan, George Baker, Walter Bumphus—illustrating the influence of his ripple effect on so many. A perhaps overlooked side benefit of the book, is the documentation it provides of an important period in the history of the development of community colleges; documentation that as an emerging sector of higher education we often overlook and underappreciate because of our habit of focusing on our students over finding the time for reflection.

Each chapter brings to life Dr. Roueche's values, passion for community colleges and our students, and his intellectual range and vision. He was a true student of community colleges. As Terry O'Banion writes in an early chapter, Dr. Roueche ignited a "chain of events" with his perspectives on developmental education, leadership, accountability, teaching excellence, partnerships and diversity. In nearly every way, his ideas set forward the footprints upon which Achieving the Dream, the organization I now lead, was founded. He is the unheralded father of the student success movement. His placing such a high priority on teaching and learning with his books, *Teaching as Leading* and *Practical Magic: On the Front Lines of Teaching and Learning* centered teaching and learning in the reform work of the 1990s and early 2000s, a priority that is being renewed in our work now. I was so taken with his work that during a period in my presidency, I handed every new faculty member received a copy of *Practical Magic* during faculty orientation. His vision for the Center for Community College Student Engagement ensured that the community college student voice is centered in our improvement efforts. Hundreds of community colleges now use the tools from the center, including the CCSSE and SENSE surveys, to drive their work around student success redesign.

At a time when our field is once again facing an urgent challenge to prepare a pipeline of talented leaders for a new generation of community college leadership, there are important lessons in this book for many of us, especially aspiring students of community colleges and those leading colleges, reform networks, leadership development initiatives, and community college graduate programs. While it will be impossible to replicate Dr. Roueche's visionary leadership, we can look to replicate and scale ingredients of his active and cohesive design of the CCLP program and its affiliate organizations.

Dr. Roueche was known for quotes that became the common language of the CCLP program. I found another favorite in this book that I will add to my leadership presentations: "The status quo is going backwards."

Dr. Roueche is a man who continuously and rigorously challenged the status quo. He carried a generation of leaders along with him, injecting just enough disequilibrium into our growing understanding of our work as community college leaders, to ensure our relevancy as a sector. He is, indeed, as Terry O'Banion describes him, a rare "leader who disturbs the universe."

After reading the book, you will feel compelled to step up on the shoulders of Dr. Roueche to do your part to take on the challenge of filling the field's void left with his retirement to ensure that we are working collaboratively to design conditions to prepare, mentor and support the success of the wave of new leaders entering our colleges, some now filling the shoes of Dr. Roueche's CCLP alumni presidents.

Karen A. Stout
President and CEO, Achieving the Dream, Inc.
President emerita, Montgomery County Community College (PA)

Preface

Martha M. Ellis

Everyone who knows John Edward Roueche has a favorite story about John. Maybe that is because John is a great storyteller himself. John fully understands that a good story has the power to stay with you long after the lecture has faded. The chapters in this book explore the influence of John E. Roueche (fondly known as JER) on community colleges in the United States through stories and research from his more than 50 years in the community college vineyards.

The book documents the influence of John on individual lives and the community college movement. Woven throughout the book are testimonies of how lives were changed because of the doctoral program at the University of Texas at Austin (UT). There are stories of how John influenced the growth, expansion, and maturity of community colleges through his writings and thousands of presentations. Readers will find stories laced with humor and passion. Within each story is a lesson grounded in the values and principles Roueche expresses regularly to everyone who crosses his path.

This work is a collection of voices on the impact of John from many perspectives. While segments of his life history are included in the chapters, this is not a biography. The snippets from his life reveal how and why John came to be an advocate and crusader for community colleges and their leaders, faculty, and students.

Throughout the book, one sees his positive approach to every challenge that comes his way. With each move, he truly turns lemons into lemonade. Perhaps the most incredible example is his retirement from UT and move to National American University (NAU) to start a new type of doctoral program. In 2018, NAU decided to sunset the doctoral program, leading John to move this innovative program to Kansas State University (KSU). Many may say he has luck or good karma; that may be true, but John works hard; develops relationships; makes connections; thinks incessantly; and cares deeply about the students, faculty, and leaders of community colleges.

John is ambitious. That ambition propelled his talent, knowledge, and skills to incredible success. This ambition and success were recognized early and often by others. For example, he never applied for a job, as he was recruited for all of his positions in higher education.

Roueche honors others and eagerly shares their successes with his vast network. John is always the central figure in any room. While his reputation and personality seem larger than life, he quickly engages others to share in the moment with him. His generosity in sharing his time and knowledge is well documented in the following chapters. Perhaps you have been to lunch with John and have seen him leave a $20 tip for a $25 tab when he learned the waitstaff was a student at a local community college. Care and concern for his fellow travelers in this journey of life are genuine and pervasive.

He has received hundreds of honors and awards and is referred to as a legend in his own time. Paradoxically, he is most honored for what he has contributed rather than the awards he has received. The awards, certificates, and honors were proudly framed and displayed on the walls of his office. What was more prevalent on the walls, however, were pictures of people: John with students, colleagues, and friends.

John has a deep commitment to relationships, as documented throughout this book. The importance of people in his life leads him to approach controversy with creative ways to solve problems rather than engage in conflict or debate.

John has faced challenges. The trials faced with some colleagues at Duke, the dean of the College of Education at UT, and the abrupt closing of the NAU program are documented in several references in this work. Whether friend or skeptic, all agreed that John has influenced community colleges, educated hundreds of successful community college leaders, and provided a voice for thousands of community college faculty and students.

The authors of the chapters are his colleagues, community college leaders, and graduates from the doctoral programs at UT and NAU. The voices of his children provide insights into John as a father. Unfortunately, his second wife and trusted professional partner of 41 years, Suanne, passed away before the book began. Two brief chapters in the book provide insights into Suanne and her contribution to the Roueche and Roueche collaborative.

When embarking on a speaking tour to community colleges throughout the nation, John would often say he was leaving on a round of "Brother Love's Traveling Salvation Show." Indeed, John is an evangelist of love for community colleges, knowing that the education these colleges provide is the economic and social-mobility salvation for so many lives, particularly those who have been traditionally disenfranchised by educational systems.

This book follows the professional chronology of John's life from childhood to Mitchell Community College; University of California, Los Angeles; Duke University; UT; NAU; and KSU. A brief résumé and lists of his awards, articles, books, research, and professional responsibilities are included in the appendixes.

Themes throughout the chapters paint a picture of this man. Hopefully you, the reader, will smile, laugh, reflect, and enjoy the life and influence of John Edward Roueche.

Introduction

John E. Roueche: A Leader Who Disturbs the Universe

Terry O'Banion

Two community college leaders walk into a bar. . . .

True story: It is March 2018 at the annual convention of the League for Innovation held at the Gaylord National Resort in National Harbor, Maryland. I am sitting in the resort's Belvedere Bar nursing an overpriced and poorly made negroni when I hear "Dr. O'Banion." A tall young man, Keith McLaughlin, introduces himself and says, "I was in Block 58 in Dr. Roueche's program at UT." I ask Keith to join me, and we are soon joined by his friend, Ted Lewis, who had planned to meet Keith in the bar. Ted introduces himself by noting that he was in Block 64 at UT.

Keith says, "I'm buying." I switch to a martini, Ted orders a martini, and Keith orders a glass of chardonnay. We begin sharing our John Roueche stories, and we are soon deeply connected through a number of networks, overlapping experiences, shared values, and a revered history in which our mutual friend, John Roueche, is the nexus.

When John was a graduate student in the Higher Education Program at Florida State University in Tallahassee, one of his professors asked him if he would be willing to drive a visiting speaker to nearby Wakulla Springs, where a special conference was being held. The visiting speaker was B. Lamar Johnson, who directed the Community College Leadership Program (CCLP) at the University of California, Los Angeles (UCLA), and who founded the League for Innovation in the Community College in 1968. During the drive over and back, Professor Johnson and John became good friends and remained so for the rest of Professor Johnson's life. John even joined Professor Johnson at UCLA from 1967 to 1969 as associate director of the Educational Resource Information Center Clearinghouse for Junior Colleges and associate research educator.

In 2001, John Roueche came to Corning Community College (New York) as a keynote speaker, and the president asked a young staff member in Enrollment Services if he could pick up John at the Syracuse Airport. Keith McLaughlin agreed, and he and John engaged in a rich conversation during the four-hour roundtrip. According to Keith, when he dropped off John for his return flight home, John was getting out of the car, when Keith suddenly asked him if there would be any chance that he might be admitted to the CCLP at UT directed by John. Keith reported,

> Dr. Roueche responded to my question with much less surprise than I did, and he matter-of-factly said he thought there would be a very good chance I could be admitted to the program. I honestly believed he was just being polite and would forget who I was as soon as he stepped out of my car and headed into the airport. But, not Dr. Roueche!
>
> A few days later, I received a large envelope in the mail with the CCLP application and program materials, along with one of those hallmark gracious notes from Dr. Roueche thanking me for picking him up at the airport and encouraging me to apply to the CCLP program. That trip to the airport almost 20 years ago was a turning point for me, both personally and professionally. An entirely new world of opportunity the size of Texas opened up to me, and my "territory" has been enlarged and enriched because of Dr. Roueche's influence and impact on my life. I cannot thank him enough.
>
> Everywhere I go and the people I serve along the way—from my ongoing work in leadership roles in the community college to volunteer mission work in Haiti—are a direct result of the chain of events that started with meeting Dr. Roueche and the gift of a lifetime he gave me to be part of the CCLP legacy. (McLaughlin, 2018)

Today Keith is the provost of Morton College in Illinois.

As a visiting professor for more than a decade in the Texas CCLP, I was almost always picked up at and returned to the Austin airport by a doctoral student in the CCLP. In this process I had many rich conversations. I was able to expand my own network of significant friends, a number of whom I hired at the League for Innovation. John knew what he was doing in this strategy to connect aspiring leaders with established leaders—a lesson he learned well as a graduate student at Florida State University, when he chauffeured B. Lamar Johnson to Wakulla Springs.

Ted Lewis did not pick up John at an airport, but his experience with John proved life-changing, as it has for hundreds of other aspiring leaders. For 15 years Ted had been an instructor at Collin County Community College in Texas. His first move into administration was as the founding dean of Cy-Fair College in Texas. Ted reported,

> Shortly after Cy-Fair College opened, our college president and two other administrators, who had been students of Dr. Roueche's in the CCLP, encouraged me to apply to enter the program. One went so far as to contact Dr. Roueche's assistant and set up an appointment for me to meet with him. When I traveled to UT and entered the Sanchez building, I was both inspired and intimidated by a banner stating, "Welcome to CCLP, the #1 Community College Leadership Program in the Nation." However, when I walked down the hall to Dr. Roueche's office, the intimidation diminished as I was warmly welcomed by him as if we had already known each other.
>
> Over the years, I have learned a great many lessons from Dr. Roueche: to practice patience and humility, to at all times strive for greatness and not worry about who gets credit for accomplishments, to expect excellence and constantly inspect what you expect, that leadership is to always do the right thing, and that your character is defined by how you act when no one else is watching (Lewis, 2018).

Today Ted Lewis is the provost of Bluefield State College in West Virginia.

These chance meetings and engaged conversations with John Roueche are not unusual; it has been happening for decades in convention hotels all across the United States. These meetings and conversations in which John Roueche is the main character are but one indicator of the admiration and adulation his students and colleagues hold for him. Hundreds of his students and colleagues could tell similar stories. It is not hyperbolic to say that John Roueche has had more impact on aspiring community college leaders than any person in the history of the community college.

THE CHILD PRODIGY AND THE PRODIGIOUS ADULT

There was standing room only in the Western Avenue Baptist Church that Sunday morning in Statesville, North Carolina. Pastor Davis was thrilled at the steady increase in attendance over the past few weeks; everyone wanted to see the miracle. Pastor Davis gave a moving introduction punctuated with a goodly number of "Amens" from the congregation. Then, dressed in a starched white shirt and blue short pants, Little Johnny Roueche, age five, came to center stage and began reciting Bible verses by heart. Sometime later, Pastor Davis stopped him and brought the miracle to an end with a triumphant prayer; he knew Johnny Roueche could have gone on for hours. John Roueche was a child prodigy, and he has lived up to his early promise to become a prodigious adult.

John Roueche is the most productive and the most recognized community college leader in the history of the community college movement. There are numerous listings of his accomplishments in the chapters in this book. In a nutshell, here is that list, followed by an analysis of each category in terms of impact:

- Publications: Author of 39 books and more than 175 articles and chapters
- Speeches: Keynote speaker at more than 1,300 colleges and universities and hundreds of state, regional, and national conferences
- Grants: Recipient of more than $40 million for research and projects
- Graduates: More than 600 doctorates—one-third women, one-third minorities, more than 200 presidents
- Awards: Recipient of 40 national awards for distinguished service and leadership

Publications

No other community college leader has written so much and so well about the community college than John Roueche. He is also one of the most collaborative authors in the community college world. Of his 39 books, Suanne Roueche has been a coauthor on 12 books, and George Baker has been a coauthor on 9.

A cursory examination of his bibliography reveals that teaching and learning has been his highest priority. All his books have had impact on teaching and learning, but two stand out: *Teaching as Leading* (1990) and *A Modest Proposal: Students Can Learn* (1972). In *Teaching as Leading*, he proposes that teachers are not just there to provide instruction but to also have an important role as leaders in creating a college culture and managing many of the key functions of the college. In *A Modest Proposal: Students Can Learn*, one of his earliest books, John challenges the common wisdom of the day and creates a mantra for the community college that became a core value of the contemporary community college: Given the right environment, support, and instruction, all students can learn.

John has written 12 books on developmental education and at-risk students and has become a national spokesperson on this issue. *Salvage, Redirection, or Custody? Remedial Education in the Junior College*, John's second book written in 1968, is a blunt analysis of the failures of remedial education and a call heard throughout the community college world for reform. John wrote the book at the request of the American Association of Junior Colleges (AAJC). The report documents that remedial courses (reading, writing, and math) were the most offered courses in the nation's community colleges. His findings indicate that no more than 10% of the students placed into remedial English, math, or writing courses ever completed the course or progressed into college-level freshman courses.

Edmund Gleazer Jr., CEO of the AAJC, and his board were alarmed at these findings and worried about publishing the book as an association; up to this point, it was common practice to present only the positive side of the community college movement. It was a crucial moment for AAJC, but Gleazer and the board met the challenge and published it. The book became a major catalyst for community colleges to make good on the promise of the open door.

In 1984, John's study, *College Responses to Low-Achieving Students: A National Study*, made a major contribution to developmental educators by documenting practices that work. In *Between a Rock and a Hard Place: The At-Risk Student in the Open-Door College* (1993), he showcases 12 community college programs recognized as successful in serving the needs of at-risk students, reviews the impact of limited resources and a growing high-risk student population on community colleges, examines successful programs and strategies, discusses faculty selection, and reviews program evaluation criteria and methods. His most recent book on developmental education, *High Stakes, High Performance: Making Remedial Education Work* (1999), continues his decades-long commitment as an advocate for improving programs for underprepared students.

Today John is known primarily for his work in developing leaders for the community colleges, not only through his professorships at the University of California at Los Angeles, Duke University, UT, National American University, and Kansas State University, but also through his writings on the topic. He has written three books and numerous articles and chapters on leadership. His opus on leadership, *Shared Vision: Transformational Leadership in the*

American Community College (1989), is a seminal work that has influenced generations of leaders and reflects the core values he has taught in his courses on leadership.

As a renaissance scholar, John cannot be contained by these categories of his books. He has written three special books regarding studies he made of the Community College of Denver (Colorado), Guilford Technical and Community College (North Carolina), and Miami-Dade College (Florida). In addition, he has written seminal works on adjunct faculty, the entrepreneurial college, the private junior college, diversity, institutional research, and accountability.

His 1971 book, *Accountability and the Community College: Directions for the '70s*, created quite a stir among national community college leaders who resisted facing up to the challenge of accountability, but the book triggered a major reform effort and recognition that community colleges needed evidence to back up the promises they had made to the nation. Forty-seven years later, community colleges are still struggling to live up to the challenges John sets forth in this book.

Through his leadership programs, his research, his speeches, his articles, and especially his powerful books, John Roueche has been a leader whose response to poet T. S. Eliot's question "Do I dare disturb the universe?" (Eliot, 1915, ll. 45–46) is a resounding affirmative. Many of his books have been controversial, challenging the common wisdom and status quo in community colleges. Armed with evidence from his research on leaders, programs, and practices, he has shed light on our failures, giving the community college world a wake-up call. He has always included in his books prescriptions, examples, and recommendations on how our colleges and our students can be successful. By disturbing our universe, John has had more of an impact on positive change than any other leader in the community college world.

Speeches

It would take a dissertation to analyze John's speeches and determine their impact on the thousands and thousands of people who have made up his audiences. He has been the keynote speaker at more than 1,300 colleges and universities and hundreds of state, regional, and national conferences; it is not hyperbole to claim that he has been the most popular speaker in community college history.

John's range of topics is enormous, extending way beyond the numerous articles and books he has written. He can speak spontaneously with great knowledge about any issue in the community college world. His greatest gift as a speaker, however, is not so much about the topics as it is about his style of speaking.

John has a great sense of humor that naturally punctuates his message to the delight of audiences. In his early years, he told a terrific story about his experience as a student addressing a question on the final exam. It became a classic and was the best story I have ever heard a speaker share. Several friends asked to use the story in their speeches, but it did not work for them because John told the story with such panache that no one else could come close to his delivery.

In addition to his special style, John never uses a note or a PowerPoint, which to this day astounds me. I learned early never to follow him at the podium. He uses many brief stories and experiences to make his point, and he has a way of engaging the audience with such questions as "Are you with me?" He is a natural-born speaker and a natural-born teacher.

Grants

John has been one of the most successful recipients of foundation and federal grants in the community college world. He has received grants from

- the Lumina Foundation,
- the Ford Foundation,
- the Houston Endowment,
- the MetLife Foundation,
- the Pew Charitable Trusts,
- the W. K. Kellogg Foundation,
- the Sid W. Richardson Foundation,
- the Fund for the Improvement of Postsecondary Education (FIPSE), and
- the US Office of Education.

With these funding sources as well as others, John has expanded and enhanced the CCLPs he has directed. He has received $23,651,953 for research and development grants alone.

John has received millions more in fellowships and scholarships to support the tuition and fees of his graduate students. No other CCLP in the nation has had its students supported with so many resources. And a major source of support for his students comes from the various scholarship funds he has set up with his own personal contributions. His generosity is legend.

 Graduates from John's CCLP at UT include

- the current and former CEOs of the American Association of Community Colleges,
- the director and two former directors of the Center for Community College Student Engagement,
- the director and two former directors of NISOD,
- two former directors of the League for Innovation, and
- the current CEO of the Commission on Colleges/Southern Association of Colleges and Schools.

Graduates of John's programs have served as presidents of some of the leading community colleges in the nation, including

- Cuyahoga Community College (Ohio),
- Austin Community College (Texas),
- Sinclair Community College (Ohio),
- Tarrant County College District (Texas),
- Grossmont-Cuyamaca Community College District (California),
- Johnson County Community College (Kansas),
- Alamo College (Texas),
- Western Governor's University (Texas), and
- countless others.

In addition, hundreds of vice presidents and deans have been graduates of the program, and more than 30 graduates have been professors of community college leadership programs in universities.

Awards[1]

Just a listing of some of his national awards provides a stunning record of how John has been honored by his colleagues. Some of his awards and honors include

- the 2016 Harry S Truman Award from the AACC, the highest award given by the association;

- the 2012 Lifetime Leadership Achievement Award, the first such award given by AACC;
- the first-ever 2012 Diverse Champion Award from the publishers and editors of *Diverse: Issues in Higher Education* for his lifetime support and contributions to increased diversity in American community colleges;
- the naming in 2012 by the AACC Board of Directors of their national leadership initiative: the John E. Roueche Future Leaders Institute;
- having the Community College Association of Texas Trustees name their trustee training initiative in his honor;
- having National American University name its graduate center in Austin after him: the Roueche Graduate Center;
- having the League for Innovation in the Community College name its excellence award after him: the John and Suanne Roueche Excellence Awards;
- the 2011 O'Banion Prize for Leadership in Teaching and Learning from the Educational Testing Service (he shared this award with his wife, Suanne);
- the National Distinguished Leadership Award from the American Association of Community and Junior Colleges; and
- the 1988 B. Lamar Johnson Leadership Award from the League for Innovation in the Community College.

John has also been recognized by the University of Texas with

- the University of Texas Distinguished Faculty Award;
- the University of Texas Teaching Excellence Award; and
- the University of Texas Career Research Excellence Award, the university's top research prize.

While John has never considered himself a researcher in the traditional sense, the Career Research Excellence Award was the first such award received by a faculty member in the College of Education at the University of Texas—and that from a committee of university faculty representing the hard sciences, engineering, law, and medicine. John and his coauthors received more national research awards than any of his colleagues in the College of Education: more evidence of his ability to "disturb the universe."

A LIFETIME PARTNERSHIP BEGINS

I said earlier that John Roueche has had more impact on aspiring community college leaders than any person in community college history. As my best friend and great colleague, he has had enormous impact on me.

I first met John at Florida State University when we were both Kellogg Fellows in the Higher Education Program; we both had also been awarded a Florida State Fellowship—the only ones in our program to receive both awards. I think we both must have showed promise! We had early professional experiences that were quite similar:

- John received his PhD from Florida State in 1964, and I received mine in 1966;
- John's first job in higher education was as a dean of students at Gaston Community College in North Carolina; mine was as a dean of students at Central Florida Junior College; and
- we both started as assistant professors of higher education in 1967—John at the University of California at Los Angeles and I at the University of Illinois.

We have enjoyed a professional partnership and a close friendship for 54 years.

The first time I saw John, he was entertaining a group of students in our program at Florida State with a story, and he had a parrot sitting on his shoulder. I don't remember the story, but I remember the parrot and wondered who John Roueche was. I thought at the time he was just a kooky iconoclast. Little did I know he would become one of the most significant leaders in the history of the community college—a leader who would disturb the universe of our world.

Our early friendship deepened when we both agreed to join Nova University's pioneering program to bring the doctorate to various regions around the United States. Along with a band of others who freelanced for Nova as professors, John and I served as provocateurs to challenge university policy and practice to improve services to students. We each served as dissertation chairs for some of the leading community college presidents of the day. John also adapted Nova's practice of taking the program to the students, which is a key feature of the Kansas State University program he directs today.

Partnering with John was never all work and no play. With his delightful sense of humor and his spirit of adventure, we greatly enjoyed our time together as friends. John is a great storyteller and loves to tell the story of the time we were participating in a Nova conference for doctoral students in Hawaii. He and I had apparently been out one evening walking the beaches and talking, when we walked into the lobby of the hotel where a student greeted us with "Dr. O'Banion, I am looking forward to your speech." I responded that I looked forward to seeing him at the speech tomorrow morning. He replied that the speech was scheduled in 30 minutes, at which point John and I realized we had been out all night long. I made it to the appointed hour, and John ends the story by noting that the person who was to introduce me failed to show up. Neither of us remember what the speech was about.

John capitalized on a grant from the W. K. Kellogg Foundation in 1977 to expand scholarships for his doctoral students, establish the National Institute for Staff and Organizational Development (NISOD), and create *Innovation Abstracts* as a benefit of membership in NISOD. It was a brilliant use of foundation funds, in that John created through NISOD a means of collaboration between academe and practical needs in the field.

NISOD became a laboratory through which his doctoral students could interact with leaders in the field, network with those leaders through internships, and enrich the connections at a national conference that became one of the most important and substantive conferences in all of education. With more than 700 community college members, NISOD also became a network through which thousands of community college faculty and administrators benefited from publications, conferences, and services.

John has a very special quality of dreaming big and implementing big. As T. E. Lawrence (Lawrence of Arabia) notes, "All people dream, but not equally. Those who dream by night in the dusty recesses of their minds wake in the day to find it was vanity. But the dreamers of the day are dangerous people, for they may act their dream with open eyes and make it possible" (Lawrence, n.d.). John is a daytime dreamer, with his eyes wide open, who knows how to implement his dreams.

With this major Kellogg grant, he not only dreamed big about what he wanted to accomplish, but he also created a practical strategy to ensure his dream would continue far into the future. Grant funds were used to entice community college presidents to become paying members of NISOD by offering reduced payments for the first three years of membership. For example, annual dues were $200 the first year, $300 the second year, and $400 the third year; from fourth year on, dues were $500 a year. By the fourth year, colleges had experienced the benefits of being members of NISOD and were happy to begin paying $500 for their annual memberships.

Innovation Abstracts, a weekly report on innovations written by community college practitioners, was also created as part of this Kellogg grant. At its peak, NISOD published and mailed 85,000 copies of *Innovation Abstracts* each week, and 150,000 copies were mailed electronically on a weekly basis. Suanne Roueche played a major role as the longest-serving director of NISOD and first editor of *Innovation Abstracts.*

Our first major partnership was a W. K. Kellogg grant between the League for Innovation and John's program at UT to further enhance our leadership programs. Our mutual friend, Nancy Armes LeCroy, played a major role in drafting the proposal. With its part of the funds, the League created the Executive Leadership Institute (ELI), an annual institute of 30 to 35 aspiring leaders who had already earned the doctorate and who wanted to determine if they were ready for the presidency.

John and I designed the ELI and facilitated the first four institutes before hiring Brenda Beckman as director. Through 2015, 865 aspiring presidents had participated in the Executive Leadership Institute. Forty-seven percent were women, and 24% were minorities. Forty-two percent became presidents of community colleges. The League continues to sponsor the ELI today, which is in its 30th year.

In addition to ELI, the League also began publishing *Leadership Abstracts* in 1988 with the UT program as a twice-monthly report distributed free to all community college CEOs in the United States. John and I coauthored the very first *Leadership Abstracts* in January 1988 and, with some sense of what loomed ahead for community colleges, said:

> Our colleges require leaders who care equally about quality and access. Such leaders must be able to instill and inspire this concern in all faculty and staff members, if community colleges are to see dramatic improvement in student persistence and graduation rates in the years ahead. Such presidents will seek to identify, recruit, and select faculty and staff who truly believe in the mission of the community-college individuals who want to make a difference in the lives of the students they teach. These presidents will lead their institutions in adopting sound educational policies and practices to end the unacceptable attrition rates so common in today's community colleges. They will hasten an end to irresponsible "right to fail" policies in favor of policies that promote and provide students with the right to succeed. These leaders will collaborate with faculty and staff to create campus cultures that value learners and the teaching-learning process. They will care about the numbers of entering fresh-

men who persist to graduation, and they will be able to answer the basic
questions concerning educational quality in their colleges. (O'Banion and
Roueche, para. 11)

With our funds from this grant, John and I also began to cosponsor a national
conference we dubbed "Leadership 2000" that became the national conference for community college leaders for almost a decade. Attended by thousands, we were able to recognize national leaders identified by John in a
national study of leaders, honor women and minority leaders, and honor the
W. K. Kellogg Foundation for its contributions to the development of community college leaders.

One of the most important projects for the League in this grant was the
creation of the League Alliance, an organization of more than 600 community colleges around the world dedicated to innovation. John, with his usual
generosity, suggested we use his creation of NISOD as a model for creating
the Alliance, and he helped convince the W. K. Kellogg Foundation of the
value of this idea. The Alliance became, as NISOD did, the self-supporting
foundation for our leadership programs, and they continue to function in that
capacity today. NISOD and the Alliance may be the two best examples still
in existence after 30 years of how grant recipients have used grant funds to
leverage and support the continuity of their programs.

Our next major project together focused on Expanding Leadership Diversity (ELD). Building on the success of the ELI, John and I worked with the
W. K. Kellogg Foundation to create a new program to increase the number of
minority leaders. This year-long program was initiated in the 1989–1990
academic year for approximately 20 faculty members and midmanagers who
aspired to senior-level leadership positions. The program included two intensive week-long seminars held on community college campuses; a third seminar was held in conjunction with the Leadership 2000 conference. In addition
to the seminars, participants worked with a mentor, prepared a long-range
professional development plan, held an internship at a community college,
conducted research on a community college issue, and expanded their professional networks.

The program was funded by the W. K. Kellogg Foundation for nine years.
By 1999, of the 202 participants in ELD, 29 had become presidents; the rest
had become vice presidents, deans, or program officers. ELD was a resource-
intensive program that could not be continued without foundation funding,
but it did create a model of how more minorities could join the ranks of
leadership. Following ELD, both the League and the UT program continued

to expand leadership opportunities for minorities by enrolling them in the UT doctoral program, the ELI, and the National Institute for Leadership Development—a program that has prepared more than 6,000 women for leadership positions (O'Banion, 2016).

Our friendship and partnership continued through the Community College Leadership Program (CCLP) at National American University, where John served as director of the CCLP and president of the Roueche Graduate Center. John asked me to join this effort as chair of the graduate faculty and chair of the National Community College Advisory Board. At the first formal graduation ceremony for the CCLP on June 8, 2018, 34 graduates received their EdDs; 26 were minorities, and 29 were women.

As of 2018, John has been working as an advocate of community colleges for 58 years, and I have been working alongside him for 57 years; together we have contributed 115 years of our lives to the community college movement. We plan to continue our work as long as our health permits.

SUMMING UP A RENAISSANCE MAN

The title of a featured article in the May 22, 2012, volume of *Diverse: Issues in Higher Education* is "John Roueche—Community College Renaissance Man." It is an apt appellation for John, who is definitely a "man for all seasons" in the community college world. And it is a real challenge to sum up this dynamo of a leader who is constantly "disturbing our universe."

In the 117-year history of the community college movement, John stands out as the most prolific, creative, gifted leader and educator in the community college world. No former or current leader comes close to matching his record, and we are not likely to see his kind ever again.

The personal and professional traits admired in John Roueche become for us a basic leadership template that may prove useful to leaders and leadership programs—and certainly to the thousands of educators who admire John's work. In the simplest terms, these elements include the following:

1. Practice honesty and consistency with colleagues and constituencies.
2. Faithfully keep the promises you make to students, networks, foundations, leaders, and donors.
3. Embody the core values of the community college movement by demonstrating openness, service, fairness, and respect in your day-to-day work.

4. Cultivate and enjoy humor as a bridge to relationship building.
5. Give generously of your own talents and resources to further the work.
6. Develop stamina and career productivity through healthy life choices.
7. Intentionally build relationships across traditional boundaries that tend to isolate groups and perpetuate prejudice.
8. Cultivate ties with similarly strong peer organizations, emphasizing collaboration rather than competition.
9. Emphasize the core truths you espouse through speaking, writing, teaching, and mentoring.
10. Be field-based to the core, connecting continually to the groups you serve.

How very fortunate for the community college movement and for all of us who have worked in the community college vineyards that John Roueche decided to cast his lot with the downtrodden segment of higher education—the People's College, Democracy's College. With his extraordinary talent, John could have been

- president of a flagship university or flagship community college,
- CEO of a Fortune 500 company,
- a popular televangelist,
- head of a major foundation, or
- governor of North Carolina.

But the community college was clearly John Roueche's calling, and our students, our colleges, our communities, and our nation are all the beneficiaries of his career choice.

Those who know John Roueche relish and celebrate his delightful sense of humor, his keen ability to create networks of inclusiveness, his uncanny gift for grafting vision to action, his awesome intelligence, his genuine compassion and love for humanity, and his courage "to disturb the universe." I hope the readers of this book will come to know him at least in part as I do. John Roueche is absolutely unique and absolutely wonderful.

Part I

John and His Family

Chapter One

Shaping a Legacy

Coral M. Noonan-Terry

It's no secret that one's childhood environment and experiences shape their adulthood and career, and John E. Roueche II was no different in that regard. Few realize it at the time, and most don't appreciate it until much later in life. Whether from his parents, grandfather, nanny, teachers, or the jobs he had growing up, John learned valuable life lessons that shaped his view of life, his career, and the world around him.

John Roueche was born in Statesville, North Carolina, on September 3, 1938, to his father, John Edward Roueche, and his mother, Mary Grace Harris. His little sister, Sue, was born two years after him. Statesville was a small, working-class town in central North Carolina.

At the time John was born, Mr. Roueche was working for Morrison Furniture and Fixture as a furniture designer. His job was to inspect the lumber, picking out pieces of wood that had the same grain and look for use in the construction of furniture for banks. Mr. Roueche worked for Morrison until he was drafted into the army in 1943 to fight in World War II.

John's mother, Mary Grace, worked in a local hosiery factory. Mary Grace grew up in the country, about 10 miles outside of town, which in those days was considered quite a distance, given that roads were not paved. The hosiery mill in which she worked made hose for soldiers during World War II, becoming the official hosiery mill of the army. On Saturdays, Mary Grace worked at a cleaners for extra money to support her family.

Although Mary Grace was quiet, John describes her as the "rock" that kept his family together while his father was deployed in the South Pacific.

John remembers that his mother worked day and night for the entire time of his dad's enlistment.

Although neither of his parents finished high school, they knew the importance of education, and little Johnny was a good student. In fact, his teachers tried to convince Mary Grace that John should skip a grade, but she was adamant that he needed to be in school with children his own age. John's parents bought him an Encyclopedia Britannica set, 15 volumes in all, to encourage his learning. What he didn't learn in school, he learned from those encyclopedias. Johnny started with Volume A and eventually made it through Volume Z.

There wasn't anything particularly noteworthy about Statesville, North Carolina, but to John it was home. More importantly, it was the place where John learned those life lessons that shaped him into the man he was to become.

HARD WORK PAYS OFF

John learned his work ethic from his parents. Both were extremely hard workers, and John's dad taught him how working hard can overcome challenges. In junior high school, a guidance counselor administered a new test to the students. The test turned out to be the Stanford-Binet IQ test. At that time, an intelligence quotient was a new concept. The guidance counselor told John that he scored the highest on the test and was one of the smartest boys at the junior high school, but she explained, "Johnny, I'm so sorry. You're not gonna be able to go to college." She was the *first* person who ever told John that he couldn't go to college.

Devastated and perplexed, John shared with his dad what the guidance counselor had said to him. Mr. Roueche explained to John that, even though they didn't have the money for him to attend a large public or private university, there were many colleges that he could attend. Mr. Roueche told John, "In the United States, where you're born and who your parents are has absolutely nothing to do with what you may do or may become, if you're willing to go for it and work for it." John took this to heart.

John held many jobs when he was growing up: a newspaper delivery boy at the *Statesville Record and Landmark*; a grocery store worker at Fraley's Food Fair—the largest grocery store at that time in Statesville; a textile worker at the Pyramid Mills plant; a worker at Purcell's Drug Store; and even a wobble wheel driver at Tarheel Construction Company. (It was a choice between wobble wheel driver or shoveler—and to quote *Indiana Jones and the Last Crusade*, John chose wisely.)

John explained that when he "went to college, there were no Pell grants, no college work study, no guaranteed student loans, and nobody would loan you money to go to college. . . . The job, for me, was a ticket to ride. I don't remember ever having a job that I didn't appreciate. The reason was it was the only way out. It was the way to go and explore what options I might have. I never had a bad job."[1]

John started working from age nine on his paper route to earn extra money. He continued working throughout high school and college so he could pay for college and save some extra money. His class at Statesville High School was the first one to have a 51% college attendance rate; however, it's unknown how many of his peers actually finished college. His high school buddies teased John about his desire to go to college when working at a job without a college degree paid more than being a high school teacher with a college degree.

It was true: Jobs in those days had good salaries, health insurance, and benefits. But John didn't want that one job to be the only option. He was resolute in that he was going to college. And his passion for attending post-secondary education panned out. By the time John was 45 years old, many jobs working for the North Carolina companies disappeared. A college education was the way to open a door to more opportunities.

As in all of his places of employment, John excelled in his work at Tarheel Construction Company and was offered the opportunity to become co-owner and take over the business. But John stuck with his desire to go to college and become a teacher by understanding that the construction business was "hard work and unpredictable work because, when it rained, you didn't work. When it was snowing or cold or icy, you didn't work. I thought, 'No, I think I'll teach.'"

During his tenure as the director of the Community College Leadership Program (CCLP) at the University of Texas at Austin, John would frequently share memorable quotes from his dad. John would have this look of amazement in his eyes as he would recite a quote and share how wise his parents were, even though they did not have what some would consider a formal education.

During his years at Texas, John had quite the reputation for being an early bird. If he was in town and not speaking to one of the 1,300 community colleges and universities that he had presented to, he would be the first person in the office each and every day. He learned from one of his mentors that, when you arrive early and have uninterrupted quiet time, you can do your best thinking. He expanded, "I have never written a book or an article during 8:00 a.m. to 5:00 p.m. at the University of Texas or at Duke or wherever. I've always done it before school or on the weekends."

THE GREAT ORATOR

The ability to communicate effectively is a gift and a necessity for success, and John is one of the best. Like his work ethic, John's eloquence and engaging, witty storytelling began to take shape in his childhood, and it started with his paternal step-grandfather, Alvin (A. L.) Dorris. John's biological paternal grandfather had a kidney infection and died when his father was about two years old. In the 1920s–1930s, John's grandmother raised two children by herself working two jobs, including one at the Piggly Wiggly grocery store, and 15 years later married A. L.

Although A. L. was John's step-grandfather, John refers to him as his grandfather because he's the only paternal grandfather John has ever known, and that's how John sees him. A. L. had a heart attack when John was about three or four years old. This was back in the days before bypass surgeries and stents. Having a heart attack meant that the person couldn't work again and would need to stay relaxed and calm at home—which is how A. L. became a goat farmer.

A. L. lived next door to John and his family. With A. L. being home all day, he spent lots of time with John and had a major impact on John's life. A. L. read the comics to John, which piqued John's interest in reading at an early age. John became a prolific reader and writer.

The CCLP Block Guide,[2] a 40-page hard-copy booklet published for CCLPers (the term coined for students who were in or graduated from the CCLP), prospective students and partners, and visitors to the CCLP, describes the learning objectives, expectations, and requirements of the Block experience. One section in the Block Guide, "Selected Reading," explains, "Very definitely, the final product of the Block depends heavily upon how faithfully and how astutely you devote 10–20 hours per week, upon your own initiative, to acquiring what you need from the literature." At the end of the very first day of the Block, new doctoral students were told to read a selected book before 7:30 the next morning. CCLP graduates have John's grandfather to thank for instilling in him a love of learning through reading!

The most significant influence on John was A. L.'s teaching of a Sunday men's Bible class. The class had approximately 100 men in attendance, and every Sunday A. L. would quote scripture, which impressed John:

> One Saturday, [A. L.] was working on his Sunday school lesson, and he said, "Would you like to learn some scripture and say it to the class tomorrow?" Well, by that time, I knew everybody in that class, and they all knew me. I watched him do it. I thought nothing about it. It was just—that'd be fun. I memorized four or five verses of scripture and, the next Sunday, got up and quoted them, and . . . the men came up and put a nickel or dime in my hand. I thought, "Gee, this is pretty good. First paid speech." Anyway, from that point on, every Sunday, I quoted scripture to the men's Bible class—all of it. I was to the point I was doing 15 to 16 verses. Then the pastor, Wendell Davis, got all excited about it, so he would have me come in on special occasions and quote scripture before the sermon in the big church.

John's parents were not much into religion, so every Sunday John would go to church with his grandfather and recite scripture. After his mother died, John found a picture she had of him—wearing a white jacket and shorts at the pulpit "quoting scripture. By the time I went to the first grade, I could read and write and speak before adults, and the teacher said, 'Good God. Where in the world did this child come from?'"

John, in his humble way, attributes A. L.'s influence to "opportunity and chance. I had nothing to do with who my grandfather was. I had nothing to do with him having a heart attack or loving his grandson, but that was the gift."

A. L.'s influence is clear just by looking at the CCLP Block Guide. The Block Guide details the competencies for the Block, and under the chapter "Leadership Roles" is the heading "Spokesperson." This section describes the role of a spokesperson, including keeping various segments of the community informed about a college's progress, dealing effectively with the media, and having a working knowledge of the political process at the state and federal levels. Whether leading a Sunday morning pulpit speech or directing a premiere community college leadership program, both roles require great oratory skills.

Beloved John Roueche Sayings

At the University of Texas, "Blockers" (the term used to describe the students in the CCLP cohort) would hear certain phrases from John that would resonate with them throughout their careers. And Blockers usually ended up repeating the same phrases they heard John sharing when they became community college presidents and chancellors.

The Trick Is to Make the Horse Thirsty

When John presented at workshops, sometimes a faculty member would say something like, "Well, the problem is these kids aren't motivated. Many of them are not college material." And someone else would say, "Anybody knows you can lead those horses to water, but you can't make them drink." John would respond, "My grandfather was a farmer, and my grandfather said that the trick was to make the horses thirsty, not just to lead them to water. That's the genius in teaching—or leading as well."

John went on to write a book in 1990 with George A. Baker and Rosemary Gillett-Karam entitled *Teaching as Leading: Profiles of Excellence in the Open-Door College.* John explained,

> We concluded the reason the title is what it is, *Teaching as Leading*, is that the skill sets are almost identical. How do you motivate people? How do you get people excited? How do you get people committed? Anyway, they're very similar. Now, the populations are different, but it's powerful when you can do that. It's not about how smart you are or how much chemistry you know. Can you get people in that class excited about learning it and wanting to and seeing some meaning to it?

Inspect What You Expect

John was one of the first authors to publish a book on accountability in higher education. It's difficult to think that accountability was a concept often not broached in community college literature back in the 1970s, when community colleges were sprouting up every week. John published a book with George A. Baker and Richard L. Brownwell in 1971 entitled *Accountability and the Community College: Directions for the '70s.* John reflected on his high school football career when explaining the significance of "Inspect what you expect":

> I get the ball. I carry off the left tackle. I'm running. I can see the goal line, and I'm sure I'm gonna score. It was a tied game. I get hit from behind, and as I hit the ground, the ball comes out. They recover, and we lost the game—worst memory from athletics. That night, of course, I'm very upset, and everybody's coming around trying to console because they knew that, if we'd scored, we'd

have won the game. Anyway, I'm about out of the shower and Coach Archibald comes over. He says, "Roueche"; gets a football; and comes over and says, "Take this football. I don't want to see you without this football for the next month. In class, at the dance, and on the football field, I want to see you with this football. We don't fumble. We're not good enough to be giving the other team the ball, so we don't fumble. You understand that?" I said, "Yes, sir." I carried that football for a solid month. That was a great lesson about "Inspect what you expect."

Status Quo Is Going Backward

John would say, "The point is it doesn't matter how good you are. You're either working to improve, or you are declining, and others will surpass you." This saying came from one of John's tennis coaches growing up. When teaching at the University of California, Los Angeles (UCLA), John played tennis with Arthur Ash and other student athletes at the time. John would ask his CCLP students, "Do you think my tennis skills were up or down back then?" John's doctoral students became much better writers in graduate school because they were continually writing and improving their skills, with the help of the CCLP mentors. Practice really does make perfect!

Multiple Perceptions of Reality

When referring to this book, John said, "There are multiple perceptions of reality. Mine is only one. Too bad so many people who know the true story are not around to corroborate or challenge."

Element of Truth

John once had an ethics professor who said, "There should be an element of truth in everything you do." John would laugh as he would retell his doctoral students this saying, pointing out that, to be ethical, they need to have just one element of truth.

It's Someone Else's Idea

"One of the things I learned along the way is that you're always better when it's somebody else's idea. When I'm speaking to faculty, I never talk about anything being a new idea. Well, you need a change. I said, 'This is old stuff. Harvard's been doing this for 30, 40, or 200 years. I don't even know how long.' Don't threaten people with change."

It's Amazing What Time Does to the Memory

John's English teacher at Statesville High School introduced John as the commencement speaker. John was a little curious as to what she was going to say during her introduction because they had several encounters while he was in high school. One Thursday afternoon during John's senior year in high school, the teacher brought John and three of his close buddies up to the front of the class and said, "Class, I want you to see these four boys. Nothing good is gonna ever happen in their lives."

Well, when the teacher introduced John before his commencement address, she

> got her glasses on, and she got into this long story about how she had reviewed the writings of her best students for the last 40 years. Well, nobody doubted that because she kept up with what everybody was doing. She said, "Low and behold, I am delighted to tell you that tonight's speaker is without a doubt the finest English student ever to finish Statesville High School."

And John, with his quick wit and wonderful humor, gave the teacher a big hug, walked up to the podium, and said, "Isn't it absolutely marvelous and wonderful what time does to the memory? We tend to forget all the bad things that happen in our lives." Of course, the audience, by this time, was alert.

This teacher was also someone whom John "never forgave for not wanting to write a letter for me to go to Mitchell Community College. She said, 'I'm not going to do that because you'll be in the academic backwaters the rest of your life if you go to a little junior college. That's just the worst thing. You oughta borrow the money and go to Wake Forest or something.'"

This teacher was someone who always wanted John to attend Duke, and yet, at 27 years of age, John was teaching at Duke. She later said, "I've had to really change my views about how you succeed in life, and it's really not where you go. It's what you do where you go."

After graduating with his doctoral degree, John was a highly sought-after keynote speaker and prolific writer. Although John took a typing class and even earned extra money by typing papers for college peers, one of his mentors had told him that he would save a lot of time if he learned to dictate. He was so well spoken that, every book he ever wrote, he did by dictating.

DIVERSITY AND INCLUSION

With John's dad drafted to fight the war in the South Pacific and his mother working several jobs, an African American nanny named Luticia White was hired to care for John and his sister and take care of the household chores. Luticia worked for the Roueche family for three years when John was around five to eight years old and was one of the most influential people in John's life.

Luticia's husband, whom everyone called Babe, worked at the same lumberyard as John's father. Luticia and Babe had two children, Dude and Tony, and John would play with them. The railroad track separated the white community from the black community (called Rabbittown) in the segregated town of Statesville. One-half of John's paper route was to white families, and the other half was to black families. John remembered, "I grew up with black folks, so I knew as many of them, or more of them, than I did the white folks along the way."

In junior high, one of the coaches called in John and his buddy Butch Alley and said, "You boys have gotta quit playin' with the negros. They're gonna go one place, and y'all are goin' in another, and you don't wanna be known as a negro lover."

When John came home and told his dad what the coach said, Mr. Roueche explained,

> Don't ever think that you're better than somebody else because you have not a thing to do with being born white or being born in this country because, if you'd been born anywhere else, it wouldn't have mattered how bright or talented or able you are. You're gonna have options that Luticia's children don't have just because of your skin color. You had nothing to do with that any more than they do.

It was a great lesson.

Luticia taught John about human skills and was a powerful force in helping him learn to accept other people and not stigmatize or categorize people. One of John's saddest memories from high school was on graduation day: "When Luticia came to my graduation, they wouldn't let her in. True story. No black person was allowed in. It was segregated."

In his professional life, John remembered what he had learned from Luticia and how others treated her and her family. One of John's mentors at UCLA tried to discourage John from leaving Duke for the University of

Texas job. He said to John, "Texas is not Duke. It's a good school, and that's a great program, but they don't have any minority students. It's still part of the segregated south, and you grew up in that." According to John, "Duke was already integrated when I got there. I had black students in my classes, too. When I was interviewing at Texas, they had never had an African American student. None. One hundred twenty years. One Hispanic—Alfredo de los Santos."

John took the CCLP from one graduate who was a Hispanic male, another who was a Catholic nun, and no African American students to graduating more women and minorities who have become college presidents and chancellors than any other community college leadership program in the country. John has won numerous awards for the impact he has made in "breaking the glass ceiling" by recruiting and retaining minorities and women, including the Diverse Champion Award in 2012. (Suanne Roueche earned it posthumously in 2018.)

MENTORS

The importance of a good mentor cannot be overstated, and John had an outstanding mentor during his early college years. In high school, John took two years of history classes with a football coach who would later become his wrestling coach. High school history class was a lot of memorization and was just "deadly." He remembered, "What we did [in history class] was work on kickoff returns, linebacker blitzes, and double coverage of wide receivers." Of course, this was not exactly the content one would expect in a history course.

When John enrolled in Mitchell Community College, he was told that he would have to take history. He spoke with a counselor about trying to get out of taking a history class, but she explained that the only person who could approve a student not taking history was the dean:

> By the time I got to the dean's office, I was about number 39 or number 40 in line. Everybody was trying to get the dean to make an exception on something. By the time I met with him, I really refined it. I said, "I think I learned all the history. I think I could pass that test. I'd really like to get into economics, where my heart is." I wasn't even sure what economics was. I read "economics" in the catalog. The dean said, "Mr. Roueche, I'll be honest with you. I don't like history any more than you do, but if you want an associate's degree from this college, you gotta have two years of history. Next."

It was a good thing that the dean denied John's request for an exception to history class. Had he not, John would have never met one of the best mentors he ever had and one of the key people who inspired John to be the person he is today. In that history class, John met Louis Brown:

> I went to Louis Brown's class. I didn't have a textbook. I was going to wait and see how it went because I thought, if it's as deadly as it had been in high school, I want to do something else. I'm not sure what.
>
> Louis Brown came in that day and introduced himself to the class: "I'm Louis Brown. I've been here X number of years. By the way, the reason you're studying history is that people who fail to understand the mistakes of the past are doomed to repeat them in the future. You will learn from other people's trials and errors."
>
> Then he went around the room, and he introduced every one of us by name. He had no notes. He had no pictures, and there were probably 25 of us: "This is so and so from North High School . . . from Scott's High School . . . from Statesville High School." He didn't miss any names.
>
> A few weeks later, the Browns had my history class out to their home for a hot dog/hamburger cookout. I went over to assist Mr. Brown with the grilling, and Mr. Brown said, "I want to share something with you that I've only talked to my wife about. Are you aware that, when most people are in high school, history is taught by coaches and people that have no real interest in history and not much knowledge? The real thing is the students came here hating history. I told Dean Bradshaw the other day that if these students didn't have to take it, if it wasn't required, I wouldn't have a job here." I said, "I know. I heard that, but how did you know our names?" He said, "I go down to the registrar's office." In those days, you had to have a picture on your application. He said, "I make notes, and then I review those notes before every class. The reason is—let me tell you what I've learned. I've learned that if students think for a minute you have an interest in them, they will have a whole lot more interest in you and what you're trying to teach." I thought, "Boy, boy, how powerful, how powerful that is!"
>
> Anyway, he was the guy who called me at the end of the semester. I made an A in history. I was on the dean's list. My picture was in the newspaper. My grandmother bought me a new sport coat to reward good behavior.
>
> Dr. Brown called me at the drugstore, and he said, "I want you to come down. I want to talk to you." I knew I wasn't in trouble. School was out. I go down, and we talk about the football bowl games, the basketball team, and snow day, and then he said, "I want to ask you a serious question." I said, "Yes, sir." He said, "Have you ever really thought about being a serious student?" I'm thinking, "Gee, I thought I was." He said, "You could be a

straight-A student. You just got tremendous ability." I said, "Well, but I made
the dean's list, and I think I made one B, the rest As."

He said, "No, no. I'm not talking about making grades. That's going to be
easy for you. Have you ever thought about just getting up every morning and
learning what you can just for yourself? Everybody at this college is better
educated than you. You ever thought about what you could learn from all the
secretaries and all the people? They've got families. They're raising children.
Have you ever thought about what you could learn from the faculty that you
don't know? Who would have ever thought about that? If you decide to use the
talent you've got, I can tell you something. Somebody will pay your way to
college, wherever you want to go."

You could've blown me away with a feather. I didn't know that. Nobody
ever said, "By the way, if you're a really good student, there are scholarships."
There weren't many needs scholarships, and I didn't know anything about
scholastic scholarships. He said, "Let me tell you something else. If you decide
to live your life that way, you're going to have options in your life, all of your
life, unavailable to everybody else." Bingo. Well, it changed my life. I would
become a history teacher.

Louis Brown did more than inspire John to pursue a college degree to become a history teacher. A story John often shared about the power of teachers
was at the annual National Institute and Staff Organizational Development
(NISOD) conference, held over Memorial Day weekend in Austin, Texas. In
1978, John and Suanne created the NISOD conference, and it grew to be the
largest conference to focus on community college issues from 2007 to 2012.

At the closing session of the conference, which more participants attended than any other session, NISOD recognized its Excellence Award recipients. John would share the inspiring impact that Louis Brown had on his
life. While attending Mitchell Community College, John was working in the
shipping department at the Pyramid Mills Textile Plant. John was making
good money, more than he was making at the grocery store:

> It was the last week in October, I think, and Mr. Chandler called us all together
> and said, "Inventories are building up and sales are down, and we're gonna
> have to close the mill for about six months at least." Well, I had enough money
> to finish the fall semester, but I knew I didn't have any money to go forward. I
> remember my emotions very well because it just threatened every plan to go to
> college. I was thinking about joining the National Guard. Then the Marines
> had a program called the Platoon Leaders Course, and they took college stu-
> dents and sent them to Camp Lejeune during the summer to get training. At the
> end, you went through Officer Candidates School, and you came out as a

second lieutenant, but they paid for your schooling. I was thinking about how I could do that.

I got home that evening, and Mother said, "One of the professors up there called about 30 minutes ago and said he'd really like for you to call him back tonight." I said, "Well, it's almost midnight." She said, "I know, but he said he'd be up and it was important."

It was Dr. Brown, and he said, "Somebody told me that Pyramid Mills closed today." I said, "Yes, sir, they did." He said, "You were working there, weren't you?" I said, "Yes, sir." He said, "Johnny, don't you think about dropping out of college." This wasn't a counselor. This was a history teacher. How many history teachers keep up with their students? It was a small college, but he still had 20 to 25 students per class. I said, "Well, I've got to find a job to keep going." He said, "Give me a week. I'm going to talk to Dean Allen, the dean of students, tomorrow. Just be patient. Get your homework done this week. Keep your head up, and I promise you we'll find you a job."

The following Tuesday, I arrived home. My mother said, "There's somebody on the phone for you." It was Thomas Griffin, and he said, "I'm the manager of Purcell's Drugstore down on Broad Street. Do you know where we are?" I said, "Yes, sir." He said, "Son, if you're half as good as Dr. Brown tells me you are, we should've hired you several years ago. When can you get here?" I said, "How about 30 minutes?" Well, I finished college working at Purcell's Drugstore, and I made enough money not only to pay my way through college but to also go to a master's program, all because of Louis Brown. I tell that story because it's really important to acknowledge all the things that happened that you had nothing to do with.

Learning firsthand how significant a mentor could be in one's life, John made mentorship an essential component of the CCLP Block experience. Although the mentors changed a few times during the years, the one constant was John Roueche, and starting in the late 1970s, Suanne Roueche joined the mentorship team. The CCLP Block Guide describes the doctoral experience as an "unfinished composition. Of practical necessity, the structure has been placed on the canvas already by the mentors. Calendar and economic restraints place limits upon the size of the canvas. But, most of the picture is unpainted; it will be composed and produced by learner and mentor collaborations." John mentored his doctoral students for a half-century and was a significant force in his students' lives, just as Louis Brown had been for him at Mitchell Community College, where John later became a distinguished graduate.

NETWORKING

A key component to the CCLP Block experience was networking. Every year on the Saturday night before the NISOD conference, CCLP graduates would congregate to their old graduate school stomping grounds in Austin, Texas, to meet the newest Blockers and relive their graduate years with their Block-mates. This special annual reunion was called the CCLP Fandango. Imagine more than 200 of the best and brightest in this nation's community colleges coming back to visit with John, Suanne, and the other mentors; catching up with their peers; and meeting the up-and-comers in the community college world. It was the best networking opportunity in the community college field.

John learned early on that building and maintaining relationships are vital. In a small town, one pretty much meets everyone in the community. This ability to stay connected is integral in the workplace.

John also learned the valuable message from Louis Brown about taking an interest in people and expanded it to his careers: "It's doing your home-work—finding out what you know about people. When we walked into a room, I normally knew more about the people I was meeting than their mother knew about them. That's just being well prepared." The importance of "doing your homework" was instilled into every CCLP graduate student by John.

LEGACY

John's raw emotions shine through when he reflects on the impact that his parents, grandfather, nanny, history teacher, and many others made on his storied career and life. John's wise and extremely hardworking parents; his loving grandfather, who developed his oral and written communication skills; his nanny, who instilled in him the importance of kindness, diversity, and inclusion; and Louis Brown, who gave him the drive to become a better person and taught him to care about his students as individuals, all have shaped John Roueche as a high school and college history and English teach-er; a dean at a community college; and a professor and administrator at UCLA, Duke, and the University of Texas at Austin, where he directed the most successful community college leadership program in history.

At the University of Texas, some would say to John, "You've got a Midas touch. Everything you do turns to gold." John would respond, "You guys are just totally crazy. There is luck in the world. There is chance in the world. There's circumstance. No doubt about it, but an awful lot of it is just playing." This may remind you of a famous quote from another legend from the University of Texas at Austin, football coach Darrell Royal: "Luck is what happens when preparation meets opportunity."

John's upbringing helped to prepare him for his legendary career and instilled in him the virtues necessary to become one of the most prominent leaders in higher education, and yet, his hundreds of graduate students and millions of students whose community college education was enhanced due to John's teachings, readings, and presentations are the lucky ones.

Chapter Two

Suanne Davis Roueche

Martha M. Ellis

John and Suanne Roueche were a legendary husband-and-wife team for more than 41 years. Together they helped shape community colleges across the country through coauthoring books and articles, tag-teaming presentations, and training future community college leaders.

Former American Association of Community Colleges (AACC) president George Boggs said Suanne Roueche was "one of our most important scholars and writers." Together with John, the couple conducted some of the first and best research on remedial education in community colleges, Boggs noted, and also wrote about, college effectiveness, the importance of quality in teaching, at-risk students, and part-time faculty (Daily Staff, 2017).

Suanne was a graduate of North Texas State University, where she received both her BA and MA in English. She received her PhD in educational administration from the University of Texas at Austin (UT) in 1976. Prior to beginning her graduate work, she taught English at a Texas high school, followed by nine years at El Centro College (Dallas, Texas), developing and implementing a nationally recognized developmental studies writing program.

Suanne met John at El Centro College in 1972, when he delivered the commencement address at the college. He was impressed with how Suanne worked with developmental education students, tracking them down in the student center to make sure they came to class. Suanne's passion was for addressing the needs of developmental education students.

"She was probably the first voice for underrepresented students," Robert McCabe, former president of Miami Dade College in Florida, commented during an interview about Roueche in 2014. "She was the first to look at developmental education and say 'We have to do better—that is important.' She brought focus to this issue" (Daily Staff, 2017).

A year after Suanne met John, she decided to attend the Community College Leadership Program (CCLP) in the Department of Educational Administration at UT. She and John were married in 1976, shortly after she completed her doctorate.

The writing partnership between John and Suanne began with their first book, published in 1977. She was the author of 17 books and more than 60 articles and chapters focused on teaching and learning in American colleges and universities. Her most recent publications are

- *Rising to the Challenge: Lessons Learned from Guilford Technical Community College* (with John E. Roueche, Martha M. Ellis, and Melinda Valdez-Ellis, 2012);
- *The Creative Community College: Leading through Innovation* (with John E. Roueche, M. Melissa Richardson, and Phillip W. Neal, 2008);
- *Practical Magic: On the Front Lines of Teaching Excellence* (with Mark D. Milliron and John E. Roueche, 2003);
- *In Pursuit of Excellence: The Community College of Denver* (with John E. Roueche and Eileen E. Ely, 2001); and
- *High Stakes, High Performance: Making Remedial Education Work* (with John E. Roueche, 1999).

Others include *Embracing the Tiger: The Effectiveness Debate and the Community College* (with John E. Roueche and Laurence F. Johnson, 1997); *Strangers in Their Own Land: Part-Time Faculty in American Community Colleges* (with John E. Roueche and Mark D. Milliron, 1995); and *The Company We Keep: Collaboration in the Community College* (with John E. Roueche and Lynn S. Taber, 1995).

NATIONAL INSTITUTE OF STAFF AND ORGANIZATIONAL DEVELOPMENT (NISOD)

Suanne was senior lecturer in the Department of Educational Administration at UT and editor of publications for NISOD from 2000 to 2012. She served as the NISOD director for 20 years, before stepping down in 2000. During her tenure, NISOD increased its membership from 150 to more than 700 colleges, and the participation in its annual conference increased from several hundred to more than 2,000 registrants. Under Suanne's leadership, NISOD member faculty and leaders received *Innovations Abstracts*, NISOD's weekly teaching tips publications, as well as the institute's quarterly newsletter *Linkages*.

The NISOD conference, held in Austin over Memorial Day weekend each year, became the premier professional learning event for community college faculty and academic leaders from across the globe. She and John developed the highly prestigious master teacher awards recognizing outstanding teaching by community college faculty.

AWARDS

Suanne herself was the recipient of numerous honors for her contributions to higher education and to the professional development of community college educators. A few of these include

- the AACC National Leadership Award (1997);
- two Distinguished Research Awards (1995 and 1993);
- the Outstanding Research Publication Award (1984), presented by the Council of Universities and Colleges;
- the CCLP Distinguished Graduate Award (1990), presented by the College of Education, UT;
- the Great Seal of Florida (1989), presented by the governor, legislature, and St. Petersburg Junior College for outstanding contributions to higher education in Florida; and
- the Yellow Rose of Texas (1983), presented by the governor and legislature for her contributions to the state.

She is listed in *Who's Who in America*, *Who's Who in the World*, *Who's Who in Women*, and *Men and Women of Distinction*. Suanne was recognized in 2014 by author Anne-Marie McCartan as one of the most influential women in the development of community colleges in the last 25 years.

Suanne's personal and professional partnership with John was a significant legacy in writing and with the many community college leaders they mentored together. Suanne passed away on Christmas Eve 2017 after a courageous battle with cancer.

Hundreds of people joined John in a celebration of the life of Suanne on February 3, 2018, in Austin. The number of people who attended was impressive, though not surprising knowing of the love and admiration for Suanne. What was most heartwarming to witness was the two worlds Suanne loved, Austin Assistance League and community college friends from across the United States, joining together to honor and support John and the entire family in this time of deep loss. Throughout the morning, laughter and tears flowed, as celebrators remembered the woman who affected their own lives and the lives of so many others. As Walter Bumphus, president of AACC said, "Both professionally and personally, she will be deeply missed" (Daily Staff, 2017).

Chapter Three

John's Greatest Achievement and Partnership

Terry O'Banion

John's achievements are universally recognized in the field of higher education, but John would be the first to say that his greatest achievement occurred when he convinced Suanne Davis—an instructor of developmental education at El Centro College (Texas)—to become Suanne Roueche. There have been a number of collaborative couples in the community college world—Christine and Irving McPhail, Kay and Byron McClenney, and Arthur Cohen and Florence Brawer—but there has never been such a productive and collaborative partnership as John and Suanne Roueche. Some have suggested that Suanne was the power behind the throne (and in some situations, I am sure she was), but on the whole she was a full and equal partner with John in creating a legacy that will never be equaled.

Suanne powered the National Institute for Staff and Organizational Development (NISOD) into one of the most effective networks in community college history. She keynoted at hundreds of colleges and conferences. She received 18 national awards for service and leadership. She helped anchor the Community College Leadership Program at the University of Texas at Austin as a lecturer and dissertation mentor for hundreds of doctoral students.

She was coauthor with John on 12 books and many articles, and she was always the sharp-eyed editor who tidied up. On walks in the hills around their dream home in Northwest Austin, they invented some of the most creative titles in higher education—*Between a Rock and a Hard Place, Embracing the Tiger, Strangers in Their Own Land, Practical Magic, The Company We Keep*—each with an explanatory subtitle.

But Suanne was much more than a full partner with John in creating community college history. Movie-star gorgeous (she could have been the stand-in for Tippi Hedren or Dina Merrill), her delicate beauty belied her steeled strength and her enormous compassion. As president of the Assistance League of Austin, board member of the National Assistance League, and board chair of the Center of the Survival of Torture, Suanne was a model for servant leadership.

Her compassion for animals made her a poster girl for People for the Ethical Treatment of Animals. In Austin, she earned the name "the Possum Lady" for rescuing and releasing hundreds of possums into the wild. She had a similar track record for dogs and cats—many of whom took up permanent residence in the Roueche household. I was deeply honored to have a favorite named TJ (for Terry John), to whom Christmas presents were sent for years. More recently, Suanne became the champion of potbellied pigs and donkeys and supported their survival in shelters across the country. John and close friends always teased her about, upon their death, coming back as one of her dogs; such resurrection would be a life of great luxury and love.

After battling cancer for years, Suanne passed away on Christmas Eve 2017. Even in the last years, months, and days of declining health, she never flinched, never gave up, never lowered her standards, and never suffered fools. She was always there for John, and with Suanne, there was a lot of there, there. Suanne was a force of nature with a complex character. She was at the same time delicate and tough, tender and resilient, witty and profound—but more than anything she was lovely and delightful. It was one of the great privileges of my personal and professional life to be an adopted brother of John and Suanne.

Chapter Four

John E. Roueche as a Father and a Person

In the Words of His Adult Children

Linda L. García

Many individuals who know John E. Roueche have their own stories of how Dr. Roueche has affected their lives, whether as

- a doctoral student enrolled in the Community College Leadership Program (CCLP) at the University of Texas at Austin (UT) or National American University,
- a participant of the American Association of Community Colleges (AACC) John E. Roueche Future Leaders Institute,
- a recipient of a John and Suanne Roueche Excellence Award at the League for Innovation,
- a conference participant for the National Institute for Staff and Organizational Development (NISOD),
- a scholarship recipient at Mitchell Community College or Austin Community College,
- a conference attendee listening to his impressive keynote, or
- a friend who frequents the same restaurants he does.

One thing is for sure: Dr. Roueche continues to leave an imprint on the lives of others. This includes his adult children. Dr. Michelle Roueche, Jay Roueche, and Robin Maca all share the same sentiment about their father: He is a loving, caring, thoughtful, and giving person:

Everybody that I have met who knows him just loves him. They are inspired and impressed by him. Dad always wants to help others and tries to make the world a better place.

Whatever blessings I've received in life, they all start with him. I am fortunate. If I could be half the father he is, I'd consider myself a success.

He is focused, disciplined, and consistent. I am very lucky to have him accept me and treat me as one of his own.

In this chapter, Michelle, Jay, and Robin share their personal stories about their father in their own words and the lessons they learned growing up in a blended family. They provide personal insights into who their father is as a person.

LESSONS LEARNED

A lot of the lessons that I've learned have been repeated time and time again. There's a lot of things that I find myself doing that I look back and say, "Dad wouldn't have done it that way. Dad's way was the better way." I can't tell you how much I've learned along the way.

Gratitude

The biggest thing that Dad instilled in me is a sense of gratitude and counting your blessings, especially realizing that nobody owes you anything. Anything you get, you need to be very appreciative.

Dad constantly reminded us, "No one is required to do anything nice for you in this world, so you better appreciate it when they do." Such wonderful advice. Such truth.

What makes Dad happy is just seeing people be grateful and be appreciative. One of the gifts that I gave him for his 50th birthday was an album of gratitude. I thanked him for everything that I could think of in my life, such as paying for my piano lessons, raising me in the church, and giving me confidence. I feel like confidence is one of the greatest gifts that he gave his children.

Dad reminds me to constantly thank the people who support you and who are helping you because they sure don't have to do that. Write them a thank-you note. Send them flowers. If you don't thank them and acknowledge them, then that support can certainly go away.

Relationships

One of the things Dad started with us at a relatively young age and continues to this day is that there's always going to be people in your life who are in positions of power who you may not like and who are difficult. His point is, you can't avoid it, but you better learn how to navigate it and succeed in spite of it. The focus is to learn how to work your way through it because you're going to be dealing with it for the rest of your life.

Dad regularly says, "We don't have anything to do with who our family is. Frankly, you don't even have to like them, but you better choose your friends very wisely because that's your choice."

Dad would frequently say, "Talk is easy. Saying 'I love you' or 'I'm there for you' or 'I'm sorry' doesn't mean or cost anybody very much. Showing and demonstrating it is what truly will be valued."

Respect

Another thing that has really stuck with me, something his dad (my grandfather) said to him, is kids who were less fortunate don't have anything to do with where they started. Dad said, "Don't ever think you're better than someone because of what you were given at birth. You had nothing to do with that. Don't judge someone based on race or their family's financial situation." Being born to a better-off family or having parents who care and value education, I didn't have anything to do with the benefits I was born with. That was just a gift I was given.

I remember Dad telling me a story. When he was a little boy, he would stay with a black family next door when he got home from school because both of his parents had to work. Dad was friends with the family's kid. They would do things together, and he would ask his father, "How come my friend doesn't go to the same school?" Back in the early mid-1900s, North Carolina was very racist and very segregated. My dad's father would tell him, "You're going to have opportunities because you have white skin, but you understand something right now. Nobody in this world gets to choose what color they are, and nobody is better or worse because of the color of their skin." My dad's father understood how the world worked back then and [did] not buy into any of the racist things—how enlightened my dad's father was, especially for a man who was not educated at all. I think that is really where my dad's heart for wanting to help others probably was planted.

Risk-Taking

Dad has demonstrated and certainly verbalized that there are some risks worth taking. I saw it when he pushed to bring minorities and women into the Community College Leadership Program in the early 1970s in the College of Education. It would have been a lot easier to come in and join that old-boy network. That certainly was a risk worth taking.

I look at Dad's career path, and none of it was planned out. He took chances on education. All Dad knew when he was 15, 16, and 17 [years old] is that he wanted to go to college. He had teachers and others telling him that it wasn't possible due to his financial situation. Then, when he went to college, he wanted to be a teacher. He was told that he was going to starve. His parents were disappointed because they were wondering what would be the point of going to college to be a teacher, especially if he wasn't going to make much more than working at the mill. Going to college was not some grand plan but a willingness to take some risks and try new things. Sometimes you have to go out there and take risks to really make a difference.

Working Hard

Dad said, "Position yourself to have options in life." It's something that has always stuck with me. If you do well in school, then the college of your choice or graduate school all become options. If you do well at work, then someone will notice and give you opportunities for advancement. The spirit of gratitude. The acknowledgment that there's a lot of people who don't have options. Our mission is to work hard to have options.

Dad espouses to, if you're comfortable with where you are, you'll never be as good as you can be. You have to keep striving to be better, to keep growing, and to keep raising your expectations.

Other Lessons: Quotes Heard from Dad/John

"No good deed goes unpunished."

"Inspect what you expect."

"Failing to plan is planning to fail."

"Hiring is job number 1."

"There's multiple perceptions of reality."

"Doing more than you have to will pay big dividends down the road."

"Never explain magic."

"Believe in the art of the possible."

"An ugly win is better than a well-played loss."

"Always shoot for excellence."

"Build people up."

"Nothing bad has ever happened by showing up early."

"There are no rewards for mediocrity. Strive for excellence in everything you do."

"You can bring a horse to water. You can't make it drink, but you can sure make it thirsty."

WHO HE IS AS A PERSON

Life Changer

He loves his students and the colleagues and colleges he works with. They are like another family for him. Sometimes you look at what he's achieved and say, "Wow, he must be living his dreams." He actually did not have a grand plan to get to where he is today. He truly loves what he does, and he gets energized by it.

Dad truly makes a difference in people's lives. He has dedicated his life to helping others achieve their goals. There's not a huge number of professions that really make a difference in people's lives. I think community colleges really give someone an opportunity to dramatically change their life around and get on a different course.

Think about how many lives he has changed. Think of all the students that went to UT's Community College Leadership Program. Think about all the administrators he has trained and then the impact that those people had on their schools and their students. That must be thousands upon thousands of lives that he has either directly or indirectly made better. Also, think about the scholarships that he and Suanne have given to community college students to help them have access to education, better careers, and better lives. It's been thousands and thousands of lives changed. I just find all of that incredibly inspirational.

Dad was so intentional when he started his program at the University of Texas at Austin—making sure that it had people of color and women. His colleagues and mentors said, "You're going to ruin your program by doing that." Dad was just so intentional of making it inclusive and realizing that nobody gets to choose what color they are when they come into this world, but he wanted to give everybody the same opportunity.

Iconic

As well known as Dad is in the community college world, we can still go out to dinner in Austin and Dallas, and it's generally OK. But when we get together at a community college event, it's like dining with the Beatles. It was at the AACC conference when we tried to meet up. Being able to sit down and just be with Dad was tough there at the hotel. But realizing that we're on his playing field and that he's so valued there is pretty neat to see. It's also fun.

As the NISOD (National Institute for Staff and Organizational Development) conference started to grow and I realized that he was the host, I was in awe of the recognition that people had for Dad. My understanding of who he was professionally just grew and grew. It hit me even further once I moved to Houston in my early 20s, when I was picking up some dry cleaning and told the clerk my name. A couple of women there asked me if I was part of the Austin Roueches. It turned out that they were both former CCLP students of his.

I had a booth at the NISOD conference for over 20 years. I was so lucky to watch Mom and John do their magic onstage, speaking to the many attending and to see lines quickly form of people waiting to see, take photos, sign books, and talk with them. These people showed their love, admiration, and how important these two people were to their community college family. It also made me so proud to see their tapings on the television and share with my friends and teaching colleagues that my parents were so accomplished.

He is like Johnny Carson. It doesn't matter the room size he's in. He commands the room. My dad has that type of impact.

Dad would have the CCLP (Community College Leadership Program) students over for house parties. I saw students gravitate towards him. I saw his name published on books and in articles. I saw him interviewed on TV. I think when it really hit was when he took me to a college with him. He was the keynote speaker in front of several hundred people. He was the guy that people came to see.

His memory is incredible. When I went to conferences with him and he sat with a table of people he never met before—he would eventually know everybody's names. His memory is incredible.

Brilliant Speaker

I always knew Dad was special. Occasionally on Sundays when I was very young, he would preach at the church. Seeing him speak was impressive.

Dad's just the most brilliant speaker I've ever heard in my life. Nobody holds a candle to my dad. My dad never uses notes, index cards, an outline, or a PowerPoint. He's always doing it from memory. If there are any other speakers out there thinking that, "Oh, well, I'm a great speaker, too," my thought is they should try talking for two hours with no notes and being able to quote presidents, various books, authors, and studies like my dad. I've never seen anybody else who could rival him at the podium.

I vividly remember one of the first times I heard him speak. I had gone with him to some convention where he was the keynote speaker. He began his speech on the importance of excellence but then veered into a hilarious story that did not seem related at all. As the audience laughed hysterically, I secretly wondered if Dad had lost his place in his keynote. Would he be able to get back to his point? Shame on me for doubting! He brought the end of that story right back to his original theme and tied everything together perfectly with a bow! He knew exactly what he was doing and how he was going to bring it back around. I've never seen anybody else able to do that.

Watching Dad speak is mesmerizing and inspirational. Whether he is speaking for 10 minutes or 2 hours, Dad never hesitates. He never loses his train of thought, and he never stumbles to find the perfect word. He is a great storyteller. He's able to incorporate stories to keep you interested and engaged. To this day, he is simply the most amazing speaker I have ever heard! He's just a really entertaining storyteller.

One of the things that he says when he speaks is "Are you with me?" He's constantly making sure that the audience is paying attention.

Loving

Dad has a heart the size of Texas. He gave us every advantage in life—putting us through college and grad school and making sure we had reliable cars and safe places to live.

When I was a child—elementary and junior high years—the thing that really stood out was just how loving Dad was. You wouldn't see him without getting a hug and a kiss from him. It really provided a lot of confidence that your father absolutely loved you, had your back, and was there for you. Frankly, that love has never stopped. Having somebody who wasn't afraid to show emotion and feelings was really impactful to me.

As a child, I had never seen my dad cry. Not once in 18 years! The night before I left for college, Dad took me out to dinner. It would be several months before we saw each other again. As we were saying goodbye, he began to cry. That will always be one of the most cherished memories of my life.

As a child, Dad was really busy in getting his career going. He was busy grading papers or writing or doing something, but he was never too busy for the kids. This established a belief in working hard but never forgetting priorities.

Generous

Dad is generous with his time, his resources, his thoughts, and his love and support. What has always stuck out to me and what I r eally admired is that he bought his parents their very first home so they can have a better place to live. He did this in the 1970s, when he was 30-something years old. Frankly, I don't think many kids could or would do that for their parents. The fact he did that for his folks has really stuck with me and is something I admired. He is probably the most generous person I ever met. He'd give you the shirt off his back, but heaven help the person who tried to take it from him. He's very generous, but he doesn't want to be taken for granted.

My husband and I took in two girls who had no place to live. While those girls were living with us, Dad always sent them birthday gifts, Christmas gifts, and spending money. He never met them. He just wanted to help them have better lives. With Dad's help, we put those two girls through school. One finished her doctorate and works at Emory University. The other earned her master's degree and is teaching. Dad is really generous and wants to help others.

Encourager

Dad was also amazingly encouraging. He really convinced me at a young age that I could do or be anything that I wanted to be. He had a lot of belief in me. That gave me a strong backbone at a young age.

No matter what I did, whether it was playing in a recital or whether it was a paper that I wrote in school or whatever, Dad would say, "This is really excellent. This is really well done. You can do anything."

Dad always focuses on playing to your strengths. Neither he nor I can fix anything, but he always encouraged you to excel in the areas where you've got some ability.

Hard Worker

Dad grew up in abject poverty. I don't believe his parents even finished high school. They were very poor. Dad is a self-made person. He put himself through school.

When Dad was growing up, there weren't student loans. There weren't a lot of scholarships available. His dad was a woodworker in a mill in North Carolina. He had teachers tell him it's basically too bad for you that the die is cast. Everybody just assumed that he would end up going to work in the mill in North Carolina, as well, since his parents didn't have any money. The fact that he went out and broke the cycle of working-class poor is something that I can never repay. And, I'm not sure whether I would have had the same fortitude that he did to be able to do it—to go to college, work your way through, pay your parents' rent, and then go to graduate school.

If I'm remembering correctly, I think it was when Dad was in college—he was perfectly content making As and Bs. One of his professors pulled him aside and said, "Do you have any idea how good you could be if you would apply yourself?" Dad said, "What are you talking about? I'm getting As and Bs." This professor said, "You could make straight As. Your education could open doors for you and change your world." Having a professor expect more of him and say, "If you gave this your best and if you really applied yourself, you could be something special," changed Dad's destiny.

Characterized by High Expectations

Dad also was clear on setting expectations. On my way off for college, he walked me out to the car as I was about to drive away. He handed me a $100 bill. He knew me well, so he said, "Definitely have fun in college and enjoy yourself, but don't ever forget why you're there. I'll pay your way, but if you come home any semester with less than a three-point grade point average, then the next semester will be on you." He set clear expectations. He knew what I could do. He wasn't going to be supportive of me just going off to have a beer party in college for four years. The good news is I never had to pick up a semester on my own. Knowing that Dad had higher expectations and expected me to perform, I think that made the difference. I was proud of myself. Dad started talking about if I could graduate with a four-point grade point average and what all that would mean. I was thinking, "Let's stop a moment and celebrate small victories instead of counting on four years of this."

I was a day or two away from getting my first car when I was in 10th grade. I was awfully excited about it. Unfortunately, my geometry teacher called Dad and told him that I was not performing the way that he or she would like. That new car purchase fell through. It wasn't actually a new car, but it was a new car for me. He told me that I wasn't getting the car until I got my grades where they need to be. I had to wait. It seemed like an absolute eternity.

What really stood out is how trusting he was of me. How he treated me like an adult, beyond my years. It probably would be deemed too much in today's overprotective world. He gave me a lot of freedom, but he held very high standards. He had increasingly high expectations.

His generosity came with high expectations. He made it abundantly clear that, if we did not work hard and excel in school, he would withdraw his support. Not only did we learn our tremendous work ethic from him; we also learned to pay our blessings forward to those less fortunate.

Good grades were always a goal, and you didn't think otherwise! As kids, when we made As in school, Dad would give us money for every A earned. I remember Jay and I tried to negotiate. We would ask Dad, "Well, what will you give us for Bs?" He said, "You don't get anything for a B. Make As. Again, I'm not going to reward anything that's not excellent."

The fact that Dad always tied his generosity into expectations, and the second that you wasted this, the generosity would stop. Jay, Robin, and I were taught that there is a reward for hard work. It was not something that we were entitled to receive. In fact, Dad gave me a Rolex my freshman year of college because I kept a four-point grade point average. I wear that watch to this day because I just feel like Dad's always with me.

Friend/Mentor

Dad is my best friend. He was best man in my wedding. He is still a sounding board and advisor to me. I really feel blessed that we've built an adult relationship where you have meaningful, real, two-way conversations. We try to be there for each other in good times and in bad. We talk almost every day. The fact that he can dedicate 30 minutes or more a day just to talk to his son is something I truly value.

Dad and I could be perfectly honest with one another. Not everything I told him was necessarily something I was proud of. I knew, even if I was some-what off the rails and I could tell him, then it wasn't the end of the world.

He is truly happy for your successes, and he is there to encourage you when you're down. He hurts for you when you're hurting. That's the kind of relationship that you can't find very easily.

He also taught us to save money and invest in real estate. Having cash on hand (or easily accessible) when opportunities arise is always a smart thing.

Humorous/Fun

I believe I was in middle school. John, Mom, Jay, Michelle, and I were in the car. I think it was a Cadillac then—with a big backseat—and I'm not sure where we were going at the time. We were on the highway when John announced that we were driving at 100 miles per hour. The kids were all amazed and excited, and Mom wasn't. It was shut down real quick.

Several years ago, we were showing John how to download his music CDs onto Mom's computer. After we instructed him about how to use the mouse, he proceeded to lift the mouse and wave it into the air at the computer, thinking it would work from there. At the time it was quite funny, but there was no way we could show him how humorous it was to us. It was one of his first computer lessons. He's come a long way!

The thing that I always have appreciated was he and Suanne had such great humor amongst themselves and with us. We could all be very cynical and sarcastic with one another. What always got us laughing is when Dad and Suanne would disagree on a particular factual issue. They both were 100% convinced that they were accurate. Only one of them could be. Watching those discussions [was] good fun.

Most of all, as a child, Dad was just fun, whether it was play wrestling or making jokes. We've always had an awful lot of verbal humor in the Roueche family. He never seemed to take himself or others too seriously. He was always playful and gave as good as he got. If one or both of us don't spend a good portion of it laughing, it's a rare conversation. It's always a terrific time with Dad.

There was also the time I realized that, while he occasionally would say things with absolute conviction and had me scared to death, he didn't neces-sarily mean them. When I first got my license, he'd say, "If you get a speeding ticket, you're going to have to lose your license for a little while and not drive." That really tried to keep me on the up-and-up for a period of time. But, as we were going through the Arizona desert and I was dutifully driving 55 or 65 miles per hour—whatever the speed limit was at the time—he was getting frustrated at our lack of progress. Dad encouraged me to step on the gas pedal. I told him, "Well, Dad, suppose we get a ticket." He said, "Well, we'll let this one slide."

I was traveling somewhere with Dad, and he was grading dissertations during our flight. Secretly hidden in the middle of one of those long dissertations, a devious student had penciled in the question, "Are you still reading this?" Dad wrote in capital letters, "YES." I guess that student learned not to doubt him either!

Dad used to love to scare us. He would hide. If we were walking through the house, he would hide and jump out at us and scare us.

Dad was in his hometown visiting Mitchell Community College. He went out to dinner with somebody who was on the school board. At dinner, they were talking about the elementary school that they were building and how the city was growing. The guy confided in Dad that they were going to name the school Roueche Elementary School. Dad was tickled knowing that his name would be there in his hometown forever. The next day he sees the guy, and that person is just blushing red in the face. He said, "John, I'm really sorry, I was premature with saying that we were going to name it Roueche Elementary School." Dad said, "Oh, did some of your fellow board members not like the idea? Was there some issue that I should be aware of?" The guy said, "Well, unfortunately, to get an elementary school named after you, you have to be deceased." Dad responded that he would just as soon not have a school named after him. He'll continue to live his life for a while.

When I was in middle school, I went with my parents to hear live music quite often. They took me to see John Denver, and it opened up my eyes to have a broader love of music and respect for the singers and musicians. We also went to a restaurant/pub, which had a musician named Mickie Clark, who I love and still sing a few of his songs today.

For many years, our routines with Mom and John were going on long walks with our dogs and to our favorite restaurants quite often, since we spent three to four nights a week with them. Steve and I have never lived too far away from John and my mother, Suanne. Steve always said Mom and I were still tied at the umbilical cord—ha! We enjoyed spending time with them very much. Great fun and memorable, important times were also spent on family vacations in our favorite places [Jackson Hole and Carmel].

Longhorn Fan

Watching the Longhorns makes my dad happy. I made the mistake of calling one weekend. I called my dad to say hi. Unbeknownst to me, the Longhorns were playing. Dad answers the phone and says, "I'm watching the Longhorn game. UT is playing. I'll talk to you later." I'll have to make sure and check all the sports channels before I call him again.

Dad had a friend out in California going through a divorce who had wanted to unload his 280Z car relatively quietly and quickly. Dad and I flew out to Southern California to purchase the car and drive it back together when I was 15 years old. Then, we had to be back soon for the UT football game.

Animal Lover

One of the first dogs that I remember my dad getting was a Doberman named Duke. This was the sweetest dog. Dad was going to go get Duke's ears clipped the way they do for Dobermans. I begged him and said, "That's so mean. Please don't do this to Duke." I don't remember how old I was, but I was just crying. Dad never got his ears clipped. Here was this Doberman running around looking like a Beagle.

Here's an example of Dad's generosity and his love of animals: He had a dog named TJ. TJ was short for Tramp Junior—if I'm remembering correctly. Robin found this dog at a 7-Eleven convenience store. She could tell that something was really wrong with it and that it was starving. When she got up close to the dog, it looked like somebody had kicked this dog underneath its chin so hard that his bottom teeth had gone up through the roof of his mouth. He couldn't open his mouth to eat or to drink, so he was at death's door. Robin rescued the dog and took it to the veterinarian. The vet said, "This dog is not going to make it through the night." Well, they did some intravenous fluids, and the dog did survive. The next day, the vet called Dad and said, "We're going to have to implant a new jaw." Dad said, "Do it." They spent thousands and thousands of dollars on this dog to give it a jaw. Every time we drove by the vet's office, Dad would remark, "Do you see that BMW the vet is driving? I paid for it!" He was referring to the thousands of dollars he spent on TJ's surgery.

Dad loves animals. I think he would adopt every animal that he could.

Consistent

He loves having a clean car, inside and out. Outside of work, John watches football, reads, and goes to movies. He does not like surprises. Everything is planned and discussed. He likes to listen to a music CD straight through, not random songs. Again, no surprises.

CONCLUSION

The stories shared by Michelle, Jay, and Robin about the lessons they learned and who their father is gives readers a personal perspective of John E. Roueche. Many readers will find themselves nodding their heads in agreement as they read these stories—they, too, have experienced a glimpse of John's lessons, generosity, encouragement, love, humor, and much more.

This chapter concludes with one more story of John E. Roueche. It's a story shared by his daughter Michelle of her father's singing voice:

> Dad had a beautiful soprano voice when he was a little boy. He had a solo with the Statesville Boys Choir. He said when his voice changed nobody wanted him to sing after that. These days, he sounds more like Johnny Cash. Occasionally, he'll sing to me on my birthday, if I'm lucky.

The next time you see John E. Roueche, ask him to sing for you!

Part II

From North Carolina to the University of Texas at Austin

Chapter Five

Teaming with John Edward Roueche

The North Carolina Story

George A. Baker III

"More is thy due than more than all can pay."—Shakespeare, *Macbeth* (1970–1972)

"We are informed by the past." —Jon Meacham (2018)

"A successful man is one who can build a firm foundation with the bricks (blocks) that others throw at him."—David Brinkley (2019)

I first met Dr. John E. Roueche at Duke University in the spring of 1970 after having just survived what seemed like a half-decade in combat in Vietnam. Deploying with the First Marine Brigade to South Vietnam in the spring of 1965 and surviving without injury there for a complete 12-month tour, I (senior captain of the Marines) would meet the very demanding 36th president of the United States, Lyndon B. Johnson (LBJ), at the carpeted Camp David arrival ramp for the helicopter designated as Marine One.

In order to complete the requisite background checks for this position, every rock in my past was uncovered and evaluated by the Secret Service, FBI, CIA, DIA, and so on in order to gain direct White House security clearance to the president of the United States (POTUS) and his family. As a newly assigned executive officer of the presidential mountain retreat, I, along with the family, became part of a treasured place that President Dwight D. Eisenhower renamed Camp David from "Shangri-La." It was the place LBJ's daughter, Lynda, would eventually choose to spend her honeymoon.[1]

In those days, survival was secondary to protecting the president, his family, and distinguished guests from harm. I focused on not doing something that would get me fired by LBJ. After more schooling in 1969, my focus shifted to surviving Vietnam again upon redeployment. In combat, after many missions and a Purple Heart, I eventually made it home to my family, who lived near Durham, North Carolina, at the time. As a reward for several years of service, and on orders from the White House, my next task was to be enrolled in Duke University's doctoral program for higher education administration, which eventually led to me meeting John Roueche.

NORTH CAROLINA: THE EARLY YEARS

North Carolina is an important common denominator in this story of two lives. It is a state of 100 counties and one that is 600 miles across, stretching from Murphy in the west to Manteo on the Atlantic, facing the Outer Banks in the east. By 1860, it was the immigration choice for the southern and western expanse of the United States and had been heavily populated during the 18th century by Germans and Ulster Scots, who would later provide a stable labor force for the northeastern cotton mills that popped up near the Appalachian Mountains and nearby rivers.

Also from this state, without wealth or a portfolio, came an individual one might compare to Thomas Wolfe or Martin Luther King Jr.[2] Young John Roueche would survive the long, fearful, and rationed days of World War II. Later, people would remark on John's ability to persevere and how his motivation and drive were stronger than others in the organizations he led. This was also evidenced by the hundreds of publications John produced during his career. Personally, his writing style reminds me of a cross between J. D. Salinger and John Steinbeck, both writing from their cultural heritage.[3]

John's childhood seems to have shaped him into the successful person he became (as well as myself and others so fortunate), with a competency set I would carry for the remainder of my days. He wrote directly to me,

> I was born in Statesville, NC, Sept. 3rd, 1938. My father worked in a furniture factory, where his father, my grandfather, died of kidney disease when my father was only two years old. My grandmother remarried many years later to Alvin Dorris, who was a furniture designer. . . . Hence how my dad ended up in the furniture factory. My mother worked in a hosiery mill in Statesville. My early years were spent playing with lots of other children in my neighborhood. The bombing of Pearl Harbor changed everything. My father, who was 24 at

the time of the attack, was drafted early in 1943, and after finishing basic training at Ft. Bragg, was shipped to the South Pacific. I don't think I saw my father until his arrival in spring 1946. [A] Neat thing that happened to me was the arrival of Luticia White, my black nanny, who arrived at our house every morning before 7 a.m. to look after my sister and me since Mother began her shift at the hosiery mill at 7 a.m., Monday through Friday. Mom also worked at the laundry/cleaners on Saturdays to keep food on the table for my sister and me. Well, Luticia was the kindest and most gentle person ever. Whatever goodness or kindness I now have I attribute to the love and unconditional acceptance by Luticia and her family.

Boys of that ilk rarely had much of a cosmopolitan view of what their future lives would require of them. The view of most mill families of that time was that their offspring would complete high school and get a good job, probably as an extension of their after-school and summer jobs, working in the cotton mills, JC Penny's, or hopping curbs at one of the eateries, catering to the working folks who happened to have a prewar Chevy, Ford, or Oldsmobile. By any measure or macro-analysis, John Edward Roueche would become the essential pioneer, human potential developer, researcher, and the most important individual to the development of community colleges in America and Canada in the 20th century.

John's tenacity is well known, but so are his kindness and his values, which also seem to have developed during his early years. According to John, Sunday school was the opposite of freedom—more like one's responsibility to family and God. It was there that the young JER, who was an early reader, got the job of reading from the Old Testament—the Ten Commandments—and the New Testament, with the hope of salvation.

In the hometown of Mitchell Junior College, John received a good, basic education, which was designed to allow him to succeed in life and in higher education. After a time, it was evident that he had something in mind beyond that imagined by his locals and cosmopolitans, which was the desire to be somebody and to serve others in the glory of God. In correspondence with me, he explained,

In the Sunday school class, it was the practice for me to recite several verses of scripture. The men in the class applauded, and several handed me dimes and nickels, which probably had some long-term effect on my motivation. From that Sunday on, I believed that many things happened during this time that had great impact on my values, motivation, etc. My step-grandfather lived next door to us and taught the men's Bible class at the Western Avenue Baptist

Church. I spent every day with my grandfather, an absolutely kind and gentle man. One Saturday, as he was preparing his Sunday school lesson for his class, he asked me if I would like to learn some scripture and recite it to his class on Sunday. Well, I had watched him do this Sunday after Sunday for a long time and thought it would be fun. He had no learning objectives, of course, but just great interest in his grandson's development.

In those days many read and reread the *Saturday Evening Post*. People didn't much read the president's words but looked at Norman Rockwell's pictures of the four freedoms and the people who looked like them.[4] They were reinforced through their perceived values, even if at that time in the middle of the war, they didn't see the likes of John's Luticia anywhere in Rockwell's paintings.

Surely the young JER saw and mused over these lily-white visions depicting freedom from want and fear, of speech, and of religion and wondered if the other so-called colored groups were included in those personal freedoms from the fears so associated in that time of national peril. In fact, later, as understood by an older JER, "Our democracy looks much different today. In the 1940s, the United States was almost 90 percent white; today racial minorities make up more than a quarter of our population, and by 2044 the United States will be a minority-majority country."[5]

Surely, as other boys in elementary school during wartime, JER wanted to grow up quickly to join the fight, probably flying sleek fighter airplanes over Tokyo or Berlin. In segregated schools in a small mill town in North Carolina, he was free to speak his mind within limits and free to worship every Sunday, if only in his grandfather's Baptist church. With parts of two generations working, he was free of hunger, with a big breakfast, a brown-bag lunch made by an African American nanny, and supper consisting of what was left over from Sunday dinner; the leftovers in the icebox after the big Sunday meal might stretch until midweek. The boys and girls across the several states realized that their fathers were fighting for the Constitution's granted freedoms, and those times required sacrifices by way of wartime rationing.

The young JER developed the lifelong habit of thrift, resulting in his financial resources today. It is perhaps 1 person in 10,000 who would travel JER's route from whence he came to where he leads an entire movement, called democracy's human experiment, in upward mobility for now close to a half-century.

JER'S experience at Mitchell Junior College (1956–1958) provided an opportunity for citizens of his ilk to attend college at home and, if successful, find a way to complete the baccalaureate nearby.[6] JER's next stop was Lenoir-Rhyne University, a Lutheran liberal arts college in Hickory, North Carolina, where he graduated with a bachelor of arts in 1960. He then matriculated at Appalachian University with a master of arts in 1961. In his educational development, JER had not wandered too far from home. That home is a major influence on him. He was an early recipient of a Kellogg grant and graduated with his doctoral degree in 1964.

In 1968, JER completed his first major work. It is *Salvage, Redirection, or Custody? Remedial Education in the Junior College*, which he wrote for the American Association of Junior Colleges. In that work, he challenges junior college administrators to throw off that *administrative cloak* and become educational leaders. This new publication became central to his coursework and service work at Duke.

Later in the Regional Educational Laboratory for the Carolinas and Virginia (RELCV),[7] his students and laboratory staffers were proud to accompany him to Kittrell College,[8] which is on the Tar River in eastern North Carolina, where he received the Distinguished Service Award (DSA) from the African Methodist Episcopal Church. In 1975, this private junior college, along with so many nonstate and locally supported colleges, did not survive, but due to LBJ's Great Society and the work of Dr. John Roueche and his graduates, such exclusively black colleges as Kittrell closed because of the college's raison d'être (i.e., the Jim Crow years) and the federally mandated integration that allowed qualified students to enroll in colleges and universities of their choice.

Many other junior colleges became state-supported community colleges in the RELCV federally assigned states of North Carolina, South Carolina, and Virginia. Initially, and later as the National Laboratory for Higher Education (NLHE), Dr. John Roueche began his national effort to influence and improve the performance of North America's two-year colleges. At one point, around 1964, he served in the trenches as assistant to the president and the dean of students at Gaston Community College in Gastonia, North Carolina. At Gaston Community College, he gained crucial experience, learning about the operations of a medium-sized community college of North Carolina in a statewide system steadily growing toward more than 50 community colleges.

TWO WORLDS CONNECT

The time was spring 1970. The flowers were in bloom, and the Duke campuses were near their boiling points with general student unrest, something rather new. Students were protesting, showing their unwillingness to die for a White House administration that, from their perception, seemed to care little about the injustice of the lottery draft system for those poor and unconnected students who, unlike their connected brothers, were unable to receive draft deferments for such deformities as bone spurs. Ugly fights with the administration over discrimination affected the environment, and midrange social changes, such as the minimum wage for domestic workers at Duke, were compromised when the Vietnam War seemed to have no end in sight.

The spring semester had begun, and looking for a head start, I sought out the department chairman of the education administration in the College of Education. This occurred after a false start with the chairman of the Counseling Psychology Department at a preenrollment session that reminded me of Senator Dan Inouye (pronounced "in no way") from Hawaii. During the Watergate trial of President Richard Nixon, Senator Inouye indicated that there was no way he could let POTUS off the hook for crimes and misdemeanors during the Watergate crisis.

After listening to the stuffy professor in the Department of Counseling about the so-called five-year departmental imprisonment, which included two years of internship, I, with less than a two-year US Marine Corps (USMC) pass, realized I did not want to go down that road and detoured two flights down to the educational administration. For the remainder of my military and educational leadership career, I would thank John Roueche for the road not taken. For those at Duke University Graduate School, during those unsettling days, thanks were given especially to John Roueche and his many graduate students who lived through those times and embraced the Chinese proverb "May you live in interesting times."

Dr. Allen S. Hurlburt, who reminded me of Hollywood actor Burl Ives in girth and gate, saw the young and dynamic JER as his adopted son and had a way of reducing the stress of the unknown with his pleasant demeanor.[9] After hearing the story that three months of learning might be found somewhere in overtime and so as not to lose the dead time from late March through May, I found pre-intern work and an assumption that the venerable old campus would remain standing through the camped-out student maelstrom and bonfires that burned through the night.

"Doc" Hurlburt related that the RELCV had a working relationship with Duke and three lab divisions, which existed to carry out the provisions of the Higher Education Act of 1965. The vice president of the university and several professors were framing out programs under the broad provisions of the update of the Morrell Land Grant Bill of 1862. This higher education bill and others constituted LBJ's forward projection of John F. Kennedy's vision, called the Great Society.

President Johnson had the referent power to make things happen in the US Senate, but close associates in the Senate warned that his passage of the bills involving desegregation and voting rights for the disadvantaged would have the effect of moving the South to the political right for a century. History documents that those fears have impeded the work of such community college advocates as John Roueche and the thousands he has influenced, but they have not had the effect of changing educational opportunities for those learners willing to put their shoulders to the grindstone and lead effectively when the opportunities are afforded.

Transformational leaders like JER and his followers, such as George Boggs and Walter Bumphus (both presidents of the American Association of Community Colleges); Belle Wheelan (who leads the Southern Association of Colleges and Schools); hundreds of presidents, chancellors, and distinguished professors; and Terry O'Banion (from the League for Innovation), were leaders in this movement who clearly laid out the path for students and staffers and aided in rolling the boulders away from impeding progress. As frosting on the cake, all in this dimension continued to guide followers and leaders as necessary, as former graduates and staffers were guided to weave their way forward toward the end of their student-centered careers.

Back in Durham and at Duke University in the spring of 1970, with a definite push by Doc and his selling job, I was guided toward the special and unique program headed up by Professor John Roueche, former professor at the University of California, Los Angeles (UCLA). JER was a researcher and change agent and one of the designers of the Education Resources Information Center for junior colleges that would store and categorize information relating to undergraduate higher education in the United States. Soon in that framework, his graduate students would be going to retrieve the writings of two-year college advocates dating back to early days of the 20th century. Those who had dual roles of both graduate students and program staffers or administrators in Duke Graduate School and the NLHE had dual responsibilities. With Dr. Roueche's temperament, they were often able to pilot-test assigned projects in his classroom, as well as for the other graduate faculty in Duke's Community College Leadership Program (CCLP).

That first matriculated day, the batting average headed up several notches as I walked out of the meeting with the six-year-younger professor from Statesville, North Carolina, with an offer for a pre-internship, a job in the Junior College Division of the RELCV. On top of that, I quickly found another jarhead, retired colonel Dick Brownell, USMC. Being introduced around the office, a star was born when I met the then Barbara Washburn, another learner and staff member in the Junior College Leadership Program. She started by helping with my dissertation and staff projects and then became a lifelong friend.

Eventually after a 21-month, nose-to-the-grindstone adventure, a doctorate in hand would take me to three keystone assignments at the Marine Corps Combat Education and Development Command at Quantico, Virginia. These included curriculum coordinator/professor at Amphibious Warfare School, director of the Marine Corps Instructor Management School (IMS), and assistant chief of staff of academics for the Marine Corps Development and Education Command (MCDEC). These two last jobs would be implementing the Department of Defense (DOD) curriculum and instructional modeling (ISD) that was and is to this day employed to train faculty and administrators in the expanding consortium at RELCV (and later the NLHE) for the DOD. [10]

Something probably never to see the light of day in this K–16 world is the DOD's competency model, developed by trained field specialists, where the competencies for an entire field, such as engineers (E-4-9), are analyzed across the several services with a single source manager assigned. Then all services congregate their specialist and equipment there for the application of enhanced competencies with the newest cutting-edge technology. Hello Southern Association of Colleges and Schools?

These two well-earned positions at the Marine Corps major command, while performing at one rank above the appointed rank, led in 1974 to the first student/professor role in history at the Naval War College in Newport, Rhode Island. Not only would my newly found mentor guide and direct the experiential learning at Duke University, but Dr. John Roueche would voice his interest and support, communicate, offer powerful advice on personal performance, and visit me, his former student, at Quantico when the old bulls (senior colonels), in the forms of Brutus and Cassius, sharpened their knives to fight the DOD directive that all training and education would henceforth be designed and presented under the mastery- and competency-based format.

And similarly, the framework of the John Roueche philosophy employed in his CCLP at Duke and later at the University of Texas at Austin (UT) and the National American University Roueche Graduate Center was employed in the development of future transformational and mastery-oriented leaders. This administrative leadership, faculty development, and curriculum development model was very similar to the one developed in the Junior College Consortium of the RELCV back in the helicon days of the 1970s.

The role of the NLHE's Community College Division was to pursue the development of community colleges in its cohort in three dimensions: the leadership of the executives in accepting and embracing, by a signed commitment, the totality of the three-pronged approach of the NLHE; the development of officers for innovation and planned change; and the retraining of academics, officers, and their faculty, with emphasis on first-semester students.

Dick Brownell, Bart Herrscher, and George Baker, with JER's overall leadership guidance, took care of the leadership development component.[11] Stewart and Rita Johnson, formerly from UCLA, organized the teacher improvement component, and Oscar Mink led the institutional change officer, labeled the EDO—the educational development officer. The goal was to get the member colleges from the three base case states to participate collectively in all three components in order to gain the synergy that these programs would generate in student success. It was believed that, by accepting these ideas across the institutions, it would help the colleges raise all boats. Not only would the most competent students perform better, but also the average and below-average students would be challenged with mastery- and competency-based ideas from an effective and productive instructor.

Certainly there was a great deal of midnight oil and data crunching with RELCV's ancient IBM 360 completing the work at Duke University, but its probability was highly enhanced by Dr. John Roueche, who at the same time became a professor, work leader, lifelong friend, and someone who would have a major hand in my work, progression, and professional support, even to this day in retirement at age 86 in Greenville, South Carolina.

I graduated in the last days of 1972, with a cherished degree and supporting letter to the commandant of the Marine Corps. On the first day of the spring semester, I was able to report to the new job at Quantico on the banks of the majestic and historical Potomac River two days later. "Doctor-Major

Baker," as the first in the doctoral USMC education program to return to duty with the program completed, would be destined to join one of the lifetime legions of close followers, good friends, and colleagues with his enabler, who would become "Mr. Community College" for the next half-century and beyond.

Several nationally recognized community college professors and administrative leaders gained that recognition with JER. For example, Dr. Barbara (Washburn) Mink, dean at Mitchell College (1971–1973), was a program specialist at NLHE from July 1969 through July 1971. She and NLHE program administrator Barton Herrscher (president, 1970–1974) went at different but overlapping times to John's Mitchell Community College. The Statesville news reported that they were there to improve the performance and success of the students assigned through systematic instruction and evaluation of progress.

Jim Hammons followed as a program associate at NLHE. He later became professor of higher education at the University of Arkansas. In fact, many higher education, public school, and community college leaders grew from their experiences in the NLHE.

BREAKING THE MOLD OF GRADUATE EDUCATION

The fully functioning adult in John Roueche would come to understand that, in his professional bureaucracy, both pedagogical and rational concepts were fighting for space and recognition among perceived but unequal equals. His grandfather certainly reminded him of the dehumanizing autocracy of the Nazis' Final Solution, where second-class citizens in Europe were placed in cattle cars and driven to their deaths by furnaces and gas chambers in concentration camps.

In a turn-about-fair-play concept, the Japanese, whose government had decided to declare war on the United States by attempting to destroy the Pacific fleet at Pearl Harbor on the island of Oahu, would suffer the prejudice of the GIs in the Pacific during World War II. Even the families of Nisei (Japanese and other Asians fighting in combat on two continents) would be subjected to concentration-like camps in the good ol' USA.

Sometimes such preconceived notions would find homes in such rational places as higher education. It was not enough that the top 100 universities, such as Harvard, Yale, and UT, would comb the applications of their potential undergraduate and graduate students to find the top 1% of articulated quantitative talent, which they often did regardless of a legislative edict. In contrast, the programs looked for a rainbow of potential talent with motivation and drive to "be somebody."

While leading programs at Duke University, where the founding fathers would never have imagined it, John and a team of professors produced well-trained and well-developed academic and instructional leaders of mixed ethnicities and both genders. The model conceptualized at the Duke University Program of Educational Administration, teamed with what was later known as the NLHE, provided an early-teamed, experiential learning environment for a cohort of future community college presidents, chancellors, and educational administration (leadership) professors, which placed Duke University at that time as one of the few higher education universities practicing such leadership concepts; it would become the model at UT and North Carolina State University, in addition to 1,200 community college programs in the United States and Canada.

A Formosan native, Peter Ku (later the distinguished chancellor of the Seattle Community College District), completed his college degree in his birthplace and, with his top quantitative score, came to his graduate program concerned about meeting the lofty goals of Duke University. On his first paper in JER's CCLP, Peter received a C primarily for not showing leadership and participation in group work. After a pub meeting with Dr. Roueche and his fellow students, even if graduate student Ku's spoken English was wanting, he became a member of a dedicated team of students organized to pull all cohort members across the finish line.

Such student teamwork broke the mold of graduate education at forward-leaning Duke University. In analyzing and debriefing students after orals and employing basic statistics principles taught in the department, the student leaders, including Peter Ku, could predict to a very high degree of probability the range of questions employed by Professor X in the subsequent scheduled graduate student oral.

It is not that Professor Roueche taught this behavior as such. A basic tool employed by the students was to reduce uncertainty and focus on what the professors thought to be essential. Peter Ku related, "I really did not understand American culture and my classmates, and Dr. Roueche's patience and support were crucial to me while I was at Duke, but he also had a huge influence in launching my career in educational leadership" (Ku, personal communication, 2003).

It would be the exploding Vietnam years in the early 1970s when I, who eventually wrote about my experiences with JER, was a student at Duke University (1970–1972) and a program associate at the NLHE during the same period. Not quite dry behind the ears from college experiences as vice president for general education at a technical college in South Carolina, I, a worn-out change agent, was brought by my teacher, brother, mentor, and friend to UT in 1978 and was presented with responsibilities far beyond my readiness.

Dr. Roueche intimidated his colleagues at Duke University and UT in several ways. He earned the highest student evaluations for every semester because of his teaching; published more than the sum of his departmental colleagues altogether; and provided services at the NLHE, which became a model for the remaining public schools and higher education entities in the RELCV.

Several of his colleagues stultified and retired early in disgust; their cold lectures based on three-decades-old theories did not meet the needs of those hungry for mastery concepts, a structured syllabus, and evaluations of their own student progress. Developmental theories, competency-based concepts, and technological progress were evidence to the point that, to remain in the top tier of enriched, private universities, universities would need to invest in young talent. It was paramount to the alumni, the board, and the advisors— Duke needed to change.

After Dr. Roueche accepted a full professor position at UT at age 31 and the retirement of Dr. Allen Hurlburt, the father of the community college system in North Carolina, Duke University's Department of Educational Administration closed down and reestablished aspects of the program in the College of Arts and Sciences. In the Education Administration Department at Duke and later at UT, the tenured professors had vested interests in the status quo, and in a single voice, the chorus would sing, "It is not that we loved that experiment less; it is that we loved our vested power more."

This is my analysis, and surely there were strategic reasons for closing the CCLP at Duke University. At the college level, there was no one qualified to lead the program as had Drs. Hurlburt and Roueche. Additionally, as I would discover later, cohort models at major universities, other than in business and perhaps law, constantly challenge the staffing and operating models of these programs.

The liberal arts programs remain pyramidal, in that a great deal of under-graduates are admitted and about half will make it to the upper division; of that number, the very best typically are selected and encouraged as master's students. Those groomed and selected assist in the teaching in the department. Above this level, a few doctoral students are admitted, with about one-half coming from the outside. This handful of doctoral students are retained in the department, taking on teaching and research projects with their assigned major professor.

Dr. Roueche and his rainbow cohort threatened the status quo, and the facilities, research, and public school professors likely felt insecure in accepting leadership of dissertation research conducted by higher education candidates. A similar thing happened when Dr. Roueche retired from UT in 2012. While the major research had come out of the CCLP, the teaching model in the CCLP was 7 to 10 students per professor, and the other 75% of the college was producing about 25% of the research and very few doctoral graduates.

In another game changer, at Duke and at UT, the student research was cutting edge, and as a part of the training, student teams worked the curriculum and became writing teams for sponsored research. While this was a great experience for the students, it threatened the other educational departments, who by their departmental head count of tenured professors held the numbers in promotion, recognition, and the power of the block vote. Often, the dean and department heads would need to horse trade even to get earned recognition for the smaller departments, such as educational administration.

At the "Forty Acres" (a nickname for UT), JER fought for and often "paid ransoms" to get the boat spaces that he needed to adequately run his program. In his day, awards authorized by the faculty senate were extremely hard to come by and typically not based on performance. After all, by this time, JER had become a full-fledged Texan; poker bluffing and horse trading in that environment is a cultural prerogative.

Since 1970, Dr. Roueche has spoken to more than 1,300 colleges and universities on the topics of teaching and leadership from the Roueche curriculum vitae. By taking a conservative approximation of 500 per visit, that amounts to 650,000 people. Considering that there might be some repeats in the same institution or at conferences in these numbers, this calculation amounts to more than a half-million people.

In these sessions, which aimed to positively influence behavior, the message was always clear: The process of leadership, regardless of the situation or context one finds themselves in, is a set of qualities or characteristics attributed to those who are perceived to successfully employ such influence.

His message is clear: Quality leadership occurs in the classrooms and institutions as well as at home and follows one all the days of their lives.

During JER's almost 50 years in higher education, he was able to persuade grantors, both public and private organizations, and individuals of about 30 different grants totaling many millions of dollars to support organizational development and student learning. He was always able to bring forth new ideas to benefit public and private education. He did these things in such a way as to enhance the goals and personal philosophies of the grantees and their trustee roles.

At that time, my exposure to JER's operating style was a great lesson for me. The competencies learned from Professor Roueche were also powerful persuaders in my later role as program director of the CCLP with former governor of North Carolina Robert Scott at North Carolina State University (1992–2002).

In 2012, which was arguably the twilight of his UT career some seven years ago, JER had a featured article on the website for *Diverse: Issues in Higher Education*, where he shared his early motivation to succeed with the staff writers. In the 1950s, the world had not recovered from the worldwide depression, and in Statesville, North Carolina, such things as jobs were hard to come by. As with most born at that social level in that post-Depression era, jobs were hard to come by and JER chose to stay at home and enroll at the local junior college.

With a $100 scholarship, he managed to skillfully help his birth family and save enough money to attend Lenoir-Rhyne College (1958–1960), where he taught English and history before enrolling at Appalachian State University (1961). There, he graduated and taught for a period of time. It was in this environment where JER would begin to form a set of ideas that would take him forward to his zenith at UT in 1970.

Meanwhile in the summer of 1961, the dean at Appalachian offered an opportunity to attend Florida State University as a part of the enhancement. JER was offered one of the rare Kellogg fellowships for community college leadership with the expectation that this young scholar would fill one of the blossoming opportunities for leadership executive officers in Florida, one of the other southeastern states. From a sociological perspective, this early national experience clearly assisted him in becoming a cosmopolitan with a global perspective.

There in that graduate experience in 1961, JER met and became lifelong friends with Terry O'Banion, who set off on his own rocket career that, along with JER's, rivals anyone spanning the 20th century and the first two decades of the next. Upon JER's retirement from UT, Terry praised John Roueche's fantastic and dominating role in the history and development of the North American community colleges (Pluviose, 2012). Terry said, "In the 110-year history of community colleges, no one has come close to equaling the record that he has established. And I can't imagine anyone in the next 110 years reaching that." As his number 1 student and friend, I second that motion!

After more than 40 years of leadership, service, and achievements in community colleges, John Roueche was honored by the AACC, the Association of Community College Trustees, the Phi Theta Kappa Honor Society, the Center for Community College Student Engagement, and NISOD. In the May 2012 issue of *Diverse: Issues in Higher Education*, there were about 45 half- and quarter-pages in the 58-page issue thanking the Roueches for their years of service in the advancement of framing the so-called community college movement to its lauded role in the 21st century.

So, the southern culture in which John Roueche grew up in central North Carolina would be one written about and would become curriculum in the great universities of learning, such as the University of North Carolina, Chapel Hill. There, student Thomas Wolfe would develop skills for writing critically about his hometown in Asheville, North Carolina, and nearby, JER would capitalize on Duke's reputation of being one of the first great universities to integrate. He would build on that idea with the first community college program east of the Mississippi River and marry the program with the mission of the Higher Education Act of Texas from President LBJ; the aim was to provide better lives for immigrant Hispanics as well as other ethnic populations in America and women.

The poor southern boy from Stonewall, Texas, on the Pedernales River would be joined by the poor boy from central North Carolina's cotton mills, and both would grow up as protectors and rich employers of free speech as they sought and researched the benefits of the right to a free education in America. LBJ would advocate for the Morell Land Grant Act, which in 1862 had authorized the selling of lands of the great western expanse to finance free public education.

We pushed for low-cost junior and comprehensive community colleges. Later, with the growing influence of the American Association of Community and Junior Colleges, founded in 1920, many bought into the NLHE's ideas that college presidents must be accountable for the success of their students: the Association of Community College Trustees, early nationally recognized and innovative community and junior college leaders (including such close allies as Edmund Gleazer, Lamar Johnson, Dale Parnell, Bob McCabe, Richard Hagemeyer, and Tom Hatfield), and other early adapters who were two-year college chief executive officers.

An extension of the Federal Commerce Department's argument was that public organizations must adapt to the idea that the wealth of the nation and the success of its people depends on the measurable outcomes of both its industry and the development of its people. In the Confederate South, for example, community and junior college presidents knew in their hearts that community college doors must be open for all students who, as culture would dictate, had parents who were often trying to make ends meet and could not afford college, resulting in not encouraging their offspring to consider that course of action.

AFTERTHOUGHTS

As a historical aside, after I returned to the Marine Corps and at a level well above my pay grade, one or more of the economists in the government got the idea that, with advances in computer science, not only could a man be put on the moon, as was done in 1969, but also the Department of Defense could save billions over time by consolidating training into one branch of service that would reduce the burdensome cost of combat readiness. At the time, I was the assistant chief of staff for the Academic Center of the Education and Development Command at Quantico, Virginia, with the power of the commanding general and the commandant of the Marine Corps and full authority to implement all aspects of the curriculum and instructional model at the strategic, operational, team, and individual levels.

It would take a constitutional amendment sponsored by Abraham Lincoln; a four-year Civil War, with tens of thousands killed and maimed; almost a century of Jim Crow laws; and Martin Luther King Jr.'s, John F. Kennedy's, and his brother Bobby's assassinations to lead to the bifurcated society that remains today. John studied American history in high school and world history in college, but somewhere in adolescence, he began thinking about modeling his favorite teacher, Mr. Louis Brown, an endeavor to make his way forward as an intellectual history scholar. Before that, John Roueche would recall with interest and wonder at the teaching and learning in his own domicile.

In 1996, the Mitchell Community College Endowment for Excellence was established, and from that time, its famous former student and his bride, Dr. Suanne Roueche, supported the foundation with sufficient funding to support 10 needy college students. In 2002, the Roueches, in honor of JER's former history instructor, pledged $100,000 and endowed a scholarship at the college formerly named Statesville College.

At the presentation, John and Suanne spoke eloquently about their life-long quest to prepare students for the challenges of life and the associate careers they were persuing. John, speaking from his own experience, reported that Professor Brown gave him a "gift that no one could ever repay." Louis asked him, "Have you ever thought what you might accomplish if you learned everything that you possibly could?" Dr. Suanne Roueche replied, "Somehow this support and the culture at Mitchell will help the students see themselves in ways they never thought of before" (Mitchell Community College, 2019).

Dr. John Roueche would not want anyone to forget the grease that made the machine go in the collective programs: that is, the wonderful, creative, and key concept called supporting staff. John's Libby (deceased), Ruth and Reid at UT, my Judy, Dawn (deceased) at North Carolina State University, and the legions of graduate student research teams drove the funded projects, which resulted in numerous books, chapters, articles, and instruments to form a secret weapon in dominating research production in several higher education institutions. With timely student success theories, organization, and competitive spirts, the collective colleagues could only look for thirds and honorable mentions in the three categories of research, teaching, and internal and external service to the field.

WORDS OF WISDOM NEVER FORGOTTEN

John took Professor Brown's words to heart, and he marks the Brown experience as one that drove him to live his life in a manner that, when a person gives it their best, they will always have options throughout life. It was a very distinguished and career-fulfilling option that my mentor took masterfully in 1992. An opening occurred in 1991 for the only other distinguished chair in community college leadership ever created by the chancellor and his team at North Carolina State University. They sought a national figure in order to deliver a program to duplicate the one Roueche developed for UT. JER offered his full support, as I was a full professor at UT and was now competing with 100 responders. When I retired a decade later, JER sent me a letter expressing the heart of this unbelievable person. He honored our 22-year close and mutually supportive relationship along with a "Hook 'em Horns" photo!

Chapter Six

John Edward Roueche and the Texas CCLP

George R. Boggs

For more than 70 years, educators from around the world were drawn to a program on the campus of the University of Texas at Austin (UT). It was almost as if some mysterious, magnetic force attracted people who had a desire to learn about community college leadership and gain credentials that would open doors for career advancement in the fastest-growing and most exciting sector of postsecondary education.

The UT Community College Leadership Program (CCLP) opened in 1944 under the direction of Clyde Cornelius (C. C.) Colvert. It was the nation's first program designed to prepare community college leaders. The first graduates became some of the most recognized leaders of the early junior colleges in Texas and beyond. In those early days before the civil rights movement, most of the students were men, and there was little racial diversity.

During the 1960s, community colleges were expanding rapidly across the United States, and communities were struggling to find the people who were capable of developing and leading these new colleges. To address the leadership crisis, the American Association of Junior Colleges (now AACC) gained the backing of the W. K. Kellogg Foundation to support the development and expansion of CCLPs at 12 major universities throughout the United States, including the program at UT.

When C. C. Colvert handed the leadership of the program to John Edward Roueche in 1971, he gave John a directory that listed all of the graduates with their contact information. C. C. advised John to keep track of the program's graduates as he had done. "If a graduate is deceased, we know where he is buried," C. C. said. Dr. Roueche became a full professor at age 31, younger than all but one of his students and the youngest person to lead a national community college graduate program. He was one of the youngest full professors in all of American higher education. He would lead the Texas program for more than 40 years.

Of the 12 Kellogg-funded CCLPs, the program at UT lasted the longest and produced the most community college leaders and scholars. In his study for the AACC, Lee Betts ranked the Texas CCLP first nationally for its qualitative impact on American community colleges (CCLP Alumni Directory, 2012). Dr. Gregory Vincent, vice president for diversity and community engagement at UT, gave credit to the CCLP for its first-place *US News and World Report* ranking among public colleges of education (Smith, 2012).

When Dr. Roueche retired in 2012, *Diverse: Issues in Higher Education* reported that he had led the nation's most highly regarded training ground for community college presidents. The article went on to say that Dr. Roueche was set apart from his peers, not just for his prolific writing, groundbreaking research, and exceptional teaching on community college practices, but also for his uncompromising commitment to diversity and inclusion (Smith, May 22, 2012). The UT CCLP graduated more women and minority presidents than any other program of its kind in the country.

THE PATH TO TEXAS

When C. C. Colvert announced his retirement in 1970, faculty in the Department of Education identified John Roueche as a potential successor because of his research track record when he was at the University of California, Los Angeles (UCLA), and the reputation of the program he had built at Duke University. Dr. Roueche was an associate professor in the Department of Education at Duke and had built the community college program. He was leading the junior college team of the Regional Laboratory for the Carolinas and Virginia (RELCV).

Prior to Duke, John had taught or cotaught community college courses at UCLA with B. Lamar Johnson, and he was able to use his background in community college leadership development and scholarship in building both the programs at Duke and the RELCV. Much of his research had resulted in reports and books published by the American Association of Community and Junior Colleges, which later became AACC (Roueche, April 29, 2018).

Although there were some experienced community college presidents who were being considered for the position at UT, the dean and faculty leaders in the department believed John was the candidate who could best build on the legacy of the program. When the dean called Dr. Roueche to offer him the position of tenured associate professor and leader of the Texas CCLP, John replied that he was flattered but he was already approaching tenure at Duke. He indicated that he would be happy to work with and assist whomever was selected to lead the Texas program. The dean said he would need presidential approval to offer John a full professorship. The president agreed, and Dr. Roueche, at age 31, accepted and became one of the youngest full professors in American higher education (Roueche, April 29, 2018).

DEVELOPING AND REALIZING A VISION

Before accepting the position at UT, John met with university president Norm Hackerman. Dr. Hackerman was very supportive of the CCLP, but he asked John to consider developing a national network that community college trustees across the country could make use of when they wanted to hire a president or that presidents could use when they wanted to hire vice presidents or other administrators. The Texas CCLP was well known in Texas, but John knew that developing a national network would take additional faculty and more resources than the program had. He began to seek grant funding to expand the reach of the program. The first success was a federally funded Education Professional Development Act (EPDA) grant (Roueche, April 29, 2018).

Another early success was a W. K. Kellogg Foundation grant to build a program that would assist community college faculty to be successful in teaching the great diversity of students who attend the open-access community colleges. The grant enabled John to bring to Texas one of his doctoral graduates from Duke, George Baker, to teach in the program and begin what would become the National Institute for Staff and Organizational Development (NISOD).

When the program officer at the Kellogg Foundation recommended that the interest on the grant be used for CCLP student scholarships, John was informed that it was against university policy and that the interest would revert to the university's general fund. John took the case to the university president, who thought it would be a great idea to use the interest for scholarships. This would not be the last time John would take the program's case to the person who would say "yes" (Roueche, April 29, 2018).

Soon after Dr. Roueche began at UT, the younger faculty in the department approached him to ask if he would consider becoming chair of the Department of Educational Administration (now Education Leadership and Policy). He knew that such an assignment would take time and attention away from developing the CCLP. When another faculty member who wanted to become department chair came to John to ask for his support, John asked for his support in return for a new faculty position for the CCLP. The strategy was successful, and John was able to bring Dr. Donald (Don) Rippey onboard as an additional faculty member in the CCLP (Roueche, April 29, 2018).

In 1973, Dr. Roueche invited Val Wilke Jr., the new executive director of the Sid Richardson Foundation, to visit the CCLP. Val was so impressed with the program and the excitement of the students that he proposed funding for Sid Richardson scholarships. The Richardson Foundation later funded a faculty chair position in the CCLP.

When the Houston Endowment expressed an interest in providing funding to support the CCLP, the university president had to cut through the bureaucracy in order to accept the grant. Over the years, Dr. Roueche was able to bring in $40 million in grant funds to support the CCLP, the students, and related programs and initiatives, including NISOD, the Community College Survey of Student Engagement, and Achieving the Dream (Roueche, April 29, 2018). (Chapter 10 of this book provides a detailed description of these programs.)

John Roueche inherited the program begun by C. C. Colvert, but he expanded it, developing the program's reputation outside of Texas, building its financial resources, and setting a precedent for enhancing the diversity of both the students and the faculty (Manzo, 1996).

ATTRACTING AND SELECTING STUDENTS

I first met John Roueche in March 1981. He was a featured speaker at the annual conference of the Administrative Association of California Community Colleges. His speech was engaging and inspiring. I was an associate dean of instruction at Butte College in California and was given the assignment of securing speakers for the fall faculty convocation. After hearing Dr.

Roueche speak, I decided that Dr. Roueche's message was an important one and that he would be an ideal presenter for Butte College. Fortunately for me, Dr. Roueche accepted the invitation to come to Butte College that fall.

The 1980s were challenging times for community colleges in California, and Butte College was no exception. The financial effects of the 1978 passage of Proposition 13, the property tax limitation initiative, were beginning to be felt with program cuts and stagnating employee salaries. The Butte College faculty had recently unionized in response to the 1975 Rodda Act that authorized collective bargaining.

As in most institutions at the time, Butte College faculty and administrators were not accustomed to adversarial negotiations, and relationships were deteriorating. The hostility in the room between faculty and administrators was palpable as Dr. Roueche was introduced, but it took just a few sentences before Dr. Roueche had the attention of everyone in the room. Faculty and administrators were drawn together by his message about the important work of teaching and learning.

After 13 years as a faculty member and administrator in a community college, I decided that I wanted to do more and have a greater influence on the development of these institutions. For that, I believed I needed a doctoral degree. The time that I spent hosting Dr. Roueche at Butte College convinced me that the CCLP at UT was the best match for both my values and aspirations. Granted a sabbatical leave from my position at Butte College, I drove across the country, along with my wife and three young sons, to Austin and joined 16 classmates in the CCLP Block of 1982.

Several other CCLP alumni have similar stories of hearing Dr. Roueche speak at a conference or college and becoming inspired by the potential of studying with him. Some students were referred by their college presidents or vice presidents who saw potential in them as future leaders or by friends who were CCLP alumni. Others met Dr. Roueche at one of the annual NISOD conferences and attended a session that Dr. Roueche presented about the CCLP. Some students attended an intersession taught by the CCLP faculty before being admitted to the program.

Jerry Sue Thornton, a student in the 1982–1983 CCLP Block, said her decision to leave her administrative post and move from Illinois to Texas hinged not only on the program's curriculum but also on the impact that the alumni were having in the field: "I had a set criteria . . . to determine which (program) would be best for me, given my goal to be a college president" (Manzo, 1996). All of the students were attracted by the program's reputation; its supportive, cohort-based model; and the opportunity to participate in the premier CCLP in the country.

In her 1996 article on community college leadership development, Kathleen Kennedy Manzo notes that Dr. Roueche's forte is to spot talent. Not all applicants were granted acceptance into the program. Students were expected to do well on the graduate record examination (GRE), but Dr. Roueche did not believe a high GRE score was the most important criteria. The faculty looked for students who had excellent human relations skills and an ability to listen (Roueche, April 29, 2018).

THE BLOCK

Dr. Roueche gives credit to Larry Haskew for designing the Block: the block of time when the CCLP students were together in classes in the fall. Dr. Haskew had taught in the program with C. C. Colvert and had been dean of the College of Education (Roueche, April 29, 2018). Students eventually referred to themselves as "Blockers" and identified themselves as belonging to particular Blocks designated by year or sequential number.

George Baker describes the Texas CCLP in his 2012 book, *The Making of a Marine-Scholar*. On Monday through Wednesday mornings of the fall semester, the doctoral students took Administrative Functions in Education—Junior College Administration (EDA 682G) and Community College Problems (EDA 383). On Monday afternoons, the students took Organizational Theory in Education (EDA 382M). On Tuesday afternoons, the students took Seminar in College Leadership and Decision-Making (EDA 395). On Wednesdays at lunch, the students had a brown-bag colloquium. All of the CCLP students took this same block of courses, collectively called "the Block" (Baker, 2012).

The Block guide describes the experience as a constellation of individual students, each of whom would be a resource for all of the others, as well as an independent acquirer of cognitive and affective behaviors. The CCLP was intended to be a device both for conducting and causing learning experiences. Each entering cohort of students was thought to be an unfinished composition.

In the first week of the Block, a situational temperament sorter, designed by Dr. Baker, was administered to the students. After completing the instrument, students were classified into one of four dominant leadership profiles. Students also completed the Leadership Competency Assessment Instrument to determine entering competencies. In addition to heavy reading assignments in all of their courses, students had to prepare for presentations of simulations and case studies. As a final examination for the Block, students completed a paper in which they discussed leadership competency gains through the 16-semester-hour Block experience (Baker, 2012).

The most demanding aspect of a Blocker's first semester was learning to write effectively. Students would write a weekly feedback report, in which they would document their learning and evaluate classroom presentations. Feedback reports were read by each of the professors and were always marked up with grammatical corrections, criticisms, praise, and suggestions. Many of the comments were supportive, and several challenged the students to think more critically or to express themselves more clearly.

Some guest speakers were popular with the students, while others were criticized by the students in feedback reports in one way or another. Dr. Roueche would remind the students that each speaker brought expertise to the Block and that the students could learn from all of them. Criticisms had to be backed up with theory to support observations. Terry Calaway, a 1998 graduate of the program, said, "We [had] an opportunity on an almost daily basis to meet with some of the best people in the world on community college issues" (quoted in Manzo, 1996). Dr. Roueche and the other professors wanted to expose the students to chief executive officers who had differing leadership styles and values and served in many different cultures.

Blockers were expected to host the guest speakers—that meant providing transportation, introducing them in the class, and having dinner with them. George Baker (2012) notes that students attended at least one dinner per week to honor a visiting president or chancellor. The dinners provided informal time with the visiting leaders, enabling the students to get to know them personally.

The CCLP students were required to take additional coursework in subsequent semesters, including data analysis and research design. A unique aspect of the program was a required, nine-semester-hour internship, along with a three-semester-hour reading course with an assigned mentor. The internship required that students "shadow" a president or other top-level administrator on the senior leadership team of a college. Students were also required to work on projects with each member of the leadership team. Students taking the internship course were required to write weekly reports on their experiences, which were read and graded by their mentors. (Chapter 9 in this book describes the internship program.)

Students invited professors to serve on dissertation committees, so the faculty had heavy loads of student dissertation work to supervise, as either chairs or committee members. Once students began dissertation research and writing, they could take three, six, or nine semester hours per term until they had completed and successfully defended their dissertations.

PROGRAM GROWTH AND DIVERSIFICATION

In the early years of the CCLP at UT, the program lacked diversity in both its faculty and students. Until Dr. Roueche arrived in 1971, only one woman and one Hispanic male had graduated from the program. No African Americans had been students in the program. Over the next several decades, the program dramatically increased the number of female and minority students, with the strong support of the university presidents (Roueche, April 29, 2018).

In partnership with Dr. Terry O'Banion, who was president and CEO of the League for Innovation in the Community College, Dr. Roueche began concentrating on building the field of diverse candidates. Dr. Roueche faced opposition at first at the university, as some colleagues cautioned him that he would ruin the program by bringing in women and minorities. The faculty believed that women were not serious about their studies (Roueche, April 29, 2018). However, Dr. Roueche convinced skeptics that diversifying the program would make it a pacesetter and that traditional criteria for program admission were not necessarily appropriate measures of student success.

Before affirmative action was being promoted, the CCLP sought out and accepted women and persons of color—black and brown—to enter the program. The concepts of commitment, generosity, counsel, appreciation, and connectivity were intertwined into the student experience. In the decades of the '70s and '80s, while students of color still faced institutional obstacles, their success rate in the CCLP was 100% (Valverde, 2018).

By 1981, the CCLP cohort majority was female; in 1996, the cohort was predominantly made up of students of color (CCLP Alumni Directory, 2012). If anything, the growing diversity of the program created a richness, as students learned from each other. Between 1987 and 2007, 60% of the students were women or students of color (Manzo, 2007). Dr. Roueche made it a point to highlight female graduates and graduates of color in national publications (Roueche, April 29, 2018). The program gained a reputation for accepting and graduating a diverse group of students. Many of them would assume significant leadership roles in community colleges and national and state associations.

The Alumni

In order to describe the program accurately, I e-mailed a survey to the CCLP alumni. Because many of the graduates have retired or moved, obtaining current contact information was a challenge. I sent e-mail messages to the last-known e-mail addresses listed in the UT CCLP Alumni Directory published in 2012. I asked classmates to contact other alumni they knew and encourage them to complete the survey. I also posted the request on the CCLP Alumni Facebook page. I received 48 responses.

The respondents felt strongly (9.54 average on a 10-point scale) that their experience in the UT CCLP was instrumental in their career advancement. They entered the program as faculty members, counselors, directors, coordinators, division chairs, associate deans, assistant deans, deans, and vice presidents. After completing the program,

- 21 respondents (44%) became presidents,
- 3 became chancellors after entering the program as graduate students or assistants,
- 1 tutorial supervisor became dean,
- 1 program director became vice president,
- 1 graduate student became dean,
- 1 adjunct faculty member became program manager,
- 1 program director became department chair,
- 1 faculty member became department chair,
- 1 foundation director became dean,
- 1 faculty member became provost,
- 1 faculty member became dean,
- 1 faculty member became vice president of a regional accrediting agency,
- 1 financial aid director became associate vice chancellor,
- 1 faculty member became chief of a state agency,
- 1 business manager became executive vice president,
- 1 director of institutional advancement became executive director and CEO,
- 1 department chair became director of an advanced technological education center,
- 2 faculty members became executive directors,

- 1 development officer became senior vice president,
- 1 assistant became executive director,
- 1 executive director became associate vice president,
- 1 college trustee became executive vice president,
- 1 department chair became president; and
- 1 Navy retiree became a vice president.

In addition,

- 2 UT CCLP graduates became presidents and CEOs for the AACC,
- 2 became presidents and CEOs for the League for Innovation in the Community College,
- 4 became executive directors for NISOD,
- 2 became executive directors for the Center for Community College Student Engagement, and
- 1 became secretary of education for the state of Virginia and later president and CEO of the Commission on Colleges for the Southern Association of Colleges and Schools.

The respondents considered Dr. Roueche to be a mentor to them (8.6/10 average), with many contacting him to seek career advice (5/10 average). Nearly all of the respondents have mentored other leaders, and most had recommended the UT CCLP to others. A few of the respondents are published authors who have themselves contributed to the understanding of community college issues.

A Distinctive Program

The uniqueness of the CCLP was that it combined rigor and support. The faculty challenged the students, but they also cared for them and pushed them to succeed. Their goal was to prepare all students to be successful and courageous leaders who could take risks and inspire those around them to make a positive difference for the institutions and students they served. Every aspect of community college leadership was covered in the curriculum.

According to Dr. Leonard Valverde, former chair of the Department of Higher Education at UT, the program features were, in many ways, a reflection of John Roueche's beliefs and values (Valverde, 2018). Once students were accepted into the program, the commitment to make them successful lasted even after graduation, as success was defined in practice as well as in the Block. Connectivity meant one was in the field learning about the current and changing conditions and bringing in leaders from the field to engage with students, which provided multiple benefits.

The cohort concept was powerful because it required people from different backgrounds to get to know each other firsthand and form lasting connections. Dr. Valverde notes that Dr. Roueche kept in touch with alumni to provide counsel about their future moves. Further, by building a high-quality program, he was able to capture external resources to support the program activities, expand and enhance its operation, and add value for students (Valverde, 2018).

Program requirements that the alumni found most memorable include the cohort structure, interactions with visiting scholars and leaders, visits to colleges, and written weekly feedback reports. The cohort itself was a learning community, and most Blocks developed strong and lasting friendships.

Each cohort was responsible for organizing its own Block governance that included assigning responsibility for transporting and introducing guest presenters, purchasing and delivering refreshments, and organizing social events. The faculty expected the students to plan and administer many of the details of the program. The program encouraged a spirit of collaboration rather than competition among the students.

Nearly every week, the Block hosted guest presenters that included the most respected leaders and scholars in the community college movement. The guest presenters were diverse in every respect. The alumni commented that they appreciated seeing successful leaders and scholars who looked like them. The presenters were different in other respects—some were extroverts, while others were introverts. Some made organized presentations, while others were storytellers. Students discovered that there are many types of leaders and learned that it was important for the leader to match the culture of the community served by the college.

The alumni identified the college visits as a highlight of the program. Teams of students were assigned to visit specific colleges and submit written reports analyzing the colleges' strengths and issues. In many ways, these visits were much like mini-accreditation visits, as students interviewed college leaders, faculty, and staff and reviewed college documents. The student teams then worked together to prepare reports of the visits for the faculty. Like the weekly feedback reports, the entire CCLP faculty read the visitation reports.

CCLP students were required to complete some courses outside of the program, including classes in research, data analysis, and organizational behavior. Also, students must pass qualifying examinations to advance to candidacy for their doctorates. The collaborative relationships that were developed in the Block carried over to these courses, as students helped each other to understand the assignments and prepare for the qualifying examinations.

Student and Graduate Support

George Baker (2012) notes that John Roueche began his tenure at UT with a pot of $200 or so, but he worked hard to squirrel away enough scholarship money to provide each needy student with the resources to complete the program. The alumni of the program have many stories about how Dr. Roueche helped them to overcome financial or personal challenges. The program is demanding, but the faculty, led by Dr. Roueche, were supportive and encouraging.

Dr. Walter Bumphus (a CCLP alumnus, former CCLP faculty member, and president and CEO of the AACC) said the Texas CCLP was "probably the most rigorous program anywhere. But the expectation is that you are going to go through the program and do well. The professors don't take pride in how many people they flunk out; they take pride in how many people they help to succeed" (quoted in Manzo, 2007).

Some of the students needed help improving their writing skills and were referred to the University Learning Center, where tutors were available to assist them (Roueche, April 29, 2018). Of course, the faculty provided plenty of feedback on the weekly reports and papers. The professors all read everything, and they were in class as students made presentations. Students who entered the program not having written much in their prior educational or work experiences or with little oral presentation proficiency soon developed strong writing and speaking abilities.

Support from the faculty often extended beyond the classroom. One of the students told how Dr. Roueche helped him to transition from a career in the Navy to academic life, even helping him and his wife to find housing in Austin. Another student who was a single mother told how John and Suanne Roueche would pick up her daughter at school and look after her while students were traveling to complete assignments to visit colleges. Many students talked about how John and Suanne Roueche opened their home to students.

Myrna Villanueva, a student in the Block of 1995–1996, said she was concerned about the financial challenges of leaving her position at Cuyahoga Community College in Ohio to study in Texas. She told Dr. Roueche, "I would really like to eat when I get there." Dr. Roueche's reply was, "If you get here, we will take care of you" (Manzo, 1996).

Dr. Don Rippey would tell students at the first class meeting that they were now and forever connected. That connection extended from one Block to the others and between faculty and students. In particular, Dr. Roueche would often check in on graduates. He had a unique ability to guide people through decisions. He always provided words of encouragement and support. Discussions were warm, meaningful, and educational. Belle Wheelan, a CCLP alumna and president and CEO of the Southern Association of Colleges and Schools Commission on Colleges, said that her best experiences with Dr. Roueche came after the program, when he became a mentor and friend: "He was always open and honest, even when you didn't want to hear the advice" (Wheelan, February 18, 2018).

Another CCLP alumna and college president said that Dr. Roueche was much more than a teacher; he was a friend during difficult times. While traveling with Dr. Roueche, she told him that she had just found out that her husband of 27 years had been diagnosed with terminal cancer. Dr. Roueche comforted her and helped her to develop a communication plan for her faculty and board of trustees.

The Faculty

Dr. Roueche recruited a strong team of faculty members to join him in the CCLP. Dr. Donald Rippey (former director of Roswell Community College in New Mexico, former president of Columbia Basin College in Washington, and former president of El Centro College in Texas) joined the CCLP faculty in 1974 and served until his retirement in 1994. Dr. Rippey took leave from the program to serve as interim president of the University of Texas of the Permian Basin in 1982–1983. Dr. Roueche's wife and partner, Dr. Suanne Davis Roueche, served in Dr. Rippey's place as a faculty member for the Block of 1982.

Dr. George A. Baker III joined the CCLP faculty in 1978 after a distinguished career in the Marine Corps. Dr. Baker first met Dr. Roueche when he was leading the CCLP at Duke University. Dr. Baker discovered that he and Dr. Roueche had similar upbringings, and both had a burning desire to be somebody and take advantage of every opportunity to prove their worth through effort and performance (Baker, 2012).

After coming to Texas, Dr. Roueche recruited Dr. Baker in 1978 to join him to supervise a new Kellogg Foundation–funded initiative, which would become NISOD, and teach in the program. Dr. Baker taught in the program until 1992, when he left to assume the Joseph D. Moore endowed chair in community college leadership at North Carolina State University. Dr. Baker also served as the director of the National Institute for Leadership and Institutional Effectiveness, a consortium of colleges and universities that promotes institutional effectiveness and continuous quality improvement.

When Leonard Valverde joined the faculty in the Department of Educational Administration, he was the one and only person of color in the department of all white males and no women. Additionally, he was the youngest and sole assistant professor among all of the tenured and full professors. His specializations were instructional programs, student support (particularly for students of color), and organizational elements. Later, he became the department chairman and tried to incorporate CCLP elements into the other department degree programs (Valverde, 2018).

Dr. William Moore joined the CCLP faculty in 1995 and served as A. M. Aiken Regents Chair in junior and community college leadership until his death in 2006. Prior to coming to UT, Dr. Moore served on the faculty at the Ohio State University and was president of Seattle Community College.

Dr. Donald Phelps joined the CCLP faculty in 1994 and served as the W. K. Kellogg Regents Chair in community college leadership until his death in 2003. Prior to joining the CCLP faculty, Dr. Phelps served as president of Seattle Central Community College, chancellor of the Seattle Community College District, and chancellor of the Los Angeles Community College District.

William (Bill) E. Lasher joined the Department of Educational Administration at UT in 1988 when he became associate dean of the College of Education. He taught originally in the higher education program rather than the CCLP. Starting in the mid-1990s, he was invited to lecture in the CCLP on higher education budgeting and finance. In the mid-2000s, an external evaluation committee recommended that the higher education program and the CCLP should work more closely together. Dr. Roueche then invited Bill to join the CCLP faculty and help with the Block.

Bill said that he saw all the CCLP players at the time in action. He said that, because of John Roueche; the leaders that he brought in to speak to the

Blockers; and the major contributions of Dr. Suanne Roueche, Dr. Don Phelps, Dr. Bill Moore, and later Dr. Walter Bumphus, the students were provided with an outstanding doctoral education. In Bill's words, the students "became part of one of the most important professional networks I know" (Lasher, 2018).

Dr. Walter G. Bumphus joined the CCLP faculty in 2007 and served as the A. M. Aiken Regents Chair in junior and community college leadership and department chair until 2011, when he became president and CEO of the AACC in Washington, DC. Dr. Bumphus is a graduate of the CCLP and served as president of Brookhaven College in Texas, chancellor of Baton Rouge Community College in Louisiana, and president of the Louisiana Community and Technical College System before joining the CCLP faculty.

Other scholars and leaders who taught courses in the CCLP include

- Dr. Suanne D. Roueche
- Dr. Kay McClenney
- Dr. Byron McClenney
- Dr. Martha Ellis
- Dr. Coral M. Noonan-Terry
- Dr. Margaretta Mathis
- Dr. Manuel Justiz
- Dr. Vincent J. Gregory
- Dr. Terry O'Banion
- Dr. Barbara Mink
- Wilhelmina Delco
- Amado Pena

Drs. Kay and Byron McClenney, Mathis, and Noonan-Terry are graduates of the CCLP.

JOHN ROUECHE, THE MAN

Valverde (2018) declares, "As a person, John has many highly desirable character attributes, more than most people." Roueche's lasting attributes, as noted by Dr. Leonard Valverde, are commitment, generosity, counsel, appreciation, and connectivity. Dr. Valverde (2018) notes that John provided support to both faculty and students, allowing them to meet their goals and obligations: "John lends assistance without being asked and always gives more than required. He gives wise advice and analysis of difficult problems. He recognizes past efforts and lets others know of your contribution. He extends himself beyond his surroundings and bridges gaps and separations."

Many of Dr. Roueche's colleagues, friends, and former students say his professional achievements are topped only by his humanity and humility. Jerry Sue Thornton, president emerita of Cuyahoga Community College in Cleveland, Ohio, and a CCLP alumna, describes Dr. Roueche as always being "willing to go above and beyond the normal work of a professor to help his students. . . . And, you never graduate. You continue to hear from him" (Smith, May 22, 2012). Dr. Terry O'Banion describes John Roueche as the "last renaissance man in the community college field. We will never see his likes again. In the 110-year history of community colleges, no one has come close to equaling the record he has established. And I can't imagine anyone in the next 110 years reaching that" (Smith, May 22, 2012).

Chapter Seven

Lessons in Leadership in Two Acts

Walter G. Bumphus

If honors were currency, John E. Roueche might arguably be the wealthiest man in higher education. Over a career of almost six decades, this educator, author, innovator, and entrepreneur has been lauded by entities as diverse as the Council of Universities and Colleges and the Texas Navy (yes, there really is one). It is, however, what he has *contributed* rather than what he has *received* for which community colleges and academia writ large will be forever indebted to this legend of a man.

During a 35-year relationship, I have been privileged to observe and learn from John as a teacher, mentor, colleague, and friend. My appreciation of his contributions was substantially deepened when I assumed the current role as CEO of the American Association of Community Colleges (AACC). Interacting with more than 1,100 disparate institutions provided me the opportunity to gauge John's impact more broadly. This chapter characterizes—from a personal and national perspective—key areas where John has had a lasting impact. It is a daunting and humbling experience.

CCLP CLASS OF 1983: ACT 1

Like many Community College Leadership Program (CCLP) colleagues, I applied to the University of Texas at Austin (UT) program after serving progressive, administrative roles at community colleges in Arkansas and Maryland and at Murray State University in Kentucky. The UT program had an impressive track record for turning out successful graduates who quickly moved into higher administrative positions, including college presidencies. A long-term friend, Dr. Jerry Sue Thornton (then a dean at Triton College), had applied to the program and was convinced it was the right place and the right time in both of our careers. To say it was one of the most fortunate decisions in my career would be an understatement.

From day 1 as members of the class of 1983, students felt surrounded by greatness. Not only was John a legend in his own time, but he had also recruited proven administrators: Dr. Donald T. Rippey, founding president of El Centro College, and Dr. George A. Baker, former vice president at Greenville Technical College and later endowed chair at North Carolina State University.

Because of John's prowess at generating outside resources, most, if not all, CCLP candidates were provided fellowships to allay potentially distracting concerns about tuition costs. For someone attending UT Austin on a sabbatical from Howard Community College with limited income to support a wife and four children, receiving both a fellowship and a scholarship was a tremendous asset.

Together, John and the faculty attracted a virtual who's who of contemporary community college leaders as guest presenters. These were CEO superstars who had literally built community college systems from the ground up:

- Dr. Tom Barton Jr., charismatic first president of Greenville Technical College;
- Dr. Bill Priest, the visionary driver in forging the expansive Dallas County Community College District (ultimately the largest undergraduate institution in Texas);
- Dr. Paul Elsner, a friendly competitor with Dr. Priest as head of Arizona's Maricopa Community College District and one of the most original thinkers;
- Dr. Les Koltai, chancellor of the Los Angeles Community College District during its dramatic growth period;
- Dr. Bob McCabe, head of Miami-Dade Community College with an outstanding reputation for successfully serving the most diverse student body in the nation; and
- Dr. Edmund J. Gleazer Jr., head of the AACC (then AAJC).[1]

Broadening their real-world learning experience, CCLP students heard from those outside higher education, including representatives of major foundations, such as W. K. Kellogg and Sid W. Richardson, and a series of dynamic business leaders. The list goes on and on. All were guest presenters who enriched a rigorous and strategically focused combination of theory and practice. The CCLP students had a chance to hear about and observe firsthand what great leaders thought, did, and dreamed about for the future.

The program John and his colleagues had assembled was unique for its time and powerful in its impact, providing a model that other universities would study and attempt to emulate. Guest lecturers, in their variety, reflected the community college itself—large systems, single-campus colleges, rural, and urban. Presenters with specialized knowledge and expertise—from finance to workforce training to effective public speaking—were tapped. Best practices, many of which were identified through John's prolific research and writing, were analyzed and often incorporated.

Particular emphasis was given to the essential *leadership roles*—visionary, task giver, motivator, figurehead, and liaison—as well as *informational* and *decisional roles*. The basic study guide provided to each class or "block" underscores a fundamental tenet of the program: "Leaders become leaders by being leaders" (The University of Texas at Austin, 2009).

Dr. Kay McClenney (class of 1981–1982), who would go on to lead the Community College Survey of Student Engagement (CCSSE) and play a principal role in countless other initiatives that have helped to transform community colleges, captures the impact of the shared CCLP experience:

> Participation in the CCLP was literally life-changing, in the arena of professional development and career trajectory. The combination of connection to a major national network of community college leaders, exploration of contemporary issues confronting community colleges, and development of friendships that lasted a lifetime added up to an education both lasting and meaningful. (K. McClenney, August 21, 2018)

McClenney also stresses the supportive and engaging value of the cohort approach:

> Two things made the CCLP experience exceptional. One was the cohort experience—a diverse group of people coming together and learning to trust one another to perform and produce collaboratively in a high-expectations environment (this bears strong resemblance to work in a college, or it should). Second was the combination of theory and research with almost daily interaction with colleges through (on-site) college visits, (authoritative) visiting lecturers, and on-the-ground issues via internships. (K. McClenney, August 21, 2018)

The program's outcomes—more than 600 community college leaders (including 200 college presidents) as well as CEOs of key national organizations representing community colleges—underscores the genius of its design. Dr. Sherry Zylka, a member of the last CCLP class to graduate before John's retirement in 2012 and a recently named president at Kentucky's Big Sandy Community and Technical College, echoes the value of the cohort experience:

> [During] all my previous higher education experiences I commuted to and from colleges, so I never got to experience being part of a cohesive team that looked out for each other and were supportive in ways I hadn't imagined. While our block was small compared to previous groups [four candidates], there was such a wealth of knowledge among [our group] that I still contact them and bounce ideas off them—that includes Dr. Roueche, who is an icon in and of himself. (Zylka, 2018)

By the time they completed the program, doctoral candidates were steeped in community college history and values, grounded in day-to-day realities, and well prepared for the next steps in their professional journeys. Equally important, they had forged bonds that would last a lifetime and joined a community of leaders from whom they would draw support, with whom they shared knowledge, and (on many occasions) with whom they commiserated about the vicissitudes of college administration.

As John so frequently stressed, no graduate ever really "left" the CCLP. Instead, the program provided a learning foundation that buoyed success and informed future decision-making. Together, students discovered an inherent truth, which also became part of the CCLP lore: Becoming a community college president is not for the faint of heart.

CCLP: ACT 2

In 2007, a rare "second act" at UT began for me, an experience that brought what might have been the greatest career challenge. It also presented an extraordinary opportunity: the chance to work closely with John Roueche and other outstanding CCLP faculty in a new role as a professor, A. M. Aikin Regents Chair in junior and community college leadership, and chair of the Department of Educational Administration. UT's was the only graduate program in the nation with three endowed faculty positions—the Aikin's Regents Chair, the Sid W. Richardson Regents Chair, and the League for Innovation Professorship.

My solid track record as an administrator led to the appointment of the UT chair position:

- president of Brookhaven College (1991–1997),
- chancellor of Baton Rouge Community College in Louisiana (2000–2001), and
- president of the Louisiana Community and Technical College System (LCTCS) (2001–2007).

The presidency at LCTCS was during the Hurricane Katrina devastation, a "trial by water" that destroyed major portions of the 10-college, 50-campus system and severely tested the mettle of its leaders.

Becoming a full tenured professor with an endowed chair at the flagship university in a state as large and proud as Texas, however, called for an entirely different skill set. It was seasoned by a crash course in academic politics. With John as both a model and a mentor, lessons in leadership that he had honed in building the CCLP to be the premier leadership development program in the country were quickly assimilated. Technically, John's "shop" reported to me as department chair, but the working relationship was collegial, respectful, and enormously effective. In Texas parlance, I was jokingly referred to as John's "sidekick."

Many of the most valuable lessons emanated from knowledge absorbed two decades earlier as CCLP doctoral candidates:

- the value of collaboration and partnerships,
- innovation predicated on entrepreneurship,
- open and constant communication, and
- the importance of setting high but realistic expectations.

All this was leavened by the ability to accept occasional setbacks or obstacles with grace and, if possible, good humor.

Collaboration and partnership building were as natural to John Roueche as Texas sunshine. For years he had enjoyed a robust partnership with Dr. Terry O'Banion, former president of the League for Innovation in the Community College. Specifics of that partnership are detailed in the introduction of this book. Suffice it to say, the two collaborated on multiple successful grants, bartered services and favors, and shared with Suanne Roueche's and

my roles as senior CCLP faculty. Within the university, John modeled outreach to other departments for mutual benefits, a process rare in academic
settings, where guarded self-interest is more common. It was described as
making 2 plus 2 equal 5.

Entrepreneurial thinking brought both visibility and resources to the
CCLP and the department. As the father of the National Institute for Staff
and Organizational Development (NISOD) and with Suanne Roueche, its
passionate and longest-serving director, John took advantage of a clear but
neglected marketing niche to engage community college practitioners.

John attributes much of his success to clear, frequent, and copious communication:

> I would have to say that we could never have accomplished the goals we did
> without the continued support of UT presidents, who understood from the
> beginning the importance of a program like ours. Drs. William H. Cunning-
> ham (1985–92) and Larry R. Faulkner (1998–2006) were always supportive of
> the program, providing support and assistance along the way.

Dr. Stephen Spurr (1971–1974) played a key role in allowing the early expansion of the CCLP's recruitment of women and minority candidates, a
significant factor in the program's growth. The CCLP never took a major
action, received a new grant, or enjoyed a recognition that was not shared
with the university president at the time as well as key administrators and
faculty (Roueche, August 13–September 14, 2018).

During both phases of the association with the CCLP, setting and meeting
high expectations was non-negotiable. As the administrator advocating for
the program within the College of Education and the broader university, my
job responsibilities to ensure respect, cooperation, and engagement were
made significantly easier because of the financial reserves John's operation
provided. Not only was it possible to hire six new faculty for the department,
but administration also was able to underwrite travel to national conferences
and other professional enrichment activities, an advantage that notably
broadened parochial viewpoints and deepened understanding of crucial issues.

Chapter Eight

Diversity and Inclusion in Action

Belle S. Wheelan

The 1960s and 1970s were a time of transition in this country for women and minorities, as recently passed civil rights legislation was moving organizations, including educational institutions, to increase the participation from each group in order to ensure equity in all programs. It was at the height of this movement in 1971 that John E. Roueche (JER) became director of the Community College Leadership Program (CCLP) at the University of Texas at Austin.

During his tenure, there was a concerted effort to include both women and ethnic minorities into each class of students admitted to the program. Dr. Roueche was even recognized by *Diverse: Issues in Higher Education* in 2012 with the Diverse Champion Award for his lifetime achievement in developing minority and female leaders. Several of these students were also awarded the Distinguished Graduate Award by the Department of Education at the university (Roueche, August 13, 2018). I surveyed some of those awardees to find out what brought them to the university and what influence Dr. Roueche had on their personal and professional careers.

Between 1971 and 2012, approximately 150 women and minorities were enrolled in the CCLP. Of those, 34 were named distinguished graduates, an honor earned for outstanding achievement in the community college arena. Through a selection process by faculty in the program and previous award recipients, these graduates became presidents and chancellors of community colleges, as well as chief executive officers of major associations that serve community colleges. I selected 10 of these distinguished graduates to respond to the following questions:

1. Why did you choose to attend the CCLP?
2. What skills did you learn from the program that helped you become a successful community college president or leader?
3. In what way(s) did Dr. Roueche himself assist you in your path to leadership?
4. What do you wish you had been taught in the program?
5. If you could say anything to JER now that you're out of the program, what would it be?

The graduates surveyed and the years in which they earned the distinguished graduate recognition were:

- Dr. Charles A. Green and Dr. Jerry Sue Thornton, 1988
- Dr. Walter Bumphus, Dr. Leonardo de la Garza, and Dr. Tessa Martinez Pollack, 1992
- Dr. Thelma J. White and Dr. Jowava M. Leggett Harrison, 1999
- Dr. Ray L. Belton, 2001
- Dr. Mark Escamilla and Dr. Leslie Anne Navarro, 2009

Of the 10 graduates selected to participate, 7 responded to the survey.

ANALYSIS OF RESPONSES

The overwhelming response to the question "Why did you choose to attend the CCLP?" was the strong reputation of the program. Dr. Roueche's passion for community colleges and his leadership in developing a practice-based program that resulted in successful community college leaders also echoed among the respondents:

> While enrolled in the CCLP, I thoroughly enjoyed the weekly engagement with community college leaders and advocates who shared strategies, interventions, and observations regarding leadership and management. Further, the opportunities afforded the Block to visit colleges and reflect upon the practices of successful institutions, which was of tremendous benefit. Equally important was the requirement that the cohort work as a senior leadership team. In that capacity, I was elected by the Block to serve as president and in doing so was affirmed by many colleagues who had served as administrators in higher education sectors. That interaction was invaluable. (Dr. Belton)

The respondents consistently said that it was the feeling of warmth, welcoming, and acceptance by the CCLP faculty and the success of the graduates as community college leaders that led them to apply. Additionally, in several cases, former graduates who were supervisors or professional colleagues of those surveyed had recommended the program.

As to specific skills learned in the program, respondents mentioned a variety of items, including the improvement of reading and writing skills developed in the Block and a nine-hour course where they were required "to consume (read, write, analyze, and synthesize) great amounts of information." Along those same lines, one respondent referred to the "appreciation and thirst for academic content relating to teaching and learning." This was evident in the exposure to research and data analysis required throughout the CCLP curriculum. Among the many skills I learned from the program were those connected to the appreciation and thirst for academic content relating to teaching and learning, the value of research and data, the importance of a strong network, the necessity of preparation (skill building), and the benefits of mentors familiar with the community college landscape.

Though, at the time, I frequently gnashed my teeth while attempting to eloquently describe what had been learned or read each week, the value of analyzing information and describing ways to implement what had been learned in my daily work life was the successful outcome from the Block's exercise. Not only did it cause everyone to pay attention, but it also forced each person to spend time reflecting on the relevance of the information:

> I improved my reading and my writing skills. Also, from Dr. Haskew I developed a deeper appreciation for the importance of the principles of effective management and accountability regarding organizational resources, all of which I applied throughout my career, especially as a CEO. Another area of growth and learning was the development of collaborative working skills with fellow CCLP Block partners. Finally, and very importantly, from Dr. Roueche I learned and appreciated greatly his emphasis and the importance of "causing learning, with and for students, as well as with and by the faculty." (Dr. de la Garza)

Other nonacademic skills identified include those related to the topics of leadership development, the importance of a strong network, the importance of effective management and accountability of organizational resources, the interpretation and execution of a vision, tenacity for hanging on in difficult times, and the benefits of mentors. Several respondents shared examples of ways they had incorporated these skills in their daily professional lives:

> There were residual skills that I recognized long after I graduated from the CCLP, such as the long-term support of the professors, cohort members, and other alums or graduates of the program. (Dr. Thornton)

> Vision in its interpretation and execution; tenacity for hanging on in difficult times; and the importance of owning a deeply held set of convictions—those areas in which you will not compromise at the expense of students, ethics, or excellence. (Dr. Pollack)

Additionally, the long-term support of faculty within the program, cohort members, and other alumni of the CCLP was mentioned as an asset of the program.

Question 3 specifically asked how Dr. Roueche himself assisted each person in their path to leadership. Responses included the financial support JER secured for students to be able to attend, his penchant for taking each student under his wing and providing feedback, encouragement from JER on both personal and professional issues, and providing letters and phone calls of support when graduates were attempting to secure presidencies:

> Dr. John E. Roueche was my first connection to the program through the president of Triton College, Dr. Brent Knight, who supported my doctoral application to the CCLP and personally introduced me to Dr. John E. Roueche, who assisted me in obtaining a graduate scholarship to attend the program. It was the first time that I did not have to work to pay all of my tuition, and I was provided with a wonderful opportunity to fully engage as a student. He also served as my dissertation chair and guided my research and the completion of the dissertation. After completion of the PhD, Dr. Roueche continued to mentor and support my career with great advice and guidance, as well as serve as a sponsor through letters of recommendation and as a reference. (Dr. Thornton)

> Encouragement, encouragement, encouragement . . . and a connection with the iconic Robert (Bob) McCabe, who hired me into my first presidency at the medical campus of Miami-Dade. (Dr. Pollack)

> His personal interest in me regarding my personal and professional life made for a lasting impact in the ways in which I taught and led. In fact, Dr. Roueche was the first professor to ever invite me to his home on a social/professional basis. Moreover, he was the first professor I had that I felt cared about me

personally as well. My matriculation in the program started what has now become a 35-year relationship of friendship and brotherly love for each other. (Dr. Bumphus)

Each respondent emphasized Dr. Roueche's tough love approach to success as being paramount in their own success:

Through his teachings I have come to understand the challenges and opportunities that command our daily focus as higher education leaders. From a philosophical perspective, the thing that I remember most from him was how he emphasized the imperative to be guided by excellence—nothing less. "Inspect what you expect," he would always suggest as a frame of reference. Also, I am constantly reminded of a discussion we had with respect to decision-making where he frequently stressed of me to always be guided by my personal value system. The latter has served me well in my leadership roles and is an admonition I repeatedly suggest to aspiring administrators. (Dr. Belton)

It was typical of him to patiently listen to students, provide guidance, and then give a sometimes not-so-gentle push into action—something of a Dutch uncle to guide thinking and action when needed:

His infinite patience with me, et al., gave me the assurance that I could keep going back to him with what I thought were "stupid questions." (Dr. Escamilla)

Overwhelmingly, support from JER made a lasting impression on the respondents' own successes and their adoption of a similar approach in their own professional roles as mentors to others years later:

The value of relationships, the importance of hiring the best and brightest, and that talent makes a difference in a successful college and, hence, a college presidency. (Dr. Bumphus)

Recognizing that hindsight is 20-20, the respondents were asked what was not taught in the program that, looking back, they wish had been. While much credit was given to the comprehensiveness of the CCLP, several areas were identified:

- How to deal with board members
- A more futuristic orientation to technology and its impact on higher education

- How to handle intercultural and interracial collaborations for a less splintered democracy
- A greater exposure to understanding the allocation of resources for community colleges from local, state, and federal levels and how to build a budget based on many unknown factors. This would include a more robust discussion on institutional advancement as a fundamental expectation.

While it was acknowledged that the aforementioned topics were discussed somewhere in the curriculum, it would have been extremely beneficial to have had a more thorough understanding and in-depth coverage of those areas. This would have better positioned each of the respondents for their presidencies rather than them having to learn, sometimes detrimentally, on the job.

The last question asked each respondent to tell what they would like to say to Dr. Roueche now that they are out of the program. From each respondent, a big thank-you was mentioned—for caring about the person both personally and professionally, providing a role model to emulate, providing foundational attributes necessary to be a successful administrator, believing in students even when they doubted themselves, the teachings, professional development and mentoring throughout the program and beyond, and the lifelong memories of good and bad times.

It is evident that John E. Roueche practiced what he preached and challenged each of his students to remember that they were working to make a better life for *students* who were real people and not just cogs in a wheel. His personal dedication to the success of each student was reflected in their memories many years after their CCLP experiences. Not one felt that he treated them any differently than any other student, and that was a lesson at least one respondent said would be remembered most: He worked on behalf of students, not male students or female students, not minority students or majority students, but *all students*.

Verna Myers, vice president of inclusion strategy for Netflix said, "Diversity is being invited to the party; inclusion is being asked to dance" (Myers, 2015). Dr. John E. Roueche not only threw the party but also taught each student to dance, insisted that they do so, and rewarded them for doing it well. In the words of one of the respondents, "Hook 'em Horns forever!"

Chapter Nine

Grounded in Reality

Byron N. McClenney

No other doctoral program designed to prepare students for work in the community college field was able to produce more college presidents or chancellors and vice presidents than the Community College Leadership Program (CCLP) at the University of Texas at Austin under the leadership of John Roueche for four decades starting in 1971. One of the reasons for this outcome is clearly the way he exposed the students to what was happening in the field. It was done through the engagement of guest lecturers, most of whom were CEOs, on a regular basis with members of each Block of students in their first year. It was supplemented by college visits by the Block during the first year. Finally, as an integral part of the program, each student was expected to undertake a semester-long internship in a community college.

I received the first Block of students for a college visit in 1971, followed by numerous visits over the years until 2003; I also became a regular guest lecturer over those same years. Guest lecturer assignments continued during my tenure as a staff member of the CCLP starting in 2004. Adding to the engagement was the hosting of interns, starting with the first group of students in the program. Other interns followed over the years in Dallas, San Antonio, and Denver, where I was a community college CEO.

UNDERSTANDING THE GRADUATE STUDENT EXPERIENCE

There is no better way to understand the student experience than to hear one of them reflecting on what it was like to be a part of the program. Belle

Wheelan, the current CEO of the Commission on Colleges of the Southern Association of Colleges and Schools, reflected,

In August 1982, I participated in what was then the largest "Block" of students who had enrolled in the University of Texas at Austin's Community College Leadership Program (CCLP). At the time, I had absolutely *no* administrative experience, having been a psychology professor for eight years. For the first time in a long time, I felt like a fish out of water.

The syllabus was filled with the names of seasoned presidents and vice presidents who were scheduled to visit and share their experiences with us. There was also a set of visits to community colleges nearby that would allow us to go in and evaluate their effectiveness. With each visitor, I quickly learned about dealing with such topics as the politics of higher education (both inside and outside the institution), enrollment management, operational budgets (their development and management), personnel matters, strategic planning, academic program assessment and review, and balancing all of that with the demands of a personal life and family. With each visitor, I questioned my decision to become a community college president.

As the semester progressed, I began to feel more comfortable in my environment. My classmates, all of whom had some administrative experience, made me feel less like a fish out of water by explaining various details of the topics covered. We role-played several situations where I would have to make administrative decisions based on information I had read and stories I had heard from our visitors.

Additionally, the visits we made to three area community colleges provided me an opportunity to see how other colleges performed the various functions described during my classes. Varying strategies used for the myriad of activities across the institutions provided me a "picture" of what made each institution successful. Though each was different in many ways (programs offered, funding formulas, etc.), I was able to experience the results of their work in a very short period of time. Little did I know that the reviews we conducted would be the beginning of my experiences with the accreditation process and a future opportunity for employment. By the end of the first semester, I felt much better, armed and ready to continue my journey to the presidency.

During the second semester, I had the opportunity to participate in an internship designed to actually work in the office of a community college president and witness firsthand the day-to-day life of a president. Given several issues with which my own institution was dealing, I was permitted to serve the internship at my "home" institution. My assignment was primarily with the development of the strategic plan for the institution; however, I witnessed firsthand the care and feeding of the board of trustees, the development of the budget for the next fiscal year, management of several personnel issues, and how to better manage my time in order to get everything done. The experience was invaluable.

Over the years, after I had secured my own presidency, I reflected on many of the lessons I learned in the CCLP. The most important of those was making sure that those who aspired to the presidency know as much as they could about the path they would travel. I continue to stay in touch with many of my colleagues from the program. The real-world experiences provided to me continue to have a lasting impact. As I mentor others who come behind me, I make every attempt to be as open and candid about the journey they are beginning so that they are as successful as they can be. That's what those in the Block did for me, and it has served me well (Wheelan, May 24, 2018).

Belle Wheelan held two presidencies and served as secretary of education in Virginia before assuming her current position. I had the pleasure of working with her during her doctoral internship.

I went into my professional archives to retrieve a presentation I made to the Block in July 1996 to illustrate the type of material often shared during the guest lectures. The presentation raised a number of key questions to help Blockers think about institutional assessment in a community college. Included were the following:

- Do we understand the realities and constraints within which we must work?
- Do we have a way of developing a collective vision of our potential future?
- Do we have a way to identify institutional priorities for a given year?
- Do we properly link plans with the allocation of resources?
- Have we identified our competition and defined our place in the higher education market?
- Do we have processes in place to properly inform and involve constituent groups in planning and budgeting?
- Do we have a way to learn from assessment of outcomes and apply the understandings to alter practices and processes?
- Does our budget implement the important values?

The hope was that the ensuing discussion would help the students prepare for productive college visits during their first year in the program.

My archives further yielded an actual report, corrected by Professor Roueche, on a Block 52 visit to the Community College of Denver (CCD) in November 1996. The report describes the service region of the college, along with the demographics of the area. It describes the leadership style of the CEO and provides perceptions drawn from an interview with the executive staff, along with conclusions about the campus climate. The role of faculty and the rich offerings in professional development led to the description of a process focused on faculty pay for performance that had been developed. The report describes the wide range of student support services, along with financial aid available to incoming students. The report discusses strategic planning and resource allocation processes and links these to how the institution decided on the strategic priorities for the next academic year.

Marginal notes from Roueche raised questions about the group's conclusions and indicated instances when they might have requested materials to take away from the visit. He also reinforced the points where the group reached appropriate conclusions or where they displayed particular insight into a problem.

Another presentation to the Block in November 1998 clearly reflected a shift in the field during the period since the 1996 presentation. A growing emphasis on accountability and institutional effectiveness, along with a movement to focus on learning, was observable around the country. "Potential Outcomes of Systematic Effectiveness Efforts" included an effort to push students to think about institutional change. They were asked to consider the following:

- Clarity about vision and goals
- Work aligned around vision and goals
- Communication across institutional boundaries and with "customers"
- Processes that continuously improve
- Information systems to tell everyone how we're doing
- Incentives to encourage mission-related outcomes
- Value of individual learning and organizational learning
- Benchmarking or best practices to inform future decisions

I presented outcomes from the CCD to illustrate change.

A LATER LOOK AT STUDENT REFLECTIONS

A later look at the reflections of another student showed the consistency of the impact of Roueche's efforts to keep students grounded in reality. Whereas the Wheelan piece comes from the early '80s, Cindy Miles wrote about her experience after the first half of the '90s. Miles, chancellor of the Gross-mont-Cuyamaca District in California, reflected,

> Find a partner to room with for our first site visit—we'll leave 7:30 Thursday morning and return Friday night. Your visitation report is due Monday morning. Here's the sign-up sheet. My head exploded. This was day one of the "Block," and all 18 of us strained nervously in our dress-for-success suits to quickly find roommates. Swiftly surveying the U-shaped table that would be the hub of our learning environment for the next two years, I counted an odd number of women and confirmed I was the only one not sitting next to another woman. Chip and Luke, on either side of me, confirmed their partnership as my anxiety went up. My rescue came with a gentle tap on my shoulder and the kindest voice I'd ever heard said, "Would you like to room with us? We noticed you didn't have a partner." I looked up into Stella's bright face as she gestured back to Leann, who nodded and smiled welcomingly. Little did I know that I had just passed my first Block test and met my dearest friends for life.
>
> Examining the CCLP experience 24 years later, it's tempting to view it as a well-constructed rite of passage, which transformed us in ways far beyond academics and research. We learned abundantly, and most of us became decent scholars, but our most profound lessons were in the social-emotional domain, cemented by intensive, experiential learning. Naturally, grad school invokes challenge and change. But the Block took its initiates through cultural anthropology's classic stages of Separation, Transition, and Incorporation, reflective of tribal initiations and military boot camp—some have even called it a cult. Call it what you may; it unquestionably changed many of our lives. And it worked. The CCLP has an unparalleled record for preparing women and minorities for national leadership positions.
>
> **Separation.** The CCLP required full-time residential attendance for the first year, and we came from across the country, leaving jobs, families, friends, and all that was familiar behind. The Block immersed us in a simulated college leadership world to prep us for the "real thing": daily classes from 8:00 a.m. (sharp!) to noon, mandatory career dress (no shorts and flip-flops, despite sweltering Austin weather), afternoons for other required courses and library work, and evenings bursting with reading and writing (weekly feedback reports on top of research papers), plus a hefty schedule of work groups, presentation prep (notes not allowed), management teams, site visit travel, and formal social events.
>
> **Transition.** We were given multiple, abrupt challenges—all high stakes and public—and we knew our success depended on the outcomes of the group. We were told, "Organize yourself to meet the objectives.

Form teams, determine your roles, pick your leaders, build your budget, collect your funds, and build your timeline and actions. You've got 10 days to complete your master plan." Having trouble with a team member who doesn't carry his/her weight or does inadequate work? "Figure it out. But your grade depends on them." Under constant pressure and forced to deal with difficult personalities and seemingly untenable situations, we had to confront our unconscious biases, insecurities, and flaws. We slogged through identity-testing swamps of our personal and collective differences to learn from one another, sharpen our skills, work out our disputes, and strive to forge a better collective.

Incorporation. Hands-on learning was the secret sauce. We sailed forward, and our ideas and ideals were sharpened by a stream of diverse, luminary college leaders as guest lecturers. Their insider truth telling shed light on the good, bad, and ugly of these jobs. They were our role models, and their inspiration and solace have held up over the years. ("Leadership and management require different skills." "Change is stressful and threatening and will be resisted." "All rocks are not meant to be turned over!") Many of these leaders became our mentors for high-quality internships, colleagues, and friends. Initiation into the CCLP network of graduates provided access to a powerful national web of professionals to tap into for advice, resources, and intel— invaluable leadership tools.

Clearly, the Block experience separated us from our previous place in the community, led us through a luminal stage of self-discovery, and then reincorporated us into a new world with new identities. We all were changed by the CCLP, and even if it was a cult, this cult was about breaking boundaries, building communities, and making our colleges work better for students. No doubt this rite of passage changed us for the better and for good! (Miles, 2018)

Miles did her internship at the CCD, where she was productively involved in the development of a policy on faculty pay for performance, which ultimately led to a comprehensive dissertation.

BECOMING AUTHORS

It was not unusual for the students to parlay an internship experience into the role of coauthor with John and Suanne Roueche. One example was the internship of Lynn Taber at the CCD, where she became heavily involved in the Denver Network. The Network, funded under the Urban Partnership Program of the Ford Foundation, was a consortium of colleges, K–12 systems, and community leaders coming together to work on building a college-going culture. She participated in work groups and Network gatherings and documented the way the group dealt with many issues. Due to her leadership role at the CCD, she was able to contribute significantly to the problem-solving agenda.

She then moved easily into the role of coauthor of *The Company We Keep: Collaboration in the Community College* (1995). It was a book of case studies from 15 community colleges around the country: "The colleges included here were selected because they have given the issue of community partnerships significant reflection and, subsequently, great commitment" (Roueche, Taber, and Roueche, 1995, 35). Taber's work as an intern at the CCD contributed to the chapter describing the CCD story (Roueche, Taber, and Roueche 1995, 81–92).

Another example is the experience of Mike Flores, who also did his internship at the CCD. He took a special interest in developmental education, at least in part because of the intense work being done to increase success rates and close achievement gaps at the CCD. He was able to see the breakthrough that came with finding that students starting in developmental education were just as likely to graduate and transfer successfully as students requiring no remediation.

As a result of his experience and engagement, he joined Byron McClenney to author "Community College of Denver Developmental Education: A Twenty-First Century Social and Economic Imperative," which appears in a 1998 book edited by R. H. McCabe and P. R. Day for the League for Innovation in the Community College. He also influenced the inclusion of the CCD story as one of two success stories in a book by John and Suanne Roueche in 1999. The publication of *High Stakes, High Performance: Making Remedial Education Work* by the American Association of Community Colleges (AACC) signaled the importance of issues around a lack of success in most community colleges trying to improve remediation. His reflections add depth to the earlier thoughts of Belle Wheelan and Cindy Miles:

> I have many fond memories of the time I spent at the University of Texas at Austin pursuing my doctoral degree in educational administration through the Community College Leadership Program (CCLP). I still vividly remember arriving on campus in August 1996 as the youngest student in the cohort—Block 52. Here I was fresh from completing my master's degree while concurrently working in student affairs at a university. Prior to that, I had worked at a community-based TRIO federal program for a couple of years. I had never worked in a community college. Now, I was in a program with 20 other

"Blockers" that had many more years of direct experience and had previously served as either community college faculty, administrators, or even vice presidents before arriving in the sweltering summer heat in Austin, Texas. I felt like a fish out of water those first few days, but that feeling quickly subsided as we spent the next two weeks developing our master plan document, which delineated how we would organize ourselves throughout the 1996–1997 academic year. A team of three to four "Blockers" were assigned to coordinate the logistics for each week, which could involve scheduling and then introducing community college chancellors or presidents to your classmates on campus. Other teams would coordinate site visits to several community colleges out of state, and then the whole Block would prepare a site visit report. The trips and reports were in addition to readings from the Block and other courses we took at the College of Education and the university. Clearly, the CCLP was the ultimate learning community because it provided a praxis between theory and application.

Weeks now turned into semesters, and we were encouraged by Dr. Roueche and our other exemplars to begin thinking about our dissertation topics and our internship placements. Philosophically, I always liked the phrase "community college movement" because it describes how this uniquely American institution was created to provide educational access to under-re-sourced communities and student groups. The national dialogue in the mid-1990s reflected a similar zeal with a focus on increasing success rates and closing achievement gaps among all student groups—from entry into developmental education to progression through college-level coursework and finally graduation. When I read *The Company We Keep*, specifically "Community Colleges as a Nexus for Community," by Byron N. McClenney, I knew that I wanted to spend my CCLP internship at the Community College of Denver (CCD). Here was an institution that still had that missionary zeal to serve and ensure success among all student groups. President McClenney had conducted a landscape analysis upon his arrival at the CCD and saw that few Denver public high school graduates even attended the college. He determined that something had to be done by effectuating a comprehensive plan that included partnerships with area businesses, community organizations, schools, and government. During my spring 1998 internship, I was fortunate to examine and participate at the CCD firsthand. Upon arrival, I was given the opportunity to observe broad engagement in the annual strategic planning process that sets the focus for the institution; I also helped implement the inaugural year of a nationally recognized, NASA-funded science, technology, engineering, and mathematics (STEM) summer camp and examined innovative work on campus with learning communities and scholarship programs. I was fortunate to also contribute to an article on developmental education reflective of work at the CCD.

My CCLP internship at the CCD clearly laid the foundation for my professional work throughout the last 20 years. My tenure as a community college president and soon chancellor builds on the work of Dr. McClenney and Dr. Roueche by ensuring that we preserve the tenets of the community college movement with its focus on ensuring access and success to all student groups. For me, a natural extension has been to infuse the movement with a social equity and justice framework. The focus all began at the University of Texas at Austin Community College Leadership Program (Flores, 2018).

Mike Flores was assuming the role of chancellor of the Alamo Colleges in San Antonio when he wrote this reflection on his CCLP experience.

Eileen Ely was another CCD intern who immersed herself in the student success of the equity agenda at the college. She participated in planning and evaluation activities and collected significant materials and data about student success, which ultimately appeared in a book she coauthored with John and Suanne Roueche. *In Pursuit of Excellence: The Community College of Denver* (2001), published by AACC, focuses on all of the processes leading to breakthrough outcomes like closing achievement gaps in student success: "Institutionally, the college reached a milestone in 1998–99 when more than 50 percent of its graduates and transfers were students of color (in 1985–86 it was 13 percent)" (Roueche, Ely, and Roueche, 2001, 57). Ely went on to become a college president in Washington.

Kay McClenney, in "Ahead of the Curve" (chapter 13 in this book) describes an array of initiatives created within the CCLP focused on student engagement, success, and completion. The Center for Community College Student Engagement (CCCSE), led by Kay McClenney, and Student Success Initiatives, led by Byron McClenney, were created because John Roueche foresaw what was coming in the community college sector. These initiatives became what amounted to a learning lab for CCLP students.

One of those students who was able to engage fully in the opportunities was Margaretta Mathis. She was able to build on her graduate learning experience to become assistant director of Student Success Initiatives with Byron McClenney. Her dissertation was on the transformational experience of the Community College of Baltimore County, which became a case study included in *Making Good on the Promise of the Open Door* (2011), which she coauthored with Byron McClenney for the Association of Community College Trustees (ACCT).

She became senior vice president at National American University (NAU) in the Community College Leadership Program, created by John

Roueche following his retirement from the University of Texas at Austin. Many of the other leaders of the NAU effort were longtime community college CEOs who served as guest lecturers, hosts for site visits, and hosts for internships during the four decades of the CCLP years at the University of Texas at Austin.

These examples of graduate students becoming authors as a result of their CCLP experiences are but a few, many of which could be described from the graduate student experience, grounded in reality, developed by John Roueche.

THE COMMON EXPERIENCE

These comments made by three graduates of the CCLP make clear that students experience a process of self-discovery beginning in the early days of the Block experience. From a "fish out of water" to a seasoned vice president from a community college, they all started by learning how to negotiate a group process, which serves the individual well if he or she learns how to be part of a team. Over time, the foundation is put in place for a long-term network that expands as guest lecturers, site visits, and internships enter the picture. What is experienced by the students fits the definition of a learning community, and experiential learning is at the heart of the Block as students begin to face the full range of community college issues and innovative solutions.

The exposure to a wide variety of leadership styles, along with the insights gained by visiting diverse institutions, provides an opportunity for students to sort out what feels comfortable when contemplating leadership roles in community college administration. While the Block tends to lead to common understandings about community college issues, the students are free to develop the ways they would approach problem-solving when faced with particular situations.

An illustration of Blockers talking with one another can be drawn from an earlier reference to a Block presentation in July 1996. Results of a survey about the presidency, reported in *Educational Record* from the American Council on Education (1996), were shared, and the students identified which of the 12 items they felt were most relevant. By a wide margin, the students identified "rising expectations and diminishing resources" as the most crucial issue facing presidents. They were then able to discuss how they individually might go about addressing the issue. The second-most important item selected by the students was "conflicting expectations of different constituencies," which was followed again by a discussion about how each would handle the challenge. Finally, they identified "white waters of rapid and dramatic change" for further conversation.

None of the other nine survey items rose to a level of importance in the eyes of the students. Items like "it's lonely at the top," "creep of partisan politics and ideology," "ceaselessly scrambling," "trustee activism," and "engaged in continuous selling" came close to the top three items. Their year together obviously had led to some common understandings.

Graduates of the CCLP emerged from the program with common understandings, but they also emerged with a leadership style grounded in reality. The steady diet of guest lecturers, college visits, and then the internships gave them a clear understanding of the significant issues in the field, as well as insight into innovative solutions to the problems.

Graduates also completed the program linked to an extensive network of professionals scattered around the country. They were able to observe the thought leadership provided by John Roueche, Suanne Roueche, and many others involved in the CCLP. More importantly, they understood how they could contribute to the field early in their careers.

Chapter Ten

More Than a Graduate Program

Evelyn N. Waiwaiole

I was sitting at dinner with a childhood friend this summer. She is younger than me, hip, trendy, and a professional photographer. She has shot covers for *Rolling Stone*, *People*, and *Texas Monthly*. While we were visiting, she mentioned that a friend of hers is an "influencer." She used the term as if it was a job title, and not knowing what she meant, I asked. She said it's someone who has 200,000 followers on Instagram and is able to influence the behaviors of those followers. She said it's similar to people who call themselves foodies and post reviews about where to eat (and where not to eat).

INFLUENCER

When John Roueche started his tenure as the director of the Community College Leadership Program (CCLP) at the University of Texas at Austin, social media didn't exist, and the notion of foodies or influencers wasn't on anyone's mind. But when reflecting about someone who has influenced community colleges—by researching and writing about them, by celebrating exemplary faculty and staff, by engaging leaders in data conversations, and by focusing on *all* students succeeding (not just first-time college students but *all*)—there is no doubt that, had Instagram existed, he would have exceeded 200,000 followers. Even without it, there is no question that behaviors, policies, and practices have been influenced because of him.

As the leader of the CCLP, John Roueche's vision and reach far surpassed the graduate program. The CCLP served as the umbrella for many organizations that focused on serving community colleges:

- the National Institute for Staff and Organizational Development (NISOD)
- the Center for Community College Student Engagement (the Center)
- Student Success Initiatives (SSI)

NISOD was started by John and his wife, Suanne Roueche; the other two organizations were started by Kay and Byron McClenney. When asked about having Kay McClenney bring the Center (originally called CCSSE) to the CCLP and Byron McClenney starting SSI at the University of Texas at Austin, John said,

> I do think that, aside from the talent and abilities of both Kay and Byron, it was the presence and active involvement that the CCLP had with the community college world. It was also our focus on "making good on the promise of the open door" that coincided neatly with the intended purpose and goal of the proposed CCSSE initiative. I think our strong and positive national reputation was a big factor as well.
>
> Dr. Russell Mawby, who chaired the W. K. Kellogg Foundation Board, shared with Dean Kennamer [former dean of the College of Education] as he announced the first major Kellogg grant to the CCLP, and that established NISOD. While most foundations look at what is "in the wagon" [the proposal document], he and his Kellogg associates were most interested in the "horses that would be pulling that wagon." He said, "We fund horses." I have always remembered that admonition that it is almost always the "lead horses" that make things happen and get things done. We were so very fortunate for our CCLP horses over those four decades plus. I doubt that any program in higher education ever had as many national leaders on their teams as we did during that time. Just take a look at the American Association of Community Colleges (AACC) National Leadership Awards to document that impact on the national community college movement (Roueche, July 18, 2018).

This chapter looks at each of these three organizations: their histories, missions, and roles in the community college space. The organizations were under the CCLP, an umbrella program that provided outreach, promoted research in community colleges, and encouraged student success.

NATIONAL INSTITUTE OF STAFF AND ORGANIZATIONAL DEVELOPMENT (NISOD)

The Origin of NISOD: The Napkin Story

The first organization under the CCLP umbrella was NISOD. When talking to John Roueche about the genius of NISOD, he always states that it all began on a napkin. Digging a little further, I learned that, just like most things with John, it began because of a relationship. According to John, he; his late wife, Suanne Roueche; and Arlon Elser, senior program officer for the W. K. Kellogg Foundation, were meeting for a casual and informal breakfast—just good friends catching up over an early-morning meal at the AACC annual convention. Elser asked the Roueches if they had ever thought about *disseminating good practices* to community colleges across the country. John remembers he and Suanne smiled and said, "Well, we think we do that. We write books." John recalls Elser sighing and responding with some seriousness: "Yes, but nobody reads them."

After some lively banter, the three turned to drafting the bold concept that became known as NISOD, sketching it out *on a breakfast napkin*. NISOD was born that morning—a membership organization designed to foster the sharing of innovative ideas in community colleges, to disseminate valuable print resources, and to celebrate teaching excellence at an annual conference.

The Mission

When it was created in 1978, NISOD's mission was to focus on serving, engaging, and inspiring by concentrating on quality professional development strategies and programs through relationships, resources, and recognition.

Relationships: Member Colleges

The original goal of NISOD was to offer such extraordinary, high-quality services that the organization would be self-supporting within its first five years. During NISOD's first year, it had a membership base of 51 colleges, the cost of membership was $500, and its first conference attracted 152 participants. NISOD grew exponentially over the years. By 2008–2009, the membership fee was $995, NISOD was serving more than 700 colleges from 44 states and 6 countries, and the annual conference was hosting more than

2,000 participants. By 2012, when John retired from the University of Texas at Austin, more than 750 colleges were members of NISOD, and just over 2,500 people were attending the annual conference.

Under John's leadership, serving member colleges was *job 1* at NISOD. William Law, former president of Tallahassee Community College (Florida) and later St. Petersburg College (Florida), said, "NISOD has transformed our college" (Waiwaiole, 2018). Mary Retterer, former president of Cerro Coso Community College (California) and a former Excellence Award recipient, shared that NISOD supported the highest level of community college teaching and leadership excellence in the nation (Waiwaiole, 2018).

Resources: *Innovation Abstracts, Celebrations,* and the International Conference on Teaching and Leadership Excellence

From its inception, NISOD circulated print resources. The flagship and trademark publication, *Innovation Abstracts*, focuses on weekly teaching tips. It was and still is an executive summary-style publication, written by practitioners for practitioners and distributed to more than 250,000 readers. *Celebrations* is still an occasional paper written by invited authors or abstracted from texts of presentations at NISOD-sponsored events, disseminating some of the best ideas in teaching, learning, and leading from professionals on the cutting edges of successful practices.

However, of all the resources NISOD brings to its members, the hallmark is its International Conference on Teaching and Leadership Excellence, held each May in Austin, Texas. The conference began with 152 participants and was originally housed on the University of Texas at Austin campus in dormitories and classrooms. Originally, colleges used the conference as a team-building experience. Bill Segura, who was the chancellor of Texas State Technical College from 1998 to 2011, brought teams in 15-passenger vans to be housed in dormitories for what he called "Camp NISOD."

When Steve Johnson, president and CEO of Sinclair Community College (Ohio) was asked about attending NISOD, he said,

> NISOD provided a number of important benefits to the faculty and staff of colleges across the nation. And I believe these benefits flowed to the millions of community college students across the nation. First, the convening itself brought together engaged educators from afar and helped them to connect with others who were developing innovations in serving college students. Second, the conference sessions were informative and inspirational. Finally, and likely

the most important, NISOD provided an opportunity for colleges to honor their outstanding faculty. The faculty awards, presented in a ceremony with like others across the nation, reinforced and honored the good work and results [of a] better college education (Johnson, 2018).

When asked about NISOD, another leader, Richard Rhodes, president of Austin Community College District (Texas), responded,

> My favorite conferences over the years have been NISOD conferences, inspired and created by John and Suanne Roueche. There are a number of reasons why they are so memorable. First, they are an authentic celebration of teaching excellence, recognizing the passionate and compassionate work of outstanding faculty at our institutions. Second, the breakout sessions on various topics of student success, teaching, and learning have been invaluable. Third, it is a time of team building and getting to know your faculty on a personal basis. Fourth, I always looked forward to sitting at the feet of my mentor, John Roueche—he inspires me continuously. And fifth, NISOD was always a heck of a lot of fun (Rhodes, 2018).

Recognition: Excellence Awards

NISOD began the Excellence Awards Program in 1989, and under John's leadership, this program celebrated its 20th anniversary in 2009. Each year and even now, NISOD member colleges submit the names of their exemplary faculty, staff, and administrators to receive a NISOD Excellence Award. Throughout the years, Excellence Award recipients have proudly worn their medallions during special ceremonies on their campuses as their colleges celebrate making a difference in students' lives.

Award recipients also submit quotes, describing what their profession means to them. Some of the quotes share what happens in the classroom, while others are inspirational. All of them remind people of past teachers they have had. Here are two examples:

> A former teacher once said to me that teaching was a privilege and a great responsibility, and this has always stuck. Now being a teacher myself, I am fortunate to work with colleagues who have that same philosophy. I firmly believe that great teachers, like great students, thrive in a positive and nurturing environment. We are all students at heart. (2012 recipient)

> For me, "Think, pair, and share" is at the heart of education. I am the facilitator, bridging the opportunity to learn to inspired thinkers of tomorrow; I am the

motivator, transforming individual knowledge into civic responsibilities. I im-
part confidence so that an educated person makes global differences—I am a
teacher. (2013 award recipient's application)

At the closing of the conference, the Excellence Awards video is unveiled.
Once again, this was John's brilliant way of celebrating everyone at the
conference and making the closing session at the conference the largest. In
the video, recipients share touching and humorous stories about their educational journeys, their students, and their successes. For example, one teacher
began his video by describing a lecture he gives about Vietnam. After one of
these lectures, in which he shared his personal Vietnam experiences and
mentioned the names of a few of his fallen comrades, a student approached
him to share that one of the names he mentioned was her uncle. She always
had wondered if anyone remembered him!

NISOD, full of tradition, closed each year during this time with Suanne
Roueche, the director of 15 years, reading a passage from *Jonathan Living-
ston Seagull*. The book, first published in 1970, is a fable about a seagull
trying to learn about life and flight and has a powerful message about the
value of teachers. Conference attendees left inspired, encouraged, and hope-
ful for the new academic year.

COMMUNITY COLLEGE SURVEY OF STUDENT ENGAGEMENT (CCSSE)

Just as NISOD was under the umbrella of the CCLP, in 2001, the CCSSE,
founded by Kay McClenney, also found a home under the leadership of John
Roueche. Funded by the Pew Charitable Trusts and the Lumina Foundation
for Education, the focus of the work was and continues to be student engagement. When Kay McClenney, now senior advisor to the president and CEO
of the AACC, was asked why the CCSSE was housed under the CCLP, she
responded,

> When the leadership at the Pew Charitable Trusts and the Lumina Foundation
> asked me where we should locate the to-be-invented student engagement sur-
> vey for community colleges, I responded immediately and with conviction,
> "the Community College Leadership Program at the University of Texas at
> Austin (UT)." Why? Because UT is a major research university where value is
> placed on quality and rigor of research and building the body of evidence
> about effective educational practices. Because the Community College Lead-

ership Program, through Director John Roueche and other faculty, had a large, committed network of community college presidents across the country who would be immediately available to support and advise in the work. Because doctoral students could contribute to and benefit from the new Center for Community College Student Engagement through internship placements, employment, and dissertations, making use of the research. And because John Roueche was personally and professionally committed to supporting the work and ensuring its positive impact in the field (K. McClenney, 2018).

When the founding chair of the CCSSE National Advisory Board (NAB), Peter Ewell, president emeritus of the National Center for Higher Education Management Systems, was asked about why the CCSSE came to the CCLP, he said,

> With the demonstrated success of the National Survey of Student Engagement (NSSE), the Pew Charitable Trusts was encouraged to support the development of a similar survey designed for administration at two-year colleges. This became the Community College Survey of Student Engagement (CCSSE) under the direction of Kay McClenney at the University of Texas at Austin. An added benefit of this location was the presence of the Community College Leadership Program (CCLP), directed by John Roueche, and the decision was made to house the CCSSE in the CCLP. Several important synergies emerged from this decision. First, the CCSSE provided students and researchers at the CCLP with a relevant and growing data resource through which to undertake studies of community college functioning and effectiveness. Second, graduate students from the CCLP helped staff CCSSE operations, and several later became permanent members of the CCSSE staff. Finally, conferences hosted by the CCLP (NISOD) provided convenient settings around which to plan CCSSE events, such as report releases and board meetings. These connections benefitted the CCSSE in its start-up years and continued to strengthen the survey as its reach broadened and its visibility grew (Ewell, 2018).

The CCSSE, founded on the work of the NSSE (a survey that focuses on four-year colleges and universities), had and continues to have a clear vision: The more actively engaged students are—with college faculty and staff, with other students, and with the subjects they are studying—the more likely they are to persist in their college studies and to achieve at higher levels.

The CCSSE was launched in 2001 with the intention of producing new information about community college quality and performance that would provide value to institutions in their efforts to improve student learning and retention, while also providing policy makers and the public with more appropriate ways to view the quality of undergraduate education.

At the onset, 12 colleges participated in the pilot administration of the CCSSE:

- Butler Community College (Kansas)
- Cascadia College (Washington)
- Central Piedmont Community College (North Carolina)
- Community College of Denver (Colorado)
- Hocking College (Ohio)
- Johnson County Community College (Kansas)
- Kingsborough Community College (New York)
- Kirkwood Community College (Iowa)
- Lone Star College System (Texas)
- Richland College (Texas)
- Schoolcraft College (Michigan)
- Sinclair Community College (Ohio)

Through 2018, the CCSSE had been administered to 954 colleges in all 50 states and beyond, representing more than 6 million student respondents.

The Community College Faculty Survey of Student Engagement (CCFSSE)

Shortly after the CCSSE began, conversations at community colleges about data deepened, and a desire for more tools to guide the conversations grew. The first additional survey was created in 2005, which was the CCFSSE. It was developed in response to demand from the community college field to elicit information from faculty about their perceptions regarding students' educational experiences, their teaching practices, and the ways they spend their professional time—both in and out of the classroom.

Offered as a companion to the CCSSE student survey, the CCFSSE was and continues to be an online survey that invites all faculty teaching CCSSE survey-eligible courses at participating colleges to contribute their frontline perspectives on student engagement. The CCFSSE provides colleges with an effective way to invite faculty into a college-wide conversation about student engagement and success while spurring interest in their CCSSE survey results.

Through 2018, the CCFSSE had been administered to 558 colleges in 47 states and beyond, representing more than 4 million faculty respondents.

The Survey of Entering Student Engagement (SENSE)

Launched in 2007, the SENSE was designed to help community and technical colleges focus on the "on ramp" of the college experience. Grounded in research about what works in retaining and supporting entering students, the SENSE collects and analyzes data about institutional practices and student behaviors in the earliest weeks of college. These data can and do help colleges understand students' crucial early experiences and improve institutional practices that affect student success in the first college year.

To help colleges understand the earliest experiences of their students, the SENSE is administered during the fourth and fifth weeks of the fall academic term to students in courses randomly selected from those most likely to enroll entering students. By 2017, the SENSE had been administered to 457 colleges in 46 states and beyond, representing more than 3 million student respondents.

The CCSSE and the SENSE in Action

One example of a college using data collected from the CCSSE and the SENSE is Zane State College (Ohio). The college has frequently participated in the Center surveys since 2004 and uses the survey data in much of its continuous improvement work, including accreditation. Accredited through the Higher Learning Commission via the Academic Quality Improvement Program (AQIP) pathway, Zane State has used survey data to make comparisons to peer institutions (including the Achieving the Dream consortium as well as other Ohio institutions). The college has also used survey data throughout the AQIP Systems Portfolio, specifically in these categories:

- Helping Students Learn
- Meeting Student and Other Key Stakeholder Needs
- Valuing Employees
- Knowledge Management and Resource Stewardship

For example, in using survey data to support "Category 1: Helping Students Learn," Zane State implemented two projects: "Building and Scaling Learner Analytics" and "Mandatory Advising."

The "Building and Scaling Learner Analytics" project was developed as a pilot for an early-intervention initiative and used specific SENSE items (19e, 20d[2], 20f[2], 20h[2], and 21a–c) and pre-2017 CCSSE items (4h, 4m, 9b–d, 9f, 13a[1], 13b[1], 13d[1], 13e[1], and 13h[1]) as the benchmarks against which to measure progress.

The "Mandatory Advising" project at Zane State initially used insights from a CCSSE Promising Practices special-focus item that is now on the main survey instrument as the impetus for continuous improvement. One such insight reads, "Before the end of my first semester/quarter at this college, an advisor helped me develop an academic plan [a personalized plan with a defined sequence of courses for completing a college certificate or degree and/or for transferring to a four-year college or university]." Combining survey results with data on retention and course evaluations, the college used the subsequent findings as a metric for defining success of the project in support of the AQIP accreditation category "Helping Students Learn."

In the 2011 accreditation review, peer reviewer feedback in the results section of "Helping Students Learn" recognized Zane State as having a strength for its use of CCSSE and SENSE data in assessing improvement efforts.

The Expansion of the Work

As the work of the Center expanded, grants continued to fund new and innovative work. The foundations funding these grants have included

- the Bill and Melinda Gates Foundation;
- the Carnegie Foundation for the Advancement of Teaching;
- the Greater Texas Foundation;
- the Great Lakes Higher Education Guaranty Corporation;
- the Houston Endowment, Inc.;
- the James Irvine Foundation;
- the Kresge Foundation; and
- the Trellis Foundation.

Whether funding allowed Center staff to continue to conduct focus groups, help rural colleges build data capacity, or study high-impact practices, the work grew largely due to the strong reputation of the CCLP and John Roueche.

Because of the growth, the name Community College Survey of Student Engagement, or CCSSE, no longer sufficed. With three surveys and many additional grant-funded projects, the Center had grown far beyond the original survey; therefore, in 2008, the name of the organization officially changed to the Center for Community College Student Engagement (the Center).

Student Voices

Another body of work was also introduced shortly after the launch of the CCSSE. In 2001, the Center received a grant from the MetLife Foundation to conduct focus groups at community colleges. The purpose of the work was and continues to be to better understand the students' college experience. The surveys, which provide quantitative data, are no doubt important, but the focus groups provide additional data to more fully understand the student experience.

Center staff conduct focus groups and interviews at select colleges, gathering the perspectives of students, faculty, student services professionals, and administrators to paint a more complete picture of the student experience. The surveys' rich data help colleges better understand what is happening. Information from the focus groups and interviews can help them begin to figure out why.

The Center continues to conduct and videotape focus groups and use the clips—frequently called "student voices"—to help tell the community college student story. Perhaps the most famous student voice is a young Latino student named James. In the video, James is shown three times over the period of one fall semester. In the first video clip, it's early in the semester, and he is excited to be in college. In the second clip, it's a bit later in the term, and he appears anxious and stressed. By the third clip, it is November, and he says, "School is not for everyone. I guess I'm one of those people it's not for. It is what it is." By the spring semester, he was no longer enrolled in college. When college leaders, faculty, and staff across the country see video clips such as this one, they immediately recognize their own students in James—and they want to help those students persist and succeed.

The Center has a repository of focus group clips on a wide variety of topics, including but not limited to

- registration,
- financial vulnerability,

- orientation,
- faculty,
- race and ethnicity,
- transfers, and
- students asking for help.

Because guided pathways is a topic of interest to many colleges today, a few focus group quotes about advising, career counseling, and transfers follow.

Advising

> Unfortunately, they weren't as much help as I had hoped. I mean, they registered me for the classes, but they didn't really give me a direction that maybe I could go in. They just signed me up for general courses. He didn't talk to me about making a plan; that was a personal choice. He just did what I asked and sent me home. (Student)

> So for a first-time person going to community college, you know that you have X amount of time, but you haven't really studied to find out how much time you're gonna need for your classes, your studies, and your homework. Then you're lost, really, when you go in, and that's what happened to me. I went in, and I knew the approach that I wanted. I knew what I wanted to go after, and so I went after that. But nobody said, "What about your job? What about your home? What about your children? What about the time you need to spend with your wife? What about church?" (Student)

Career Counseling

> I know there are a lot of resources, but some of them—even the good ones— get shoved under the rug. The career success center is just in the corner. I'm super involved on campus, and I still really don't know what it is. I'm just being honest. (Student)

> I'm not too sure if anybody told me about a career plan because I haven't gotten really in touch with the career plans or anything like that." (Student)

Transfers

> The good thing in Florida is that there is a common prerequisite manual that outlines all of the prerequisites for all of the majors offered through the state university system. All of the state colleges have access to that. Students actual-

ly can access that also. Our pathways are aligned with those so that, for example, a business major who needs three semesters of accounting, business calculus, and statistics has those all incorporated into their pathway—and we make sure that any common prerequisites are incorporated. Then most of our students, if they don't stay with us to complete a baccalaureate degree, do end up transferring to one of the public universities in Florida. By making sure those prerequisites are all incorporated, updated, and reviewed annually in case there are any changes, the student in the pathway is ready to go and be admitted as a junior.

We do review those common prerequisite manuals annually. We make sure that our college catalog aligns with our guided pathways so that students have the same message. There's no question about the courses they need to transfer to the university, and we even mark those that are required for your transfer to the university. This is suggested. We're always making sure that the student is well aware of everything they need to go into their junior year and be accepted. (Administrator)

STUDENT SUCCESS INITIATIVES (SSI)

Equipping Leaders: Continuing the Mission

Just as the CCLP was a place to educate, train, and prepare future college leaders, SSI (housed under the CCLP from 2004 to 2015), provided training and consultant outreach to existing community college leaders. The founder, Byron McClenney, led the work from 2003 to 2011. When Byron was asked about this work, he said,

> The creation of Student Success Initiatives fostered a remarkable opportunity for a nexus of relationships to flourish over a decade of operations within the Community College Leadership Program. The focus was clearly on student success with equity, and relationships included numerous national organizations and foundations. Engagement in what was truly a transformative period for community colleges allowed the CCLP to expand its thought leadership in the field (B. McClenney, 2018).

In total, SSI led more than $30 million in philanthropically supported initiatives that targeted the improvement of community college student success. Funders of the work included

- the Lumina Foundation,
- the Greater Texas Foundation,

- the Houston Endowment,
- the Nellie Mae Education Foundation,
- Heinz Endowments,
- College Spark,
- the W. K. Kellogg Foundation,
- the Winthrop Rockefeller Foundation, and
- the Bill and Melinda Gates Foundation.

When asked about the role of philanthropy in the CCLP, former program officer with Houston Endowment (1999–2014) and current vice president for strategic partnerships for the Texas A&M Foundation George Grainger said,

> The Community College Leadership Program at the University of Texas at Austin is rightly recognized for its consequential role in producing some of the nation's most outstanding community college leaders, research productivity, and relentless focus on student success. What is, I think, less well recognized is the influence John Roueche and his happy band of CCLP and UT colleagues had and still have on the massive investments private philanthropy makes to improve the human condition. Simply put, if it were not for John, the unforgettable Suanne, the powerhouse couple Kay and Byron McClenney, and innovators such as Uri Treisman, I am not so sure private philanthropy would be nearly as active in the two-year sector's success agenda as it is today.
>
> Perhaps my own experiences as a program officer at Houston Endowment, a private foundation deeply committed to fostering equitable opportunities for all people in the greater Houston region, can be used to make my point. For decades, Houston Endowment provided grants to colleges and universities in Texas—typically routine but nonetheless useful support for faculty, scholarship endowments, and facilities—and sponsored one of the larger recurring scholarship programs in Texas for local students to attend the universities of their choice. Around the time Houston Endowment began modestly investing some of its resources in projects explicitly focused on producing better student outcomes, we had the good fortune of meeting John Roueche. John led us to Kay and Byron, who helped us develop close relationships with state and local community college leaders and, to our great fortune, the wonderful program staff—Leah Austin and Sam Cargile, in particular—at the Lumina Foundation and the great Wynn Rosser, then president of the Greater Texas Foundation. This confluence of talent helped us begin to think with more ambition about the role of private philanthropy—and Houston Endowment—in supporting programs and strategies to improve student academic outcomes.
>
> John, Kay, and Byron's teaching us about the scope and importance of the community college sector to greater Houston's and Texas's future resulted in well over $30 million in grant making into this important part of the larger

higher education enterprise during a portion of my career at the foundation. We had the opportunity to partner or completely fund initiatives such as: Achieving the Dream ([ATD] as the largest funder after Lumina); Gulf Coast Partners Achieving Student Success (an extension of ATD that included local school districts); SENSE (we funded the development of this important entering-student survey in partnership with our colleagues at Lumina); the Board of Trustees Institute (originated by Houston Endowment and later joined by the Greater Texas Foundation, or GTF, the institute's purpose was to reorient elected trustees toward their obligation to prioritize student success); New Mathways (Uri's exciting developmental math innovation); and the Texas Success Center (cofunded with Kresge, GTF, and the Meadows Foundation). I remain convinced that these and similar initiatives and our partnerships with the CCLP and other funders have had some hand in moving the nature of the conversations in the community college sector from one where head counts and student credit hours were used as indicators of institutional health to one where students are now the center of attention across these institutions.

I am proud of the work we were able to help sponsor with Houston Endowment's resources. It all started with John, Kay, and Byron (Grainger, 2018).

The overarching aim of the funds was that institutional transformation and student success require sustained, visible leadership and relentless focus on a small number of priorities over multiple years. An overview of each of the initiatives under SSI are outlined later this chapter.

Achieving the Dream (ATD) and Beyond

In 2003, SSI, under the CCLP, was a founding partner for ATD. The mission of ATD was to focus on improving success in community colleges, particularly for low-income students and students of color. Byron McClenney, founding director of SSI, served as the national director of leadership coaching for ATD. In this role, he developed and deployed the original ATD leadership coaching model. Coaches served as advisors and, when necessary, agitators to the college presidents, representing an outsider's perspective on how to improve student success. During his tenure, he worked with 185 colleges in 32 states and Washington, DC.

When one of the original leadership coaches, Charlotte Biggerstaff, was asked about her experience as a coach, she said,

In 2003, the Lumina Foundation awarded a large grant to the Community College Leadership Program (CCLP) at the University of Texas at Austin to

become a major partner in a new student success initiative called Achieving
the Dream (ATD). Today, ATD is recognized as one of the most transformational and far-reaching higher education reform movements of all time. As an
original partner in this very visionary reform effort, the CCLP was charged
with selecting and managing "leadership coaches," each of whom would partner with a "data coach" to work with community colleges around the country
to improve student success. Byron McClenney, who managed the CCLP piece
of the work for many years, infused CCLP leadership principles into every
aspect of leadership coaching. Eighteen years later, although ATD is now a
nonprofit organization separate from the CCLP, many of the original CCLP
contributions to leadership coaching have been retained, and coaching is valued as one of the most significant aspects of all (Biggerstaff, 2018).

Achieving the Dream

Because of the work in ATD, the Developmental Education Initiative (DEI),
a national initiative from 2009 to 2012, formed. This work involved 15
colleges in six states that had been participating in ATD since its inception
and sought further support for solutions for developmental students. The role
of SSI was to provide technical assistance providers, also known as coaches,
to these colleges. Additionally, funding was provided to support the coaching
and technical assistance model; convene DEI institutes; and document college progress, strategies, and accomplishments.

Another project that had ties to ATD was the Student Success by the
Numbers (SSBTN) initiative, which started in 2011. This project was designed to build data capacity at 14 Texas community college districts and
promote an effective student success agenda. The population for the project
included Texas community colleges that had not participated in ATD. During
the final year of the project, all SSBTN colleges were invited to compete for
grants that would support continuing progress in building a culture of evidence to promote an effective student success agenda. Selected colleges were
invited to join the 2014 ATD cohort.

Board Development

The Board of Trustees Institute (BOTI) began in 2007 and was focused on
the 28 Texas colleges in ATD. The goal was to expand the reach beyond that
of the coach and the president at the college and specifically reach the college's board. The annual meeting, referred to as an institute, reinforced poli-

cy implications and practical applications of CEO and board collaboration—
based on data—to improve student outcomes.

To better understand the impact of the BOTI, Betty A. McCrohan, president of Wharton County Junior College, shared this about the experience she and her trustees have had as part of this project:

> Wharton County Junior College trustees have attended and participated in every Board of Trustees Institute. Every institute provided a unique opportunity for board members and presidents to review their institutions' student success data and then develop strategies for improvement. In a real sense, these sessions became the impetus for strategic planning at our institution.
>
> My board members particularly enjoyed the interaction and networking with other institutions. Ideas and actions of other community colleges flowed freely amongst participants.
>
> The sessions on governance were invaluable for new board members. I recall an awakening that occurred for two of our new board members following a presentation on the board's role. Prior to this, these members were conflicted about their role on the board of trustees. The use of case studies in the BOTI presentation further reinforced the difference and value of governance and administration. Each year, board members report on their experience at the BOTI and recommend improvements for the board's consideration.

In 2010, this model, in partnership with the Association of Community College Trustees, became the Governance Institute for Student Success (GISS) and was deployed nationally. Once again, the model was intended to provide training for community college boards regarding president and board relations, governance, and student success. GISS held

- full-model, statewide training in Ohio, Washington, West Virginia, and Texas;
- advanced follow-up training in Ohio and Washington;
- a condensed GISS in several more states (New Jersey, Florida, Nebraska, California, Illinois, Arizona, and Michigan); and
- smaller retreats for individual institutions.

Continuing in the spirit of board development, from 2009 to 2011, SSI worked with 13 California college boards and CEOs in the California Leadership Alliance for Student Success (CLASS). The purpose once again was to focus on leadership approaches and policies that increase student success in college. The initiative consisted of a series of institutes, a cohort-tracking project, site visits, and district activities—all designed to support and refine CEO and board leadership for student success.

The Gulf Coast Partners Achieving Student Success (GCPASS)

In 2011, the GCPASS project was funded in an effort to increase student completion and success. The focus was on the Texas Gulf Coast region, and the project worked with 11 Gulf Coast independent school districts and 8 community colleges. SSI managed the initiative and, because of its long history in providing coaching and technical assistance, provided coaching for the Gulf Coast community colleges and partnered with the Houston A+ Challenge and the Institute for Evidence-Based Change.

The model was based on three pillars to uphold early student success: college readiness, college transitions, and college success/developmental education. At the conclusion of the project, disaggregated final performance indicators showed that, in each of these pillars, certain outcomes improved— more black students, Hispanic students, white students, male students, and female students completed high school ready for college and took less developmental education classes, enrolled directly in higher education, and (for those requiring some remediation) successfully completed developmental education classes.

CONCLUSION

Rick Warren (2019) once said, "The purpose of influence is to speak up for those who have no influence." The quote references Proverbs 31:8, but in reading it, John Roueche comes to mind. When there was little conversation or mention of community colleges, he was giving them a voice. When there were few championing underprepared students, he was giving them a voice. When there were few that were talking about part-time faculty, he was giving them a voice. When there were few preparing women and people of color for leadership roles in community colleges, he was giving them a voice.

John Roueche provided a voice for so many people and so many community college issues. He used the vehicle of the CCLP umbrella to speak up for those whose voices needed amplification and to change behaviors. Whether with NISOD, the Center, or SSI, community colleges are better and their students are more successful because of the organizations that were under the CCLP umbrella and the leadership of John Roueche.

Part III

National Influence

Chapter Eleven

John Roueche and the American Association of Community Colleges

Walter G. Bumphus

FOCUSING THE ISSUES

The prescience to identify and elevate the issues important to community college leaders is a talent John Roueche has leveraged throughout his career. His published writings have been a major factor in broadening the understanding of crucial issues at the national level, and his collaboration with the American Association of Community Colleges (AACC) on key publications has benefited community colleges and their leaders tremendously.

More than half of the books, myriad articles, and reports on John's formidable résumé were published via AACC's Community College Press, *Community College Journal* (*Journal*), other AACC communication conduits, or a combination of these. On many occasions, a deep dive into certain issues was taken on at the request of AACC leadership (Roueche, August 13–September 14, 2018). Publications were often coauthored with Suanne Davis Roueche (John's life partner, frequent inspiration, and consistent editorial taskmaster), as well as Drs. George Baker, Terry O'Banion, Mark Milliron, and other higher education thought leaders.

Of his time but more often ahead of his time, John not only wrote about key issues but also sought out and elevated best practices. Where feasible, these best practices were not only captured in books but also incorporated into Community College Leadership Program (CCLP) reading assignments, *Journal* articles, and the National Institute for Staff and Organizational Development's (NISOD) *Innovations Abstracts*, disseminated electronically to

more than 150,000 community and technical college practitioners on a weekly basis. A detailed analysis of his books is presented in Chapter 14 of this
publication.

The following partial list of books and reports published by John via the
AACC highlights the confluence of issues that continue to challenge and
inspire college leaders:

- **Access:** *Access and Excellence: The Open-Door College* (1987)
- **Effective Leadership:** *Institutional Administrator or Educational Lead-
  er? The Junior College President* (1969); *Community College Leadership
  in the Eighties* (1984); *Shared Vision: Transformational Leadership in the
  American Community College* (1989); *The Company We Keep: Collabo-
  ration in the Community College* (1995)
- **Entrepreneurship and Innovation:** *The Entrepreneurial Community
  College* (2005); *The Creative Community College: Leading Change
  through Innovation* (2008); *Rising to the Challenge: Lessons Learned
  From Guilford Technical Community College* (2012)
- **The Role of Faculty, Teaching Excellence:** *Time as the Variable,
  Achievement as the Constant: Competency-Based Instruction in the Com-
  munity College* (1976); *Teaching as Leading: Profiles of Excellence in the
  Open-Door College* (1990); *Strangers in Their Own Land: Part-Time Fa-
  culty in American Community Colleges* (1995); *Practical Magic: On the
  Front Lines of Teaching Excellence* (2003)
- **Institutional Effectiveness:** *Junior College Institutional Research: The
  State of the Art* (1968); *Accountability and the Community College: Direc-
  tions for the '70s* (1971); *Embracing the Tiger: The Effectiveness Debate
  and the Community College* (1997); *In Pursuit of Excellence: The Com-
  munity College of Denver* (2001)
- **Diversity:** *Underrepresentation and the Question of Diversity: Women
  and Minorities in the Community College* (1991)
- **Remedial Education and the At-Risk Student:** *Salvage, Redirection, or
  Custody? Remedial Education in the Junior College* (1968); *Between a
  Rock and a Hard Place: The At-Risk Student in the Open-Door College*
  (1993); *High Stakes, High Performance: Making Remedial Education
  Work* (1999)

One early and groundbreaking report had a particular impact in revolutioniz-
ing thinking within AACC leadership about student access. In 1968,

American Association of Junior Colleges (AAJC) president Edmund Gleazer (who served from 1958 to 1981) and his board were concerned about reports of the increasing number of students entering community colleges unprepared to do college-level work. No credible data or other research existed to assess the extent of the problem. Gleazer contacted John, then associate director at the Educational Resources Information Center (ERIC) Clearinghouse for junior college information, operating under the aegis of the University of California, Los Angeles (UCLA), asking that he look into the matter (Roueche, August 13–September 14, 2018).

Many (if not most) colleges in those days believed the role and mission was to "provide opportunity." In fact, the colleges were called "opportunity colleges or democracy's college." John could find no one who believed seriously that the college had any responsibility for the success of any student other than welcoming them into a "right to try" or "right to fail" admissions practice.

As a result, *Salvage, Redirection, or Custody? Remedial Education in the Junior College* (1968) was published. The report documents through first-time data that the vaunted open door, considered to be the cornerstone of the community college mission, might also be a revolving door for far too many students: "Dr. Gleazer said many times the *Salvage, Redirection, or Custody?* report changed his entire way of looking at our colleges" (Roueche, August 13–September 14, 2018).

It was not the last time that John would question the status quo and invite administrators and faculty to rethink assumptions about the raison d'être of their institutions. The study brings into stark relief an issue that continues to vex community colleges decades later and that foreshadowed later national efforts focused on ensuring a balance of student access and student success, such as Achieving the Dream, the Completion Agenda, and other initiatives.

DIVERSITY CHAMPION

The role of the CCLP under John's leadership in helping to promote greater diversity among community college leaders can hardly be overstated nor its impact fully measured. For context, one must recall the environment of the times. The decades preceding John's appointment in 1971 as director of the University of Texas at Austin (UT) CCLP were years of social and political tumult—for both US education and the nation.

The 1954 *Brown v. Board of Education* Supreme Court decision effectively ended racial segregation in public schools. It was followed by

- the 1957 Civil Rights Act, helping to protect voter rights;
- the Civil Rights Act of 1964, preventing employment discrimination;
- the Voting Rights Act of 1965, outlawing the use of literacy as a requirement to vote; and
- the Civil Rights Act of 1968, providing equal housing opportunity.

All contributed to an environment of political and cultural division, acrimonious debate, and public activism, including (most notably) Dr. Martin Luther King Jr.'s 1963 March on Washington for jobs and freedom.

As the sector of higher education with an egalitarian mission and a fervent commitment to student access, community colleges were hardly exempt from the turmoil. During his annual presentations to CCLP doctoral candidates, AAJC president emeritus Ed Gleazer would recount with great emotion the challenges to the burgeoning community college movement and its national organization during his tenure. It was a time when member colleges fought for greater diversity within AAJC's leadership, and educators, foundations, and policy makers increasingly challenged the sector to provide greater access and support for underrepresented students.

The association's 1970 annual report, written the year of AAJC's 50th "golden anniversary," captures the gravity of the times with a bold and unequivocal headline: "CHANGE":

> There was not a celebration in the usual sense. Though many achievements could be marked using the normal measuring sticks of growth, expansion of programs, and involvement of greater numbers of people, 1970 was not a year for complacent contemplation of past and present progress. National events and issues, unrest, and resistance left little room or time for reflection on what had gone before.
>
> If there was any celebration, it was in terms of renewed attempts to make the work and services of the American Association of Junior Colleges more relevant to grave national issues and concerns. (American Association of Junior Colleges, 1970)

The following year, John would assume leadership of the CCLP at UT, 1 of 10 such programs funded in 1960 at leading universities by the W. K. Kellogg Foundation. Charged with grooming future leaders who would guide an increasingly diverse and socially responsive sector through succeeding generations, John felt the CCLP could not ignore the need for leaders who better reflected the populations and communities they served.

When he accepted UT's offer to succeed Dr. C. C. Colvert, who established the UT CCLP in 1944, John learned that, since its inception, only one Hispanic and one female candidate had completed the program. Something had to change. John met with Dr. Stephen Spurr, then president of the university, to propose greater outreach to attract more female and minority candidates. Over time, he partnered with Dr. Terry O'Banion of the League for Innovation to ramp up recruitment (Roueche, August 13–September 14, 2018).

To put it mildly, the decision was met with consternation and resistance among the all-male faculty and others, who asserted that such a move would diminish the quality and stature of the program. With both determination and diplomacy, John persisted in reshaping a program that would ultimately graduate more female and minority CEOs, deans, and other administrators than any other of its type, including those in my class of 1983. The move illustrated another "cardinal rule" Roueche inculcated into CCLP candidates: Never miss an opportunity to do the right thing.

Those who were part of that groundbreaking period remember vividly what it meant to be part of something historical. As each new African American candidate was accepted into the program, I and others in the CCLP were acutely aware of what "number" they represented on the now-growing list. Dr. Paul Meacham, then vice president at Austin Community College and later president of the College of Southern Nevada, was the first; I was number 6. As John would later note, "It did not take long for our students to be achieving at the top of comprehensive exams and graduation rates. Valuing diversity has nothing to do with lowering standards" (Roueche, August 13–September 14, 2018).

Years later, writing for an AACC publication in collaboration with coauthors Rosemary Gillett-Karam and Suanne Roueche to examine the urgent need for greater diversity at every level within the community college, John helped articulate in theory what the CCLP had been demonstrating in practice for years:

> The recent emphasis on community college constituencies has made us aware of an irrefutable fact: women and members of racial-ethnic minorities are underrepresented in higher education. Neither minority students, minority teachers, nor minority administrators in American community colleges are represented in numbers equivalent to those in the general population. This

underrepresentation demands our immediate attention and calls for positive action. (Roueche, Gillett-Karam, and Roueche, 1991)

The need to take concerted action to increase campus diversity was an urgent admonition John, Suanne, and others would return to repeatedly. Their advocacy mirrored the growing commitment within the community college movement. In recognition of his lifelong commitment, in 2012, John was the first recipient of the Diversity Champions Award, presented by *Diverse: Issues in Higher Education* at the 34th annual NISOD conference. In presenting the award, *Diverse* cofounder Frank Matthews commented, "This man is the only man in higher education who has cracked the code. He has single-handedly produced more Black, Latino, and women higher education presidents than any other sector in higher education" (Smith, May 22, 2012).

The centrality of diversity as an unwavering value continues to reverberate throughout the two-year sector. College mission statements commonly articulate diversity as a core value, as do the mission statements of the leading national organizations—the AACC, the Association of Community College Trustees (ACCT), and the League for Innovation in the Community College. In 2016, the AACC and the ACCT issued the *Joint Statement of Commitment to Equity, Diversity, and Excellence in Student Success and Leadership Development* to underscore their positions. Both AACC's report from the 21st-Century Commission on the Future of Community Colleges and the subsequent implementation guide reaffirm a fervent commitment to diversity.

A LIFETIME OF SERVICE

The recognitions John has received from the AACC and others parallel a lifetime of commitment and service benefiting community colleges and their students. In 1986, just four years after it was originated, he received the AACC Leadership Award, a distinction given to "individuals whose accomplishments and professional contributions to the community college field have been outstanding" (AACC, 2019a). Dr. Suanne Roueche later received the same award, as did a host of CCLP graduates and faculty.

Joining the prestigious company of US presidents, members of Congress, corporate and philanthropic giants, and exemplary educators, John was named recipient of the 2016 Truman Award, the highest award given by the

AACC to a "leader who has had a major, positive impact on community colleges" (AACC, 2019b).

With characteristic and genuine humility, John speaks of these and the many other honors he has garnered over the last 50 years as "overwhelming." In addition to the AACC accolades, he counts as a special highlight receiving the B. Lamar Johnson Leadership Award, given in 1988 by the League for Innovation and named for the man most responsible for setting him on his career path in community colleges: "He was a wonderful mentor, teacher, and (unofficial) grandfather during my early days at UCLA and beyond" (Roueche, August 13–September 14, 2018).

As the AACC ramped up its own leadership development efforts over the last decade, John and Suanne Roueche became ardent cheerleaders and consistent supporters. The AACC Leadership Suite is comprised of both the Future Leaders Institute (FLI; focused on "next steppers" seeking upward mobility in their community college careers) and the Future Presidents Institute (FPI; designed for those for whom a college presidency is an immediate goal, which serves a crucial need). Begun during Dr. George Boggs's tenure as AACC president (2000–2010), the program has expanded to serve more than 1,100 attendees during biannual institutes.

In 2013, in recognition of his substantial support for the AACC and its leadership development efforts, including a personal financial gift from John and Suanne, the AACC board of directors unanimously voted to rebrand the FLI as the AACC John E. Roueche Future Leaders Institute, a tribute to John's past and ongoing contributions. In addition to providing generous moral support, John has been a frequent presenter at the FLI and the FPI and has consistently acted as a sounding board for AACC leadership outreach, an ongoing association priority.

How does one sum up the contributions of a legend? Upon John's retirement from UT in 2012, the AACC prepared a special video tribute featuring the four (then-living) former AACC CEOs—Drs. Ed Gleazer, Dale Parnell, David Pierce, and George Boggs. The tribute was presented at the 2012 AACC annual convention; it offered high praise from leaders who had known and worked with John through community colleges' most transformational periods.

Dr. Ed Gleazer (1958–1981) said, "John went to UT, and he developed without question the leading center for developing community college leadership. These leadership programs not only developed presidents for our institutions, but they actually became research development centers, as well. John developed what the contemporary community college was going to be."

Dr. Dale Parnell (1981–1991) said, "[He is] the one, single individual that I look to to say that's the way it ought to run in training leaders and educating leaders. I can't think of any individual that I've encountered who has done more for the community college than John has."

Dr. David Pierce (1991–2000) said, "John has a passion for practices. Every time he hears of a good practice going on someplace, he pursues it aggressively and grabs it and brings it back into his leadership program. It's impossible to truly describe the impact he's had. It is unprecedented and unparalleled and will probably never be matched again."

Dr. George Boggs (2000–2010) said, "Dr. Roueche has been one of the most significant leaders in shaping the community college movement over the last 40 years. His lasting impact is in many ways hard to zero in on one particular aspect because he's had influence on so many areas of community colleges" (American Association of Community Colleges, 2012, *John E. Roueche*).

A complete transcript of this tribute is provided in Chapter 16 of this book.

LEADERSHIP AT A CROSSROADS

Community colleges are, in fundamental ways, now at a crossroads that will test their continued success, service, and relevance. At the forefront of multiple challenges is the urgent question of who will lead our institutions. AACC research indicates that an estimated 75% of sitting presidents plan to retire within the next 10 years. Such levels of attrition are mirrored in retirements among administrators below the CEO level, who in the past provided a pipeline to the presidency.

Calls to the AACC president's office announcing other imminent CEO retirements are constant and unrelenting, arriving almost daily or occurring multiple times per day. Exacerbating the volume of retirements has been the gradual loss of community college graduate programs at major universities. Only a handful of such programs remain. Primarily local, "grow-your-own" programs are aiming to help fill the leadership void. Such programs offer promise, but the limited access and potential volume of candidates are far too narrow to meet the overwhelming need.

At the national level, this tsunami of leadership turnover is a constant focus and concern among AACC board members and the association's executive leadership team. As noted, the AACC has significantly increased its FLI and FPI sessions, as well as special programs offered in conjunction with its annual meeting and at other times throughout the year. The association regularly updates its *AACC Competencies for Community College Leaders* publication, which is widely used by member colleges and other educational groups. In his role as president of National American University's Roueche Graduate Center (RGC), John Roueche continued to lead the charge, foregoing a much-deserved retirement to develop a new doctoral program with common core elements of the UT CCLP experience.

All of these efforts are commendable, but they are not enough. Not only is there too little capacity to match anticipated turnover, but also the aspiring leaders who are fortunate enough to receive special preparation are too often being rushed into some of the toughest jobs in higher education with the deck stacked against them. Simply put, not only is a community college presidency not for the faint of heart, but it is also a travesty for the ill prepared.

PAYING IT FORWARD

This narrative began with an almost impossible goal: measuring the many ways John Roueche has affected the transformation of community colleges and their leadership. Without an appropriate metric, one can only pay homage to the path John has paved and the extraordinary example he has set for all. Those who have had the privilege to learn from the "greats" bear a special responsibility to pay it forward—as mentors and as advocates.

This is a role John has spent a lifetime perfecting. We are immeasurably enriched. We are profoundly grateful.

Chapter Twelve

The Spirit of Collaboration

John E. Roueche Achieves a Shared Vision

Jerry Sue Thornton

Teambuilding and teamwork are valued as necessities for success in sports. A focus on collaboration to achieve common goals is widely regarded in business and industry, medicine, politics, and education. The concepts are nothing new, but there is a growing view and understanding that collaboration yields better outcomes and greater, more lasting results.

Rather than a traditional approach to winning by leveraging the competitive nature, collaborative thinkers and doers know that, by melding the talents, skills, experiences, and passions of many, their collective efforts can far exceed the achievements of a single person working alone. There is a reason the African proverb "It takes a village to raise a child" has surfaced time and again in modern culture, as the true importance of coming together in collaboration is recognized by many.

But what about competition and the spirit of winning? While the speed of decision-making and execution by a driven individual might seem like a more effective way to reach an end goal—and, in fact, easier than organizing the time and attention of a group—in the long term, team performance delivers more holistic solutions. With a team, solutions are more far-reaching, inclusive, and multidimensional. Problems are tackled from different angles, and answers are derived with the input of a diverse thought process. Too often, rewards, salary, and benefits have been based on the achievement of an individual. Now, more enlightened organizations are changing their recognition and promotion structures to focus more on team achievements.

The effectiveness of collaboration has been reflected time and again through the commitment to collaboration by Dr. John E. Roueche, which began early in his life as a young student. As the Sid W. Richardson Regents Chair and professor and director of the Community College Leadership Program (CCLP) at the University of Texas at Austin (UT), Dr. Roueche was before his time in realizing and showing the academic community (and beyond) how cohorts drive success. He understood that the catalyst for success meant shifting from the competitive arena to one that was inclusive, whether business and industry or the "business of education."

THE MODERN CASE FOR COLLABORATION

Today, there are countless examples of organizations that have achieved success based on collaboration rather than competition. From publicly traded corporations to nonprofits, as well as classrooms across the world, a shift toward collaboration shows how working together is a stronger, more effective way to solve problems and reach goals.

For example, the *Harvard Business Review* shares the experience of Mars, Inc., a family-owned, $35-billion global business with a commitment to collaboration (Valdes-Dapena, 2018). I have spent more than 25 years researching and practicing in the field of "team effectiveness" and conducted a project for Mars, Inc., to measure the impact of collaboration at an organization that, like many, "was full of people who loved to get busy on tasks and responsibilities that had their names next to them. . . . [T]hey were being affirmed for those results by their bosses and the performance rating system" (Valdes-Dapena, 2018).

The company developed a framework to make collaboration an attractive selling point to the independently inclined workers who were not convinced that including teammates on what had been considered individual tasks was worthwhile. "Collaboration was perceived as messy," Carlos Valdes-Dapena writes.

Mars, Inc., tested its framework in 2012 with its Mars Petcare China Leadership Team. The company asked the team to identify why collaboration is essential to business results—and what tasks would require collaboration. The group developed a "team purpose" centered on deploying a business strategy to boost growth. (In the eight years prior, Valdes-Dapena reports, this division had not met its financial commitments to the larger corporation.)

After a year of focusing on collaboration and implementing the newly developed framework, the Mars Petcare China division grew by 33%, and the dog food brand was up by 60%. Collaboration helped the team focus on what mattered most, and working relationships were improved. The company moved this "test" framework into full deployment as a management program, the Mars High Performance Collaboration Framework. "It had gone viral throughout the company," Valdes-Dapena shares in the report. "Connecting collaboration to the motives of success-minded team members is what unlocks productive teamwork."

Harnessing the desire of individuals to achieve and asking them to consider how partnerships can forward overall success of the company completely changed the trajectory. The conversation changed from "I" to "we." Dr. Roueche recognized the importance of the shift in pronouns. By changing the way students were accepted into UT CCLP, he transformed the culture of the CCLP.

Along with the traditional criteria for admission into graduate school by the university, being true to his value of collaboration, Dr. Roueche began evaluating how many times prospective students used "I" instead of "we" in their admissions interviews. If there was an overabundance on the personal versus the plural, he was not interested in bringing that student into the cohort group. This single action changed the makeup of the entering group of students and dramatically changed the ultimate working relationships within the program.

Collaboration has long been a key to success in the nonprofit sector—and one nonprofit that is known for recognizing the power of partnership, working as "we" and a global community, is United Way. Its mission is to "improve lives by mobilizing the caring power of communities around the world to advance the common good" (United Way, n.d.). United Way acknowledges that, as humans, as communities, and as a world, people rise and fall together.

There's an inherent, trickle-down effect that collaboration triggers when people gather to do good together, forming relationships to pursue goals. United Way shares an example of increasing the graduation rate at Vallejo City Unified School District in California by 11% in three years. Of course, students and families benefit from this community school's effort—but these students also have a better chance at landing better-paying jobs so they can live productive, healthier lives and support their families and neighbors. See, there is a trickle-down effect when people collaborate to make a difference.

United Way has long served as an example of how partnership can foster collective impact. In a report, "United Way and Success by 6: Growing Up with Collective Impact," published in *The Philanthropist* (McKnight and Irvine 2014), the authors share how United Way Lower Mainland in British Columbia had been "linking and leveraging grassroots coalitions" to improve early childhood development.

Partnership—collaboration—is the main ingredient in United Way's ability to change lives for the better. United Way, like other organizations that focus on collaboration, partners with companies, governments, nonprofits, and other groups to address complex problems on a global scale. And partners do not necessarily mean donors. While financial support is certainly essential, United Way's brand of partnership values ideas, volunteerism, and efforts to build communities.

Dr. Roueche knew that, when this collaborative mind-set was established early on in the academic arena, students from diverse backgrounds learned to value differences. They embraced varying viewpoints, and they could find common ground that allowed them to achieve goals:

> Having observed the approach to graduate schools in higher education for more than 40 years, I am convinced that the collaborative philosophy and execution are preferable to any other methodologies. When I notice that a candidate for a job was in a doctoral cohort program, I am especially interested. I think that there is a greater likelihood that the candidate understands teamwork, has participated in teamwork, and is more likely to work well with others. (Knight, 2018)

The latter half of the 20th century encompassed the founding, development, growth, and maturity of community colleges. John uniquely shaped American community colleges with the use of collaboration and the cohort group. He engaged in considerable and noteworthy research, writing, and advocacy of student success during a 50-year span that demonstrated the value of collaboration (Knight, 2018).

The benefits of collaboration have been realized in the public sector by companies that make collaboration a key focus. Randy Babbit, former Southwest Airlines senior vice president of labor relations, said, "If my fingerprints and your fingerprints are on the final product, we're much more likely to embrace it" (quoted in Wright, 2013). This remark from a *Profiles in Collaboration* interview on the Southwest Airlines community hub shares how Babbit heralded collaboration as a best practice throughout his career. Brad

Grissom, senior manager of communication and collaboration solutions at Southwest Airlines, spoke at the IBM Connect 2017 Conference and shared, "Making sure [the company] is best situated to deliver superior service to its customers is a team sport" (quoted in Davis, 2017).

In Southwest Airlines' 2017 One Report, it states, "We believe community is more than a place—it's at the heart of what brings us together." That year, the company's commitment to collaborating with community meant giving $500,000 to the American Red Cross after Hurricane Harvey and providing $4 million of travel assistance to patients in need of medical care.

Collaboration at Southwest Airlines also means partnering with organizations that share its desire to protect the planet, such as its Repurpose with Purpose initiative that upcycles, downcycles, and recycles discarded materials into useful products. For example, the company donated leather from seat covers to the Dallas-based nonprofit Dallas Designing Dreams, which provides skills and training programs for youth, people with disabilities, senior citizens, and other disadvantaged populations (Southwest Airlines, 2017).

Collaboration can also unlock solutions to even the gravest problems. Take world hunger. Ray Goldberg, Harvard University emeritus professor of agriculture and business, wrote the book *Food Citizenship: Food System Advocates in an Era of Distrust*. During a radio show on Sirius XM, he shared, "The food system has changed from being a transactional operation to a collaborative operation" (*Knowledge@Wharton*, 2018).

His work addresses why the food system is viewed with suspicion and how collaboration is crucial for moving forward. "We now have collaborations among the business school, the government school, the school of public health, and the environmental people," he shared. "We now have collaborations among the private sector, the public sector, and the not-for-profit sector that never existed before" (*Knowledge@Wharton*, 2018).

The collaboration Goldberg spoke of at the academic and community levels is changing the conversation about what can be done to make the food system "more responsive to consumers' nutritional needs, economic needs, and doing it in a way that improves the environment." Goldberg said,

> Meanwhile, as modern culture becomes more global, we are adopting tools and technologies that allow collaboration from afar. We can connect team members working in disparate offices all over the world. We can "meet" with partners across town or across the country. We can share ideas and information and grow relationships among teams in new and exciting ways. At a base level, take the use of collaborative platforms like Dropbox, Google Docs,

Microsoft Sharepoint, and other virtual file-sharing programs. (*Knowl-edge@Wharton*, 2018)

More collaboration is happening today in digital settings, and technology is allowing people to convene like never before. Dr. Roueche embraces this today with his face-to-face and technology-blended approach to the doctoral program at Kansas State University. His tremendous influence in the space of collaboration has been an inspiration for students, colleagues, and peers who recognize the power of partnership.

EARLY COLLABORATION IN EDUCATION

Rosabeth Moss Kanter (1989) advocates for partnerships both internally and externally for companies wanting to meet the challenges of the future in her book *When Giants Learn to Dance*. She calls for business and industry to be more open and willing to collaborate:

> The strategy of partnerships involves more than a mere handshake. The devel-opment of formal alliances with "external" parties also changes internal roles, relationships, and power dynamics for the organizations entering into them. The greater the sphere of cooperation between organizations, the greater the magnitude of the changes within each one, and the greater the disruption to the traditional hierarchy. (Kanter, 1989)

Clearly ahead of her time, she advances the notion of "disruption" of the traditional hierarchy, which applies to the corporate world and academia. She writes how education has pushed competition rather than collaboration, which is evident in the grading system, class ranking, scholarship awards, honors, and other recognitions; "Higher education has had a long history of infusing competition into decisions relating to administration, faculty, and staff levels of employment, as best evidenced by faculty tenure and rank. Students must not only compete for entrance and acceptance into a university but also for grades, fellowships, scholarships, and many other reward sys-tems" (Thelin, 2004).

While there were some examples of fostering teamwork and collaborative efforts within various departments positioned in universities, those remained isolated attempts at incorporating group projects into traditional means of educational delivery. It was not the norm. But this mind-set has always been a focus for Dr. Roueche. It's engaging to explore how he first sowed the seeds of collaboration and the evolution of his model as it permeated the culture of the classroom and a greater community college community. His commitment to collaborative approaches in higher education has been threaded throughout his life and is part of his value system.

Dr. Roueche's commitment to collaboration began early in his life, during junior high school, when he was engaged in athletics. His teamwork focus continued through high school—and in the 10th grade, when a knee injury sidelined him from sports, he refocused his collaborative nature into his academic pursuits. He took a team approach to studying and learning, which was quite unusual at the time.

At Mitchell Community College in Statesville, North Carolina, he honed his penchant for collaboration, understanding firsthand why community colleges are viewed as "democracy's colleges." With small classes and team projects, he engaged in learning in a different and challenging way. He wrote that his experience with students and teachers at Mitchell was supportive and the "teachers wanted the best achievement outcomes for every student" (Roueche, October 22, 2018).

At the same time, expectations of high performance were also present. Dr. Roueche said he had never been challenged in this way before. He saw the combination of collaboration and personal achievement was possible in higher education, which enriched the overall experience and learning outcomes (Roueche, October 22, 2018).

The use of collaborative learning minimizes the concept of "winners and losers." Instead, collaborative environments are supportive—everyone can win at some level. Dr. Roueche continued his education at universities that valued teamwork. At Lenoir-Rhyne, Appalachian State, and Florida State Universities, he encountered professors and students who sought opportunities to partner. At Florida State, Dr. Roueche met Dr. Terry O'Banion, one of his lifelong partners in collaborative learning and community college leadership.

Dr. O'Banion wrote about their partnership, which has lasted for more than 54 years, dating back to the time when they were both Kellogg fellows in the Higher Education Program at Florida State: "Partnering with John was never all work and no play. With his delightful sense of humor and his spirit of adventure, we greatly enjoyed our time together as friends" (O'Banion, 2016). Beyond this friendship, Drs. Roueche and O'Banion have collaborated on numerous projects, publications, presentations, and educational initiatives that have changed the lives of students.

While studying "intellectual history" at Florida State, Dr. Roueche recognized that idea generation, when guided by "like-minded people," could change the world—and even overthrow dictators. This philosophy spurred his continued interest in the power of collaboration and its ability to truly make history (Roueche, October 22, 2018).

BUILDING A CAREER THROUGH COLLABORATION

John began his career in higher education at the University of California, Los Angeles (UCLA), when he was 22. He was steeped in the community college philosophy and belief in the successes of collaboration versus competition. His views were reinforced as he witnessed the traditional institutional focus on individual performance without consideration for teamwork and collaboration. Perhaps the most obvious lessons he witnessed, where individual initiatives were rewarded or punished, came from the ways faculty members were awarded or denied tenure.

Later, at Duke University in the National Laboratory for Higher Education, Dr. Roueche seriously engaged in the concepts of shared goals and shared objectives. At the Institute on Junior College Administration, he provided leadership and direction for cohesive approaches to finding common ground—to valuing the whole. As director and associate professor of education, he created a platform to forge new ways of researching, writing, and teaching with a focus on the value of connecting people.

FOSTERING COLLABORATION AT THE LEADERSHIP LEVEL

Dr. Roueche found his "Camelot" at UT, when he was hired in 1971 to shape the CCLP. While there was a solid foundation for the CCLP, he enhanced its structure and outcomes through collaborative means. This completely changed the behavioral outcomes for graduates. Over the next 40 years, Dr. Roueche honed and shaped the CCLP to reflect his values and beliefs—respecting the ability of individuals while harnessing the power of teamwork, inclusion, and interdependency.

Understanding his role at the university as a leader and promoter of fund development, he knew his obligation as CCLP director included raising financial resources to grow and enhance the program. Dr. Kay McClenney, senior advisor to the president/CEO of the American Association of Community Colleges, observes, "Dr. Roueche's collaborative approach extended also to his remarkably productive interactions with a range of philanthropic leaders who ultimately invested many millions of dollars in his work at the CCLP. The conversations were not primarily transactional; they were about big ideas and common agendas—and how they could be realized together" (K. McClenney, September 21, 2018).

Recruiting and funding new faculty positions for the CCLP were top of mind for Dr. Roueche as a young, new director who wanted to form a team that could deliver the highest quality of coordinated teaching and learning. He increased the CCLP faculty by developing grants through the W. K. Kellogg Foundation, which provided necessary funds for an additional faculty member: George Baker, a doctoral graduate from Duke University. This addition provided Dr. Roueche with a fellow faculty member who shared his value of teamwork, and it helped him initiate the National Institute for Staff and Organizational Development (NISOD; Boggs, 2018).

Shortly after, Dr. Roueche negotiated with the Department of Educational Administration for an additional position, which resulted in hiring Dr. Don Rippey. The dynamic threesome formed a team that would teach, research, publish, and create an environment where students understood the value of working closely in groups while also giving their individual and personal best.

During this time, Dr. Roueche began to transition the Block concept from its original purpose as a block of time, where the CCLP students were together in classes during the fall semester. The early Block was formulated when Dr. Clyde Cornelius Colvert (C. C. C.) was the director of the CCLP, and the Block was later designed by Dr. Larry Haskew, who previously taught in the program and served as the dean of the College of Education (Boggs, 2018). The Block was reshaped under the leadership of Dr. Roueche, who worked closely with Drs. Baker and Rippey.

Dr. George Boggs (2018) also wrote about the Block concept established under the leadership of Dr. Roueche. He shared how UT doctoral students identified themselves as Blockers, denoting the class or group who entered the graduate program at the same time. The Block designation was often followed by the date of the entry year or possessed a sequential number, such as Block 1980 or Block 15, or both. There was great pride generated by the students for their Blocks as well as friendly competition between and among Blocks of students.

A Block guide provided a detailed schedule of courses, activities, and team composition for each group. It was a blueprint that gave students a plan for the learning and team activities they'd engage in throughout the semester and year. Blocks took the mystery out of the educational process—and encouraged doctoral students to make an investment in their intellectual growth. Dr. Boggs, president emeritus of the American Association of Community Colleges and graduate of UT, was especially impressed in the Block concept. He writes,

> The Block guide described the experience as a constellation of individual students, each of whom would be a resource for all of the others as well as an independent acquirer of cognitive and affective behaviors. The CCLP was intended to be a device both for conducting and causing learning experiences. Each entering cohort of students was thought to be an unfinished composition. (2018)

THE BLOCK AS A COLLABORATIVE STRUCTURE

While the original Block structure was beneficial in the early years when doctoral students were more homogeneous, as time progressed, new students were more diverse in every aspect: gender, racial, age, and religion. The team configurations, assignments, selection of guest lecturers, and community colleges they visited were also more diverse. This called for a transition to promote collaboration in a diverse environment and to create a situation where students could value each other's differences and learn from one another.

The notion of organizational culture is key to understanding the transition that Dr. Roueche made as he slowly but deliberately incorporated a way for diverse individuals to become better acquainted, accept and trust each other, and learn together. Dr. Roueche understood the importance of incorporating attitudes, beliefs, and values into every fiber of the Block. He also knew that creating collaborative Block experiences in graduate school would be beneficial to future leaders in an emerging community college environment, which was increasingly nontraditional, diverse, and unpredictable.

These views relate to "appreciative inquiry," which says the positive perspectives of a broad range of relationships and interactions can result in a common good. Case Western Reserve University professors Suresh Srivastva and David L. Cooperrider write in their book *Appreciative Management and Leadership*, "An appreciative process, 'appreciative inquiry,' is proposed as a way of helping members of different cultures recognize and value their differences and create a new culture where diverse values are understood and honored" (Sirvastva, Cooperrider, and associates, 1990).

The Block concept accomplished this. Dr. Terry Calaway, retired president of Johnson County Community College (Kansas) and CCLP doctoral student in Block 51, viewed the Block as a learning laboratory that brought students together from different backgrounds who may have known little about the cultures of each other. Block assignments promoted teamwork and were purposely designed for inclusion, better acceptance, and understanding differences (Calaway, 2018).

The organization that Drs. Roueche, Baker, and Rippey were shaping especially appealed to Dr. Walter Bumphus, today's president and CEO of the American Association of Community Colleges. He was seeking a university in which to pursue his doctorate degree. He said,

> First and foremost, I wanted to attend a university that by reputation had a rich history of producing outstanding leaders in the community college sector and, secondly, one that had a reputation for helping students complete their studies and graduate. I also wanted a university where students that in essence looked like me and that, being leaders of color, were welcomed and respected. Fairness and inclusion were hallmarks of the CCLP, and much of these characteristics were traced directly to its director, Dr. John E. Roueche. (Bumphus, 2018)

Drs. Suresh Srivastva and David L. Cooperrider, with other associates, note, "Formation of an organization's culture begins with the leader who is key in the establishment of the institution's practices and values" (Srivastva, Cooperrider, and associates, 1990). This conclusion was institutionalized in the transition of the CCLP Block under the directorship of Dr. Roueche. He fundamentally understood how collective experiences intentionally shape lives when communicated with precision (the Block guide) and supported by high expectations. These collective experiences generate a "return on investment" for the students involved.

While shaping the educational experience was important, Dr. Roueche also clearly articulated to graduate students that high performance was expected in group *and* individual work. Achievement was expected and understood by students—and required by the CCLP faculty. Walter addressed his selection of the CCLP at UT based on the academic results of the program derived from the joint expectations of the faculty and the delivery by students:

As I was in the process of making decisions about my doctoral graduate studies, I had a metric in my mind about where I wanted to pursue my studies. I also had thoughts about the pedagogy of the program. I eventually made my decision about the university that I wanted to attend based on the national reputation of Dr. John Roueche and the way in which he had organized the Community College Leadership Program. After confirming the positive experiences of my long-term friend, Jerry Sue Thornton, and several other program graduates whom I knew, I became convinced that the UT CCLP program was the best choice for me. (Bumphus, 2018)

Dr. Bumphus further affirmed his selection by saying that, after he was admitted and enrolled at UT CCLP, he knew early on he had made the right decision:

First, the rigor of the courses and assignments were such that I was immediately convinced that this program would yield great results in my pursuit of leadership development. Secondly, I was surprised with the collaborative nature of the assignments, work, and study groups. It was the first time that I had engaged in a learning environment based on a "team concept" as opposed to only competitive assignments. (Bumphus, 2018)

Dr. Bumphus related how his bachelor's and master's degree programs were different because they were traditional, so this collaborative doctoral experience was starkly different: "We, the doctoral students, were encouraged to work as members of a team with both group and individual accountability. This approach was very appealing to me personally and professionally, given my athletic history and career as a dean of students" (Bumphus, 2018).

Dr. Bumphus shared how he was invited to the home of faculty members—for the first time in his student career. He networked, learned, and heard from distinguished speakers. The experience was so "radically different," he said. He had become a different type of learner and felt completely inspired. "Drs. John Roueche, George Baker, and Don Rippey respected and embraced students in a way that I had not previously seen," he wrote (Bumphus, 2018).

Similarly, Dr. Belle Wheelan gained many insights and experiences from institutions, including Trinity University, Louisiana State University, and UT, as she earned degrees that would shape her future. While president and CEO of the Southern Association of Colleges and Schools Commission on Colleges (SACS), she reflected on her experiences in UT CCLP as being seminal in her development: "One of the most valuable lessons I learned in the CCLP was to collaborate with my colleagues. Whether through planning for visitors to the Block, distributing duties for institutional visits, or studying for written exams, the concept of sharing knowledge and skills has carried me through my entire professional career" (Wheelan, 2018).

Likewise, Dr. Kay McClenney, former director of the Center for Community College Student Engagement (CCCSE) at UT, vividly remembers her experience as a doctoral student in CCLP. She wrote about the first day in the Block, meeting as task-oriented, mostly Type A overachieving individuals who were skeptical about turning over their personal successes to group achievement. The cohort concept felt unfamiliar, but the individuals grew together. She wrote, "As Dr. Roueche insisted, we did just that, as evidenced through management teams for Block sessions, team reports on college site visits, shared notes from all manner of classes, group study for oral exams, and ultimately, a network of lifelong and trusting relationships" (McClenney, September 21, 2018).

These powerful observations and testimonials based on the personal and professional experiences of some great leaders in higher education illustrate how the unique insights and values of John created far-reaching impact. He is a researcher and educator, committed to enhancing the lives of students—and these are all examples of his genius.

Dr. Roueche has always exhibited an innate ability to build teams. At UT, he showed an understanding of why it is important to pair unique skills, talents, and experiences into a collective group of individuals. As a result, the cohort develops shared views, values, and goals, maximizing the opportunity for successful outcomes.

Dr. Baker confirms in his book *Team Building for Quality*, "Teams typically enjoy advantages over individuals acting alone because teams take advantage of the range of skills, talents, and expertise of all members to meet the performance objectives" (Baker, 1995). He experienced the value students gain when university personnel mobilize to grow and develop students. He played a pivotal role in the CCLP, which epitomized the benefits of a collective commitment to a common goal, where vision and action are intimately bound.

The writings of Dr. Baker center on the transformational leadership skills required to accomplish the desired outcomes of a team. This leadership creates an environment where teams can succeed. Dr. Roueche possessed a keen ability to recruit professionals who understood the power of a common vision, possessed a commitment to quality, and demonstrated a capacity and willingness to work hard and carry their load in the team.

John W. Gardner, author of *On Leadership*, promotes the value of participation and the importance of sharing leadership tasks. He writes, "The healthy community involves the participation of mature and responsible individuals. The good community finds a productive balance between individuality and group obligations" (Gardner, 1990). Dr. Roueche, like Gardner, instinctively understood that his graduate students had to develop skills in conflict resolution, mediation, compromise, and coalition building to be successful leaders.

Through team building and coalitions, Dr. Roueche created concrete activities that yielded the type of results that Gardner advances in philosophy: "Leaders must be skilled in creating or recreating the linkages necessary to get things done" (Gardner, 1990). Through the Block and cohort groups, Dr. Roueche was continuously developing opportunities, both required and optional, to put students into collaborative environments.

Dr. Roueche has written or contributed to more than 39 books and authored in excess of 175 articles and counting. A book that perhaps most represents his view of collaboration, team building, partnerships, and synergies is *Shared Vision: Transformational Leadership in American Community Colleges*, written by John E. Roueche, George A. Baker III, and Robert R. Rose. The work provides a well-documented look at the "role of teamwork and collaborative decision-making, the relationship between the institution and the individuals in it" (Roueche, Baker, and Rose, 1989). The book is chock-full of examples of leaders who work diligently "to create a common vision and [embrace] numerous opportunities of partnerships to achieve it, advocating for informed empowerment of followers to utilize their skills to achieve the shared vision" (Roueche, Baker, and Rose, 1989).

Shared Vision best expresses how John views transformational leaders and their responsibility to create a vision for excellence. "The challenge is to effect change for successful outcomes through maximizing human potential," he writes (Roueche, Baker, and Rose, 1989). The five themes that emerge in this publication undergird the transition of the Block and his belief that cohort groups yield opportunities to develop teamwork. Resulting from interviews with 50 community college CEOs (chancellors, presidents, and state directors), identified by their colleagues as 50 "blue chippers," these five themes include the following:

TRANSFORMATIONAL leaders believe in teamwork and shared decision-making. They have a bias for action, and they empower others to act. They try to develop a collaborative situation that is not dependent on any one individual for success.

THEY value people, both as members of the team and as individuals. They respect individual differences and value the opinions of others. They reward work well done. Students are a focal point of their efforts.

THEY understand motivation. They have high expectations of others and inspire them to develop their creative and problem-solving skills.

THEY have a strong personal value system. They value consistency, integrity, commitment to student learning, and openness. They model the conduct they expect of others.

TRANSFORMATIONAL leaders have a vision of what their colleges can become. They are willing to take risks and commit their colleges to new directions that incorporate the needs of their communities. (Roueche, Baker, and Rose, 1989)

REFORMING CCLP PARTNERSHIPS

Over time, as leaders and professors assumed other opportunities or retired from UT CCLP, new collaborations were formed with incoming talent. Several leaders joined the Department of Educational Administration (now Education Leadership and Policy) and taught in the CCLP. Drs. Leonard Valverde and William (Bill) E. Lasher were two professional educators in that category. Also among those new alliances were Drs. William (Bill) Moore and Donald Phelps, who along with Dr. Roueche created another dynamic threesome, as had been the case with Baker and Rippey. Later, Dr. Bumphus served as the Aiken Regents Chair in junior and community college leadership and department chair and faculty in the CCLP.

However, the most renowned partnership for Dr. Roueche was with Dr. Suanne Roueche, his wife, as they worked together in the CCLP. Her greatest contribution was the advancement of NISOD, with support from her husband. The engaging duo created formidable professional development programs for community college faculty and staff. Together, they became a force in collaborative research and publications, coauthoring 12 books. They truly brought commendable, memorable value to the community.

THE NEXT ERA OF COLLABORATION

After retiring from UT, Dr. Roueche continued his development of doctoral students through the Roueche Graduate Center, in partnership with National American University and now at Kansas State University. While the new CCLP provides a "blended approach" that calls for some in-person sessions with faculty and students, much of the coursework and assignments are offered online.

That said, the centerpiece of this doctoral program still uses the cohort structure, which brings together students from various community colleges—and these students are accepted and begin their programs together. They are closely knit together as a collective while they pursue their doctoral degrees. Like the Block at UT, students learn the value of teamwork, collaboration, and partnership. And, like the doctoral students before them (now graduates), they become part of the CCLP "family." As well stated by Dr. McClenney, "Truly remarkable are the ways the collaborative relationships intentionally develop within the CCLP and extend throughout careers and across the nation, as the students and close colleagues of John Roueche reach out to assist and support one another through professional and personal challenges, celebrations, and transitions" (K. McClenney, September 21, 2018).

On a personal level, having the opportunity to participate in UT CCLP was the best part of my higher education experience. It provided such a unique view of what education should be like for all students. For the first time, there was a new "tribe" of learners and costudents who engaged freely and openly with each other. There was trust and cooperation infused in a traditional system. It was truly a testament to the genius and heart of John E. Roueche, the most outstanding teacher and mentor that a person could have in education. It is the way that it should be for all students.

The best and lasting summary of the beliefs about collaboration and teamwork as demonstrated by Dr. Roueche is the conclusion of *Shared Vision: Transformational Leadership in American Community Colleges*, which summarizes the power of collaboration:

> Visions are only the seedlings of reality. We must value and cherish our dreams and visions, nurturing them into fulfillment. Most of all, we must remember that few of our visions can be accomplished alone. The key to the achievements that we strive for is the ability to share our visions and thus earn the acceptance and assistance necessary for turning them into reality. What is

truly important, what is lasting is accomplished together. (Roueche, Baker, and Rose, 1989)

Chapter Thirteen

Ahead of the Curve

Kay M. McClenney

What is the spark that ignites a career? What is the driving factor that provokes a leader, scholar, and teacher to see and think persistently *ahead of the curve*? John Edward Roueche (JER), a person with remarkable vision, has over decades demonstrated an uncanny ability to scan the horizon of higher education, identify emerging issues—or issues that *should* emerge—and place them squarely before leaders and practitioners in the field. Throughout his career, Roueche has powerfully led the community college field by recognizing, often long before others do, areas of potential opportunity or impending concern—and addressing them through prolific research, writing, and speaking.

MAKING GOOD ON THE PROMISE OF THE OPEN DOOR

A significant spark for John Roueche's distinguished career came from his long and productive relationship with Edmund J. Gleazer Jr., who was president of the American Association of Community Colleges (AACC) from 1958 until his retirement in 1981. Thereafter, he continued to serve as a longtime adjunct faculty member in the Community College Leadership Program (CCLP) at the University of Texas at Austin (UT), where JER was a professor and a director.

As Roueche always has been quick to point out, Gleazer was an iconic figure in the development of American community colleges. At the time of his death in 2016, an article in the *Community College Journal* describes Gleazer's tenure at the AACC: "That 23-year span saw many changes, not only in community colleges, but in the country overall. Many of those move-ments—from civil rights and women's rights to the Vietnam War—had a tremendous effect on the country's community colleges. Gleazer was in the forefront, steering the movement into a new era" (Dembicki, 2016).

For Roueche, lasting inspiration came from an article authored by Gleazer in 1970, in which he writes, "The greatest challenge facing the community college is to make good on the promise of the open door" (Gleazer, 1970). For numerous college leaders at the time, that statement was a cause of dismay and a target of criticism. As JER puts it, "Many, if not most, college leaders really believed that the provision of opportunity and access was truly the singular goal of the 'open-door college'" (Roueche, 2018).[1] For Roueche, by contrast, the notion of *making good on the promise of the open door* became the driver and the driving theme for his work.

CONSEQUENCES OF VISION

With the benefit of hindsight, it might be easy to forget how truly unwelcome visionary thought can be. For Roueche (and for Gleazer, as well), the choice to write and speak with vision and candor at times produced backlash from leaders in the field. Often, that reaction came from a sense that leaders should only be responsible for providing college access and should not be called upon to produce educational results over which they felt they had no control. Roueche's response? "Just admitting people takes no talent" (Roueche, 2018). In the end, though, the choice also brought recognition for scholar-ship, leadership, and teaching.

A CAREER IN PERSPECTIVE

This chapter highlights key areas of thought, research, and action that John Roueche identified and lifted up for the community college field and for scholars and practitioners well beyond the sector. As Roueche has authored 39 books and more than 175 articles and chapters focused on leadership, institutional performance, and teaching and learning in American colleges and universities, the discussion is necessarily limited to a small number of examples from his work. For each topic, note is taken of selected Roueche publications, of the broader higher education context, and of responses from the field.

THINKING AND WORKING AHEAD OF THE CURVE

Accountability

"We need a transformation around the purpose of college," JER asserts. "For every department, every college, there should be questions: How many students started here? How many successfully completed? How many learned? How many have jobs and earn a good living?" (Roueche, 2018).

With encouragement from Ed Gleazer, Roueche and his coauthors produced *Accountability and the Community College: Directions for the '70s* (1971), making the argument that accountability, even if threatening to educators, is a necessary professional responsibility and this need is exacerbated by public concern, taxpayer disenchantment, and criticism from policy makers. For community colleges at that time, accountability was described as featuring four characteristics:

1. Accountability accents results (i.e., emphasizing "what comes out of an education system rather than what goes into it"; ibid., pp. 6–7).
2. Accountability requires measurement (e.g., learning assessment).
3. Accountability assumes and shifts responsibility (i.e., from students to the educational institutions that serve them).
4. Accountability permeates the college community.

As to the fourth characteristic, the authors describe a comprehensive version of accountability that remarkably foreshadows the guided pathways movement of the 2010s, almost 30 years later. They argue presciently,

> Accountability implies that two-year colleges must be accountable externally to the community and that colleges must be accountable internally to the students who pass through their open door. This state is achieved when students from the community enter the college, find a program that is compatible with their goals, persist in college until the goal is reached, and then become productive members of the community. (Roueche, Baker, and Brownell, 1971)

It could well be said that accountability in higher education in 1971 was an idea whose time had not yet come. The book was met with considerable criticism from the field. The coauthors received about 200 letters asking why in the world they would be trying to stir up controversy by making college leaders responsible for outcomes that they couldn't produce. Gleazer subsequently invited JER to speak at the AACC convention, and Roueche insistently raised these questions: "Can we not take more responsibility for students? Can we not think about how we provide remediation, how we design instructional approaches? What happens to the students who leave? What is their personal future? What are their contributions to society?" (Roueche, 2018)

With various colleagues and coauthors, JER sustains the accountability theme with a series of publications extending over many years, notably including *Toward Instructional Accountability: A Guide to Educational Change* (Roueche and Herrscher, 1973) and, more than two decades later, *Embracing the Tiger: The Effectiveness Debate and the Community College* (Roueche, Johnson, and Roueche, 1997). His work continually reinforces a compelling and still-relevant theme: "Although the community college movement should be credited with pursuing the ideal of universal higher education, accountability demands that the success of that venture be judged by results. Student success (both persistence and achievement in college) is the only accurate measure of the open door" (Roueche, Baker, and Brownell 1971).

In the early to mid-1980s (and to the present), the higher education field, regional accreditors, and state policy makers have followed in JER's footsteps, with an assortment of national reports calling for heightened quality and accountability (National Commission on Excellence in Education, 1983; National Commission on Higher Education Issues, 1982; Study Group on the Conditions of Excellence in American Higher Education, 1984; Wingspread Group on Higher Education, 1993); new accreditation criteria focused on institutional effectiveness (see, for example, Commission on Colleges, Southern Association of Colleges and Schools, 1987); and legislation that set accountability requirements in many states.

Looking at progress made and at future prospects, Roueche expresses praise for excellent leaders in the community college field who have demonstrated that accountability is possible—and that *students can learn*. Still, he predicts that the demand for accountability will escalate, particularly including requirements for documentation of student success, even as states continue to retreat from providing public support for higher education (Roueche, 2018). Documented excellence is clearly possible, he has said, but it is still more the exception than the rule. There is much work yet to be done.

DEVELOPMENTAL EDUCATION: SERVING THE
UNDERPREPARED STUDENT

Given his pervasive emphasis on the promise of the open door, John Roueche inevitably became a national expert on academically underprepared students and developmental education. As early as 1967 and for at least the four following decades, JER published articles, chapters, and books addressing developmental education curriculum, pedagogy, and college performance in serving underprepared students and the pressing urgency of doing the work exceptionally well.

A crucial milestone was laid in 1968 with the publication of *Salvage, Redirection, or Custody? Remedial Education in the Junior College* (Roueche, 1968), a work once again prompted by a call from Ed Gleazer when JER was working at the University of California, Los Angeles (UCLA). The two discussed concern among community college presidents about the numbers of students needing remediation. JER found that no research had been done about the need—the sheer volume of demand.

Having called state community college directors to find leads about good programs that serve academically underprepared students, he followed up with the colleges. What he learned was that he could not find a single college that could document that as many as 10% of students in remedial courses successfully completed the course sequence. Once again, Roueche found that college leaders generally defended the poor performance by asserting that the "mission is access, that colleges can't be responsible for success"—and that students have the right to fail (Roueche, 2018).

People in the field described the remedial function in various ways:

- As *salvage*—that is, saving students, providing a second chance, offering the right to try
- As *redirection*—that is, redirecting students who didn't belong in college, who were not college material, who should be in the trades
- As *custody*—that is, keeping students off the streets, out of jail, engaged in purposeful activity

"Improving student success," JER reports, "was not an idea many people embraced" (Roueche, 2018).

JER wrote up the findings and sent the manuscript to Gleazer, concerned that the news was negative but encouraged to write about what could make college efforts more successful. Gleazer later said that dealing with reactions to *Salvage* (and also to *Accountability and the Community College*) was one of his most challenging experiences as leader of the AACC. According to JER, Gleazer told him that Roueche was his highest-risk investment.

For his part, JER continued his research and writing about developmental education—and the students whose success colleges most need to support—through at least the next 30 years.

An Enduring Partnership

It is worth noting that, in his work on developmental education—and subsequently across topics including teaching quality, student success, institutional excellence, and community college leadership—JER gained a remarkable partner in Suanne Davis Roueche (SDR), his constant collaborator, frequent coauthor, and spouse, until her death in 2017. With encouragement from Ruby Herd (who was head of El Centro College's developmental education program and later the college president), Suanne took on the task of teaching developmental writing. As JER recalls, no one ever told her she couldn't do it, so she pursued student success in developmental writing with marked tenacity, and ultimately, she wrote a textbook on the subject.

When SDR finished her UT doctorate and stayed in Austin, she became director of the community college teaching program, preparing faculty for teaching in community colleges. In 1977, the Southern Regional Education Board (SREB) reached out and asked JER and SDR to write a primer on remedial education (Roueche and Roueche, 1977), the work that became their first authorship collaboration and was followed by dozens more over more than three decades.

AND THE FIELD FOLLOWED

Over time, a number of organizations and individual researchers joined in the focus on developmental education. Appalachian State University's National Center for Developmental Education has made contributions to the knowledge base over many years, including the National Study of Developmental Education, which was conducted initially from 1989 through 1997.

The 2000s brought a veritable frenzy of activity focused on the improvement of developmental education outcomes, including the work of Achieving the Dream (launched in 2004) and its focused Developmental Education Initiative (2009–2012). The same period saw the start-up and impressive development of New Mathways (now the Dana Center Mathematics Pathways) at the Charles A. Dana Center in the College of Natural Sciences at UT and Carnegie Math Pathways, which took up residence at WestEd in 2017 following its formative years at the Carnegie Foundation for the Advancement of Teaching.

Strong state-based work includes the California Basic Skills Initiative and the California Acceleration Project. Development of the Accelerated Learning Project (ALP) at the Community College of Baltimore County served to, well, accelerate progress in achieving substantially improved results. There are many other examples of impactful state- and institution-level work.

Meanwhile, the Community College Research Center (CCRC) began producing highly significant research regarding developmental education performance and effective practice (see, for example, Bailey [2009] and other resources at https://ccrc.tc.columbia.edu/Developmental-Education-and-Adult-Basic-Skills.html). The Center for Analysis of Postsecondary Readiness (2018), led by the CCRC at Teachers College, Columbia University, and MDRC, continued producing research and analysis through 2018.

In 2015, six national organizations came together to develop and publish the *Core Principles for Transforming Remedial Education* (2015), a publication that presents design principles based on evidence of effective practices that had accrued through the work of both researchers and practitioners.

As time and research progressed, Roueche had placed increasing emphasis on institutional performance in regard to developmental education and promising educational practices that produced impressive results. In *High Stakes, High Performance: Making Remedial Education Work* (Roueche and Roueche, 1999), JER and SDR organize the growing body of knowledge and raise relevant issues, aiming to focus discussions about needed change.

In 2001 came the publication of *In Pursuit of Excellence: The Community College of Denver* (Roueche, Ely, and Roueche, 2001), which documents the past remarkable work at the Community College of Denver, where over a decade and under trying circumstances, educators took steps to eliminate differences in outcomes between students of color and white students and between students who entered the college in developmental education courses and students who did not.

The enduring theme for Roueche's work is illustrated in the dedication: "This book is dedicated to our friend and colleague, Byron McClenney, President, Community College of Denver (1986–2000), and the entire Community College of Denver team, *who lead by example and live the dream of making good on the promise of the open door"* (Roueche, Ely, and Roueche, 2001).

High Stakes

Roueche's persistent commitment to the issue of developmental education effectiveness was revealed once again in 2009, when he and Evelyn Wai-waiole chose to describe the stakes involved—the educational responsibilities, labor market demands, and societal imperatives—that insistently show "we cannot afford *not* to educate these 'at-risk' students" (Roueche and Waiwaiole, 2009).

In 2018, Roueche shared reflections about the evolution of community colleges' work with academically underprepared students: "[F]ifty years after *Salvage, Redirection, or Custody?* it is a terrific disappointment that there are still apologists out there saying that 'those students don't belong in college,' that the work of helping underprepared students succeed in college-level work cannot be done." Still, he went on to say, "We have colleges that are doing it, students who are making it. *We just haven't yet done enough of what we now know"* (Roueche, 2018).

FOCUS ON TEACHING EXCELLENCE

Constant companion to writing and research about accountability and developmental education was John Roueche's emphasis on teaching excellence. His first work for Jossey-Bass Publishers, coauthored with John Pitman, was *A Modest Proposal: Students Can Learn* (Roueche and Pitman, 1972), a book that was one of the publisher's best sellers for three years. JER reported that he was strongly influenced at the time by Benjamin Bloom, who was writing *Learning for Mastery* when John met him while at UCLA. JER's thinking developed along these lines: There are conceptual frameworks that can work in open-door colleges to more effectively serve academically underprepared students. Educators can design ways for individuals to learn what they need to learn, in proper sequence, at their own rate (Roueche, 2018). The focus on pedagogy and teaching excellence is sustained through numerous Roueche publications.

The Origins of the National Institute for Staff and Organizational Development (NISOD)

Despite the rapid expansion in the number of community colleges in the 1960s and 1970s, and despite the remarkable diversity of their student populations, there was, during most of that period, no well-organized strategy for supporting community college practitioners with strong and practical information about effective teaching and learning.

At a now-legendary breakfast meeting with the Kellogg Foundation, detailed in Chapter 10 of this book, a proposal to Kellogg was developed and funded, marking the beginning of a highly successful NISOD. The organization celebrated its 40th anniversary in 2018.

Getting good teaching materials into the hands of faculty members was a major NISOD objective, leading to the development of *Innovation Abstracts*, a weekly publication (one page, front and back) written by and for practitioners and disseminated to a huge following in member colleges around the world.

Over time, NISOD also has helped to increase the stature, dignity, and distinction of teaching in an open-door college. The organization's annual Excellence Awards have had an enduring impact, bringing national recognition to community college faculty whose heart, soul, and talent are focused on teaching.

JER's grandfather, whom he describes as a "good ol' dirt farmer in North Carolina," said to him, "You can lead a horse to water, but you can't make them drink. Your task is to make them thirsty" (Roueche, 2018). Creating and quenching thirst for information on good teaching practices was a goal for the Roueches, which is well addressed in *Practical Magic: On the Front Lines of Teaching Excellence* (Roueche, Milliron, and Roueche, 2003). The authors share the strategies of thousands of teaching professionals who had received NISOD Excellence Awards.

The Broader Higher Education Context

The field was arriving, too, at a stronger emphasis on teaching and learning. From the early-to-mid-1980s throughout the 1990s and to the time that it was dissolved in 2005, the American Association for Higher Education (AAHE) focused on promoting reform in higher education and fostering high-quality teaching and learning.

Not coincidentally, AAHE's longtime president, Russell Edgerton, was highly instrumental (after moving to the Pew Charitable Trusts) in supporting the establishment of the National Survey of Student Engagement at Indiana University under the leadership of George Kuh. Soon thereafter, in 2001, Edgerton also funded the start-up of the Community College Survey of Student Engagement (CCSSE), led by Kay McClenney at UT. John Roueche, then professor and director of UT's CCLP, was indispensably supportive of that work, as the CCSSE developed into a major national resource for assessing effective educational practice in community colleges.

DIVERSITY AND LEADERSHIP — AND LEADERSHIP DIVERSITY

To make good on the promise of the open door, community colleges must embrace diversity—and a part of that necessary process is to embrace diversity in leadership. Recognizing always the diversity in community college student populations, Roueche and his coauthors focus a great deal of attention on describing exactly how leading community colleges transformed themselves to better achieve both open access and educational excellence (Roueche and Baker, 1987; Roueche, Ely, and Roueche, 2001). Consistently, JER has said, the thing that made the difference was exceptional leadership (Roueche, 2018). So, indeed, leadership development and the development of diverse leaders has been a major part of his life's work.

When John Roueche traveled to UT in 1970 for the interview to lead the CCLP, he never believed he would get the job. JER recalled that he couldn't help noticing that there were no minorities and no women in the program. He was told they weren't there because no one would hire them as community college presidents. (Later, he learned that there had previously been one woman in the program, a Catholic nun who had become a college president, and one Hispanic man, Alfred de los Santos, who became a nationally recognized community college leader, but there had been no blacks.) In response, Roueche told faculty during the interview that they needed to become a fully integrated program and that the future of the program would depend on how well it served women and minorities.

Faculty ostensibly embraced the idea, but as JER brought in minority applicants, there was not uniform support, and there was even expressed concern about "lowering the standards" (Roueche, 2018). David Pluviose, editor of *Diverse: Issues in Higher Education*, wrote in 2012 *An Ode to John Roueche*, in which he asserts, "What's most striking about John Roueche's legacy are the epic battles he fought, and won, to recruit women and minorities to CCLP" (Pluviose, 2012).

Walter Bumphus, president and CEO of the AACC—one-time CCLP doctoral student, longtime Roueche colleague and friend, and a black man—adds his own perspective about the first Hispanic and African American students being admitted to the CCLP: "It was not a very popular thing to do, and John got a lot of criticism for that. . . . For many of us, we wouldn't be standing here today were it not for John's courage" (Quoted in Pluviose, 2012).

Once the earliest admissions of female and minority graduate students were accomplished, though, the work became easier; over time, JER's early track record built on itself, as presidents and other community college administrators across the country nominated increasingly diverse candidates for doctoral program admission.

FOCUSED COLLABORATION

In the late 1980s, JER, with his longtime friend and collaborator Terry O'Banion, then president of the League for Innovation in the Community College, codesigned and launched a set of leadership development initiatives that have served as prep school for many community college presidents, including a remarkable number of women and people of color. The Expanding Leadership Diversity (ELD) initiative (1989–1999), the Executive Leadership Institute (ELI; 1998–present), and Leadership 2000 (a national conference series), all collaborative efforts between the League and the UT CCLP, have produced remarkable results in terms of contributing to and diversifying the leadership ranks across the community college field.

CORE VALUES

From where did this focus on diversity come? Raised in small-town North Carolina, John Roueche experienced the great benefits of having a wise father. His dad insisted that he must never consider himself better or of more value than any other person. He pressed upon his son the reality that JER had nothing to do with the unearned privilege inherent in being born an American with white skin. And the elder Roueche called discrimination what it was. With this upbringing, equity and fairness became core values that have undergirded JER's career and life.

According to an article in *Diverse: Issues in Higher Education* marking Roueche's receipt of the publication's inaugural Diverse Champions Award,

> Roueche is set apart from his peers not just for his prolific writing, ground-breaking research, and exceptional teaching on community college leadership practices, but also for his uncompromising commitment to diversity and inclusion. CCLP has graduated more women and minority college presidents than any program of its kind in the country. (Smith, May 22, 2012)

A subsequent article provides, "Of the more than 500 CCLP students who completed doctorates during Roueche's time at the helm, more than 60 percent are women and people of color. CCLP graduates are among a who's who in the community college world. Through them, Roueche has affected the direction of higher education" (Smith, May 30, 2012).

Through the Roueche years, the CCLP doctoral graduation rate was in high 80s, reflecting JER's enduring commitment to access with excellence.

STUDENT SUCCESS AND COLLEGE COMPLETION

As director of the CCLP at UT, John Roueche was at the forefront in launching and supporting a new wave of initiatives focused on student success and college completion as early as 2000, well before the field at large was attending closely to data about student progress and placing priority on completion and equity. His strong support was entirely consistent with his decades-long commitment to *making good on the promise of the open door.*

As community colleges gradually came to recognize the reality that *access without success is an empty promise*, John Roueche gathered around himself a group of community college leaders, scholars, and advocates who in turn initiated a series of impactful projects focused on student success, college completion, and equity. With JER's leadership, the CCLP suite of student success initiatives in the 2000s included the following:

• The Center for Community College Student Engagement (CCCSE), founded by Kay McClenney, was operated from its 2001 origin within the CCLP, where there was immediate access to an extended and influential network of community colleges and their CEOs. The Center initiated research focused systematically on community college student engagement—the extent to which students are involved in purposeful educational activity—and on student voices about their own experiences. At the same time, the CCCSE pioneered online public reporting of survey results; encouraged disaggregation of those data by gender, race, ethnicity, enrollment status, and the like; and provided for institutional performance benchmarking. Following McClenney's retirement from UT in 2014, the work continued under the leadership of Evelyn Waiwaiole. Through 2017, the CCCSE had surveyed more than 2.9 million students (representing a population of 6.4 million) at 951 colleges in 50 states.

- In 2003, the CCLP was a founding partner in Achieving the Dream (ATD), represented by Byron McClenney and Kay McClenney in the earliest planning and throughout the organization's formative years. ATD's clear focus on student success and equity and its strong emphasis on the use of evidence and data have made a lasting impact on the community college field. For 10 years, Byron McClenney directed the leadership coaching component of the ATD strategy. Both McClenneys served as leadership coaches, working with a number of large, complex institutions through 2017–2018.

- Involving community colleges and state systems in six states (2003–2008) and codirected by the McClenneys, the Community College Bridges to Opportunity Initiative aimed to bring about changes in state policy and in community college governance and practice that would promote educational opportunities for low-income adults. One outcome was a state policy guide for increasing the number of low-income adults with postsecondary credentials in high-demand career fields, which was developed by the CCRC (which conducted the external evaluation of the initiative) in collaboration with the CCLP-based project team.

- In 2007, Byron McClenney, along with Margaretta Mathis, launched the Board of Trustees Institute (BOTI), an annual event for CEOs and governing board members from Texas colleges involved in ATD. The BOTI has, according to participants, had a remarkable impact on governing board support for student success initiatives in Texas. The work, always centered on student outcomes data, continues in its 13th year under the leadership of Cynthia Ferrell and the Texas Success Center.

- Another governing board development initiative, the Governance Institute for Student Success (GISS), was developed by the Association of Community College Trustees (ACCT) in close partnership with the CCLP's Byron McClenney. Institutes for governing board members have been conducted in a number of states, focusing on board effectiveness and, in particular, on appropriate roles for boards in promoting student success and college completion.

- Gulf Coast Partners Achieving Student Success (PASS) was a pioneering project led from 2011 to 2015 by Byron McClenney, along with Cynthia Ferrell. Nine Texas Gulf Coast community colleges, working with partner school districts, sought to align curriculum through faculty-to-faculty work, to create a college-going culture among K–12 students, to reduce the need for remediation once students reached college, and to track student progress through school-to-college transitions.
- Co-led by Kay McClenney and Byron McClenney, Student Success by the Numbers (2011–2014) was an initiative designed to help 14 Texas colleges to: (1) advance their institutional capacity to collect, analyze, and report on a variety of data depicting student progress, engagement, and success; (2) use those data to target and monitor improvements in student access, persistence, and completion; and (3) build a college culture of evidence to support and promote an effective student success agenda.
- The California Leadership Alliance for Student Success (CLASS) was established through a project led by Byron McClenney and Kay McClenney. From 2010 to 2012, CLASS involved work with CEOs and governing board members from 12 leading California community colleges. Through a series of multiday institutes, the college leaders and board members developed stronger partnerships in support of community college student success and equity.

Throughout the course of this array of student success initiatives up to the time of his retirement from the CCLP, John Roueche provided organizational and intellectual support, undertook bureaucracy blocking when needed, and ensured that class after class of aspiring doctoral students were exposed to the leadership lessons drawn from extensive work across the nation in the student success arena.

In 2018, Roueche reflected on changes he had observed in the community college field since the turn of the century. With some gratification, he noted a significant shift toward a central focus on student success, achievement, and college completion, "*at least conceptually,*" as colleges finally have accepted responsibility for more than admitting students into the institution. Still, JER worried about the evident need for high-level execution skills and for sustained commitment to large-scale institutional change. He also emphasized strongly the central role of faculty and the necessity of engaging them extensively and effectively in transformational work (Roueche, 2018).

What does Roueche foresee as the next challenge, the next level of work? Bringing change to scale, both deeply within colleges and broadly across the community college field, with a continuing focus on success for all students who enter. He knows, too, that the work will be done in the midst of a sea change: continuing funding constraints, changes in the labor market, developments in the ways people learn, and predicted demographic shifts becoming real.

LOOKING BEHIND TO MOVE FORWARD

John Roueche's first academic love was intellectual history. As far back as his undergraduate experience, he was enthralled with questions about the history of ideas. An article about JER's retirement from UT reports, "The concept of intellectual history had captivated him. 'How in the world does something as radical as the idea that people should be able to govern themselves overthrow monarchs and despots and dictators all over the world?' asks Roueche, marveling at the power of ideas" (Smith, May 22, 2012).

How can that reverence for history be reconciled with the thrust of this chapter, which focuses on Roueche's demonstrated propensity for looking so consistently forward and working *ahead of the curve*? For a person who thinks seriously, as Roueche has, about how a group of people came together to form a new and great American nation, it is not a great leap to recognize that the promise of life, liberty, and the pursuit of happiness originally was intended for white male property owners. What followed, then, was a long struggle to secure equal rights for people of color and women—and the struggle continues. In contemporary America, community colleges are a significant part of that continuing effort, as discussed in *Reclaiming the American Dream: A Report From the 21st Century Commission on the Future of Community Colleges* (American Association of Community Colleges, 2012).

What one learns from history has value, in part, for its own sake, but perhaps the greater value is in using lessons of the past to create a better future. Here a nation has sought to make good on the promise of equality, equity, and the American dream for all. In JER's own career, in his own chosen area of endeavor within that larger context, the look backward has informed and ignited a decades-long, forward-looking focus: *making good on the promise of the open door.*

Chapter Fourteen

The Books of John Roueche

Influence on Research and Practice

Tammy Adams

Over the last four decades, community colleges have faced many challenges around the areas of teaching excellence, developmental education, funding, student success and completion, diversity, accountability, and the need for collaboration and partnerships. This chapter provides an analysis of the books of John E. Roueche, identifying major trends and best practices. The examination of his writing shows how he has provided current and future leaders with a blueprint for success.

THE PROBLEM

The community college movement has transformed over the last 40 years, creating daunting and evolving challenges for leaders. The mission of community colleges to serve their communities and provide students open access to education at an affordable price brings about its own unique challenges. Training leaders to rise to the challenges facing community colleges will remain crucial for community colleges to survive and thrive in the 21st century. These challenges include

- reduced state funding,
- heightened accountability,
- the retiring of senior administrators, and
- meeting the demands of workforce training.

The traditional way of doing business can no longer sustain the health of today's community colleges. To survive, it is necessary for community college leaders to break tradition and become innovative and calculated risk takers. Today's students have many options for education, including private, public, online, and proprietary institutions. This competition requires community colleges to choose to meet the challenges or be overtaken by those that have a focus on the future (Zusman, 2005).

Due to the trends of senior leadership retiring and lack of succession planning, many of today's leaders have been thrust into leadership roles without the proper training (Ellis and Garcia, 2017). Some of these leaders lack the understanding of future trends or the depth of knowledge needed to courageously make the changes necessary to meet those challenges. Other leaders have been in the position for a lengthy tenure and have lost touch with current trends and new regulations. To be an effective leader in the 21st century, some characteristics required include

- deep knowledge of future trends in the community college movement,
- skills to motivate people,
- vision of the future, and
- courage to make the tough decisions necessary to meet the vision and mission of the community college (American Association of Community Colleges, 2017).

For more students to be successful, it is imperative for colleges to hire talented executive leaders who possess the leadership qualities necessary to move their institutions forward. In order to do so, they can look to research from leaders who have blazed the trail. Community college leader and researcher John Roueche (JER) has committed his life to championing the community college (Roueche and Baker, 1984). Leaders can continue to learn from his research-based books because of his visionary approach to dealing with the complex issues of the past and present, as well as the emerging issues of the future.

By studying community colleges who excelled in a time of crisis, JER, in his books, identifies best practices of how institutions can remain sustainable through the ever-changing climate in higher education. It is crucial for leaders to understand that they can learn skills by studying research and best practices from successful leadership (American Association of Community Colleges, 2017).

The books of Roueche reveal issues in the nation's community colleges. The themes and the timelines of his compilations allow the reader to observe the corrective actions that are suggested often before the issues have fully surfaced. Using model institutions throughout the country, these books highlight a pathway of best practice for other struggling colleges to follow.

When summarizing his books, I found that John routinely challenges college leaders to confront and overcome the obstacles that many administrators see as insurmountable. He urges leaders forward for the benefit of student improvement and examines best practices to identify how institutions can remain viable in a changing climate in higher education. Personal interviews with John and six of his coauthors provide insight into the process and thoughts of when and why the books were written—and why they are important to the community college movement.

THEMES THROUGH THE DECADES

A template, designed and developed by the educational staff of the National Archives and Records Administration of Washington, DC, was used to analyze 37 books written by Roueche.[1] The specific data collected includes

- document types;
- unique characteristics;
- the dates of the books;
- authors and coauthors, including their titles and positions; and
- the audiences for whom the books were written.

The document information collected includes three important ideas of the book, why the document was written, and the national issues occurring during the time the documents were written. The analysis of the 37 books reveals six overarching themes:

1. Developmental education
2. Teaching excellence
3. Leadership
4. Accountability
5. Partnerships
6. Diversity

Figure 14.1 shows the number of books written by theme.

Developmental Education, 1968–2001

Roueche and his coauthors wrote 12 books on developmental education over five decades, spanning from 1968 to 2001. The first book on developmental education, *Salvage, Redirection, or Custody? Remedial Education in the Junior College* (Rouche, 1968), was written as the ERIC Clearinghouse introduced a new series of information analyses on community and junior colleges; topics include issues of concern to junior college educators that warranted in-depth study. Several times each year, the Clearinghouse staff would review the problems of concern, consider the research literature relative to those topics, and prepare a report; "Remedial education in the community junior college is the first topic to accord that treatment" (Roueche, 1968).

During the 1970s, four books were produced on developmental education, all designed to provide colleges with specific strategies to use in designing and implementing successful programs for developmental students who enter the open-door college not prepared for college-level coursework.

During the 1980s, three more books on remedial education were brought about; however, these books were written to showcase programs that were successfully educating low-achieving students. JER contends, "The value of the findings of our study lies in the descriptions of workable solutions to common problems faced by open-door colleges. Further, the findings clearly

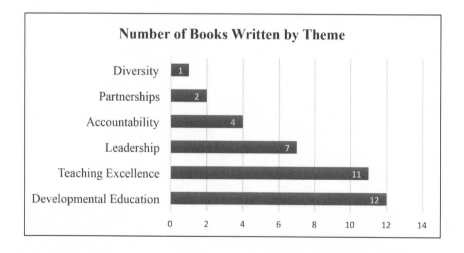

Figure 14.1.

support the contention that open access can be maintained and excellence achieved at the same time" (Roueche and Baker, 1987).

During the 1990s, two more books on developmental education were produced, both printed by the Community College Press. *Between a Rock and a Hard Place: The At-Risk Student in the Open-Door College* (Roueche and Roueche, 1993) highlights 12 community colleges and what they were doing to be successful with remedial education. *High Stakes, High Performance: Making Remedial Education Work* reviews key issues community colleges were facing and concludes with recommendations for "initiating, developing, and improving current practices in remedial education" (Roueche and Roueche, 1999). The last book by John and his coauthors on developmental education was written in 2001, *In Pursuit of Excellence: The Community College of Denver*. This book continues the Roueche pattern of taking a successful college and showcasing what they were doing right. This college had a goal and mission that "every student can be successful" (Roueche, Ely, and Roueche, 2001).

The books written on developmental education provide examples of exemplary development programs. These books allow community colleges to glean the best. The recurring message for community college leaders remains that students can learn when community colleges provide correct resources.

Teaching Excellence, 1976–2003

Roueche and his coauthors wrote 10 books on teaching excellence from 1976 to 2003, which encompassed four decades. The first book, *Time as the Variable, Achievement as the Constant: Competency-Based Instruction in the Community College* (Roueche, Herrscher, and Baker, 1976), encourages competency-based education in technical areas. This book foreshadows the emphasis seen today as states continue to encourage community colleges to embrace competency-based education. The other three books written in the 1970s encourage the instructor to look at the learning experience from the perspective of the student by focusing on student opinion, student attitudes, and student motivation.

Two additional books written in the 1980s for teaching excellence focus on holistic learning or educating the whole person. *Profiling Excellence in America's Schools* (Roueche and Baker, 1986) was surrounded by controversy, as a professor of community college teaching wrote about teaching excellence in public schools. This book was funded by a foundational grant.

During the 1990s, two books were written on teaching excellence, *Teaching as Leading: Profiles of Excellence in the Open-Door College* (Roueche, Baker, and Gillett-Karam, 1990) and *1,001 Exemplary Practices in America's Two-Year Colleges* (Roueche, Parnell, and Kuttler, 1994). Both are guides for teachers to glean the effective, pedagogical strategies innovative teachers were using in the classroom. *Strangers in Their Own Land: Part-Time Faculty in American Community Colleges* (Roueche, Roueche, and Milliron, 1995) draws attention to adjunct faculty members, who were a growing population for community colleges as they tried to meet budgets and deal with reduced funding.

John wrote about teaching excellence for four decades to provide best practices, equipping faculty to teach course content and to focus on teaching the whole student. He believes all students can learn and that, when teaching is done well, students can learn new ideas and acquire knowledge they will take with them throughout their lives.

Leadership, 1968–2012

Roueche and his coauthors wrote seven books spanning five decades (1968–2012) on the topic of leadership. The first book, *Junior College Institutional Research: The State of the Art* (Roueche and Boggs, 1968), dispels the critics who would not embrace the community college movement. During the 1980s, three books were written on leadership, mainly to help executive leadership understand challenges and changes taking place and learn to manage those changes.

In 2008 and 2012, the final two books on leadership were brought about, *The Creative Community College: Leading Change through Innovation* (Roueche, Richardson, and Roueche, 2008) and *Rising to the Challenge: Lessons Learned from Guilford Technical Community College* (Roueche and Roueche, 2012). The authors establish, "Our overarching goals were to inform practice by looking at what very successful colleges were doing, why they did it, how they did it, who was involved, what they gained (or lost) in the process, and what happened as a result" (Roueche and Roueche, 2012).

Dr. Roueche has focused on leadership issues, in both his writing and teaching for more than five decades. He highlights best practices of model leaders to showcase ideas leaders can implement to help their colleges be successful. The focus of the books is transformational leadership, which identifies needed change, creates a vision to guide the change, and communicates and inspires people to implement the change.

Accountability, 1968–1997

Roueche and his coauthors wrote four books on accountability from 1968 to 1997, spanning three decades. *Junior College Institutional Research: The State of the Art* (Roueche and Boggs, 1968) encourages institutions of higher education to use research-based decision-making.

During the 1970s, there was a focus for instructors to be leaders and be accountable in the classroom. *Accountability and the Community College: Directions for the '70s* (Roueche, Baker, and Brownwell, 1971) encourages administrators and instructors to take up the challenge of being accountable for teaching students. *Toward Instructional Accountability: A Guide to Educational Change* (Roueche and Herrscher, 1973) serves as a professional learning course to guide instructors or administrators who want to be leaders. Only one other book was written on accountability, *Embracing the Tiger: The Effectiveness Debate and the Community College* (Roueche, Johnson, and Roueche, 1997). This book is a call for institutional effectiveness to be implemented nationwide at all community colleges.

The original book by Roueche on accountability was written in 1968 and is still a best practice used in community colleges today. In the books on accountability, John again gives a call to the leadership to be accountable for

- creating excellent developmental education programs,
- developing teaching excellence in the classroom,
- developing partnerships, and
- embracing diversity in order to successfully assess and evaluate an institution's viability.

Partnerships, 1995–2005

Roueche and his coauthors wrote two books related to partnerships over two decades: *The Company We Keep: Collaboration in the Community College* (Roueche, Taber, and Roueche, 1995) and *The Entrepreneurial Community College* (Roueche and Jones, 2005). The authors believe the best practices presented in these books offer engaging strategies for becoming entrepreneurial in unsettling financial times. Roueche and Jones state, "With genuine enthusiasm for all that is possible in the entrepreneurial college, we hope this book represents a valuable guide and a first step toward transformation" (2005). These books address both the decrease in state funding of the community college and the need for college leaders to become more involved with their communities and industry partnerships.

Diversity, 1991

Roueche and his coauthors wrote one book on diversity, *Underrepresentation and the Question of Diversity: Women and Minorities in the Community College* (Roueche, Gillett-Karam, and Roueche, 1991), as a call for community colleges to hire administrators who would match the demographic composition of their student bodies.

Through the Decades

Rouche and his coauthors' books transformed from simply informing community colleges of issues in the late 1960s to being professional learning guides in the 1970s. Then in the 1980s, he and his coauthors began to produce workable solutions for developmental education and help for new and aspiring leaders. The books of the 1990s highlight examples of community colleges and what they were doing right, enabling leaders to learn and read about best practices as they faced new challenges. Beginning in the 2000s and beyond, the books again showcase those colleges performing excellently in areas where other community colleges were facing challenges.

INTERVIEWS

To enhance the understanding of the books, I interviewed Roueche and six of his coauthors. The questions provided insight to the writing process, including

- how the topics were selected,
- how institutions or individuals were identified and chosen to participate in studies,
- how best practices were identified, and
- how the community college movement was enhanced by JER's books.

I asked each interviewee the same questions and, at the end of every interview, provided an opportunity for them to speak freely about their book, the process they used, or any other topic regarding their experience that they deemed important to their research.

John Roueche's Perspective

"In your opinion, Dr. Roueche, which book or books identified and addressed the most important issues of higher education?

Salvage, Redirection, or Custody? was his first book and was written at the request of the American Association of Community and Junior Colleges (AAJCC) board and their CEO at the time, Dr. Ed Gleazer. The focus of this writing was to find out what colleges were doing with underprepared high school graduates. During the time the book was written, the board, Dr. Gleazer, and the public were upset by the large number of students who were leaving high school unprepared for college-level work. Dr. Roueche said of this work,

> What the study found was that community colleges were not doing very well with those students that they placed into remedial courses. The findings from that study were so negative and so critical that the board hesitated a long time before deciding to publish the report because they had never published anything so critical of the work of the two-year college. Because that book was negative and critical, a number of major national newspapers picked the book up and wrote editorials. The *Los Angeles Times* had a whole-page analysis of the book and what it meant, and a lot of critics were saying, "If this is the best community colleges can do, they shouldn't even offer remedial courses." But what the book did for Ed Gleazer, the president, and the executive committee of the AACC board was convince them that the colleges had to do more than just admit the students. (Roueche, August 31, 2018).

At that time in community college history, many believed that the mission of the community college was focused on access and opportunity. *Salvage, Redirection, or Custody?* confirmed for Dr. Gleazer and the board that the mission of the community colleges in the United States had to be defined as more than making access and opportunity available. John delivered a 67-page study with a key finding that floored Dr. Gleazer and his board: Less than 10% of students placed into remedial English, math, writing, or study skills at community colleges completed those studies to advance to credit-bearing coursework (Roueche, 1968).

Thus, the call that came from Dr. Gleazer to community colleges became a challenge of "making good on the promise of the open-door." When the study began, nobody had any idea what the outcome, the results, or the consequences might be. But, Dr. Roueche stated,

As it turned out, it certainly was a wake-up call for people at the national level to realize that we have got to work hard and take responsibility for students and ensure they get a good education. The real sadness is that, here we are, 50 years later, and most colleges still don't have very efficient or well-designed developmental education or compensatory education programs. (Roueche, August 31, 2018)

Walter Bumphus, current president of AACC, stated,

The report documented through first-time data that the vaunted open door, considered the cornerstone of the community college mission, might also be a revolving door for far too many students. It was not the last time that John would question the status quo and invite administrators and faculty to rethink assumptions about the raison d'être of their institutions. The study brought into stark relief an issue that continues to vex community colleges decades later and that foreshadowed later national efforts focused on ensuring balance of student access and student success, such as Achieving the Dream, the Completion Agenda, and other initiatives. (Bumphus, November 5, 2018)

The second book identified by John as having an impact on the community college movement was *A Modest Proposal: Students Can Learn* (Roueche and Pitman, 1972), which challenges the then-existing feelings and beliefs about students. This book threatened the belief of the time that not all students should be in college. The common philosophy was that many of these students should go into the military or get a job. John believed, "If you give students enough time, quality instruction, and a caring and supportive environment, they can do well" (Roueche, August 31, 2018).

Dr. Roueche referenced the work of Benjamin Bloom as being influential in the development of *A Modest Proposal: Students Can Learn*. That book received criticism from some of the good old boys who, according to John, said, "Well, he's overlooking a lot of basic research that shows there are major racial differences in intelligence and ability." John explained, "The whole point of the book was to shoot some of that down" (Roueche, August 31, 2018).

The third book identified by John as making a difference in the community college movement was *Access and Excellence: The Open-Door College* (Roueche and Baker, 1987), a story of Miami-Dade Community College, the first public community college to openly embrace the open-door concept and insist on student success and excellence. The difference was that the president, Dr. Bob McCabe, was committed to student success and worked closely with the faculty to ensure that success. Dale Parnell, president of AACC at that time, was excited to see the results of this study and an example that a college can be open-door, provide open access, and still see quality outcomes, both for developmental and general education.

The next book identified as being influential in the movement of community colleges was *Shared Vision: Transformational Leadership in American Community Colleges* (Roueche, Baker, and Rose, 1989), a study of the community college presidents in each state identified by their colleagues as being the best in helping students be successful. The book highlights the leadership skills, qualities, and educational talent characterized by top presidents. Dr. Roueche remembered, "Many of the graduate schools that offered programs in community college leadership called me to let me know how much they appreciated that study and how helpful it was going to be in getting their courses and the curriculum focused on the skills, the qualities, and the attributes that effective leaders need to be successful" (Roueche, August 31, 2018).

In Pursuit of Excellence: The Community College of Denver (Roueche, Ely, and Roueche, 2001) is the next book identified in his interview as being influential in the community college movement. This work is a study built on the model of access with excellence with the Community College of Denver. The state of Colorado required data on students, such as persistence through the first year, how many became second-year students, and how many graduated. Dr. Roueche remembered, "The Community College of Denver, at that time, had more minority students than any other institution in the state—this population included more single mothers and students on welfare, yet they were leading the state of Colorado in course completion rates, in graduation rates, and in transfers" (Roueche, August 31, 2018).

Practical Magic: On the Front Lines of Teaching Excellence (Roueche, Milliron, and Roueche, 2003) is a study of more than 7,000 National Institute for Staff and Organizational Development (NISOD) Excellence Award winners. The book identifies the qualities, attributes, proficiencies, and skills of these award-winning faculty members so that colleges have well-documented data and information about what it takes to teach at an open-door college. This study provides a guideline for staff development employees to build professional development programs for their home institutions.

When identifying books that made the biggest impact on the community college movement, JER identified

- *Between a Rock and a Hard Place: The At-Risk Student in the Open-Door College* (Roueche and Roueche, 1993);
- *The Creative Community College: Leading Change through Innovation* (Roueche, Richardson, and Roueche, 2008);
- *Underrepresentation and the Question of Diversity: Women and Minorities in the Community College* (Roueche, Gillett-Karam, and Roueche, 1991); and
- *The Entrepreneurial Community College* (Roueche and Jones, 2005).

In conclusion, John stated, "All of the books were focused on how colleges could improve and get better, but these, I think, were the ones that had the biggest impact" (Roueche, August 31, 2018).

"What topic or emerging issue would you write about today?"

To this question, JER replied, "The changing landscape in which colleges today are trying to exist" (Roueche, August 31, 2018). John then shared that community college, public regional college, and private college enrollments are decreasing and continuing to go down. The other issue is that states are slowly, deliberately, and gradually withdrawing financial support from higher education.

Today's leader has to be skilled at finding partnerships, building collaborations, and becoming a preferred learning provider with industry. There's so much training going on today in the United States, and American colleges and universities only do a small percentage of it. Roueche asserted, "If we're going to survive, we have to be working with people and in concert with others. Otherwise, we are going to lose financial support, and we cannot keep raising tuition" (Roueche, August 31, 2018).

Coauthors

I asked Roueche's coauthors, "Why was it important to write about these particular topics at the time you wrote them? Was there anything that was specific to legislation, or was it just timely?" The response was unanimous from all coauthors: While none of them could point to specific legislative changes, each one had experienced testimonies from colleagues that these writings had touched lives and changed policies and practices at local levels.

One coauthor stated, "One of the things that's great about John is he doesn't just want to articulate the problem; he wants to look at some solutions. He was big on the idea of not just understanding the problem but actually going out and finding some model colleges" (Coauthor 1, 2018). Two coauthors reported that it was important for them to write the books because they were on topics that needed to be addressed, and there was no literature available that had been written about those topics. One coauthor noted,

> One of the things that John is good about is finding important topics that are being overshadowed, so the conversation around adjunct faculty was one that indicated that fiscal constraints were getting tougher. Colleges are trying to be more innovative with their programs, and more of them were turning to part-time faculty to help with fiscal constraints. As we started diving into the literature and realizing there was nothing there, it clearly was an issue that was impacting every community college in the country. The ability to articulate and showcase models, things that didn't just make the problem worse but actually were solutions that people could begin adopting, seemed to be a really important thing to make happen (Coauthor 1, 2018).

Another coauthor stated that, during the time they wrote their book,

> More and more colleges were experiencing a disinvestment in higher educa-tion at the state level. John was discovering in the presidents that he talked to across the country . . . that so much more of their time was being spent fund-raising and generating partnerships. The entire role and scope of a community college president, John was noticing, was transforming and becoming a differ-ent kind of job. So, I think because nothing had been written about it, because John had observed that the role of the presidents was changing, and just the fact that it was clear that states were not investing at the same level as they used to, you had to think of ways to be more entrepreneurial. (Coauthor 2, 2018)

Two coauthors provided a "how to" process to answer the question of how the books came about. One discussed the detailed process of researching literature on the topic. This coauthor said, "We did both a statistical analysis and some qualitative research. . . . In the summer . . . we held a huge meeting, bringing those people in and talking about how they had contributed to our research" (Coauthor 3, 2018). Another coauthor remembered much the same process but included they would

> submit a request for proposal from a funder, private or public. We would get the funds, set up the process, write the proposal, structure the book, and devel-op our instrumentation. In one study, we took the entire cohort of students

down to Miami-Dade to help us collect the data. We would bring it back, crunch it, put it in chapters, and that's how the books were developed. (Coauthor 6, 2018)

Two other coauthors talked more about the benefits of the books. One coauthor illustrated, "It's one thing to learn the theory, but to hear from the practitioners who are out there trying new ideas, addressing the challenges that we were facing in community colleges at the time, and then to write a book highlighting some promising practices occurring across the country—that was the real benefit of the book" (Coauthor 4, 2018). Another coauthor said,

We came to the topic in a couple of ways. We recognized the many different forces that are impacting community colleges as institutions: what our mission is, how we're serving the community, the many partnerships, how we've become so global, and recognizing that many institutions are solving those new connections very rapidly and very creatively. The more we learned about what was going on within the community college world, the more we realized that community college leadership is not solely operational. It's not solely about individual leadership skills; it has a lot to do with the leaders' creativity and willingness to see things in a new way and to frame their ideas and their growth for their colleges in a new way. (Coauthor 5, 2018)

When answering the coauthor question about choosing topics, all coauthors agreed and went into great detail about how topics were identified, the important discussions that took place, and how ideas came from different places. But ultimately, it was Roueche who had the final say. One coauthor authenticated, "*Practical Magic* was written as an answer to a major milestone anniversary at NISOD" (Coauthor 1, 2018).

Two coauthors agreed that JER gave them free rein over identifying, in a draft form, the topics that they would write about. And of course, because they were going through a doctoral program, they were learning about all these things. Everybody in the doctoral program had been at community colleges, and they had faced those issues earlier in their careers. The topics really were right at their fingertips; it was not anything they had to dream up. The final topics were chosen together. They knew they wanted to highlight some of the creative things that were being done and really think about 21st-century future planning (Coauthor 4, 2018; Coauthor 5, 2018).

Two questions explored what bearing their books had on community colleges and what influence the books had on local, state, and national policy or procedures, including any examples from the coauthors. One coauthor explained,

> I think what it ended up doing was probably creat[ing] more institutional policy changes for adjunct faculty where people saw the models and said, "We've got to figure out what we should be paying these instructors and be more systematic about how we hire, orient, and involve them." A couple of examples we knew were put in place at Valencia Community College. They put an entire staff development program [together] to help engage those faculty members and have them become more a part of their college. Mesa Community College in Arizona created a virtual community for the part-timers that was so powerful, it connected to the Mesa Community College, and the full-time faculty members wanted to join this community, as well. We saw a lot of both practice and policy at the institutional level more than we saw at the state and national levels. (Coauthor 1, 2018)

Another coauthor revealed,

> At the time when I wrote, the NACCE, which is the National Association of Community College Entrepreneurs, had just come into existence several years earlier. When we wrote this book, we were invited to be the keynote speaker at their national conference. John and I did multiple keynote addresses for AACC and League for Innovation. We basically hit the road and did a number of national presentations where we introduced our concepts and stories from the book to the higher educational world. And then, of course, from that we wrote many articles. We had a great number of articles related to entrepreneurship in many of the higher education journals, which spread the word even more. John then did a subsequent book called *The Creative Community College*, which took our work to the next level. John and I came back together again and did another article, so I think it added to the literature in higher education. We had an opportunity to inform a pretty large audience of community college leaders across the nation for a number of years. So hopefully, because of our ability to get the word out, people took those lessons and implemented them at their own colleges. Of course, personally, as a college president, I've implemented them at every college I've worked at. (Coauthor 2, 2018)

Yet another coauthor confirmed,

> I have been invited to speak on the book and my experience with the book in several different locations, whether they were other community colleges in house leadership programs that were using the book all the way up to universities. I've guest lectured from the University of Texas, El Paso; in a doctoral

class; to Harvard University in their higher education program; and to community colleges throughout the state of Kentucky, as well as other colleges around the country. The book is being used as a textbook, and as a former faculty member myself, you know students will always take away something. You just don't know what unless you assess it somehow. But the feedback that we received was very positive because we were sharing real-world examples, and that's what I think a lot of us appreciate the most as practitioners: We like to hear about other practitioners, the success stories, and the challenges that they face. The fact that the book is still being sold today is a testament that there must be something of interest still in this book. The thing that I think has shaped today's higher education policy in this book are the people who have gone on to other leadership positions, like Walter Bumphus and Richard Rhodes. These men have gone on to carry their learning and their experience to a broader level, from a practitioner and a policy level. I think they are the ones who have gone on to influence today's higher education policy, probably more so than the book. (Coauthor 4, 2018)

Another coauthor went on to reflect about the 1960s, when John was a professor at Duke University and the director for the Regional Educational Laboratory for the Carolinas and Virginia (RELCV), which became the National Laboratory for Higher Education. This coauthor said,

There was a 20-year gap between what the research said educators should be doing and what they were actually doing, and what we were trying to do at that time was to close that gap. The national movement was toward accountability; they wanted accountability in the community colleges and student learning. When John was awarded a professorship at the University of Texas at Austin, he, his team, and I had the motivation that we would need to impact the community college movement in the Americas. (Coauthor 6, 2018)

BEST PRACTICES

The purpose of these 37 books by Dr. Roueche was to provide professional learning to educators aspiring to be leaders and create a resource to help them effectively provide students with the tools needed to be successful. How did Dr. Roueche identify best practices to address these issues?

The books began in the 1960s with making the readers aware of problems community colleges were facing; they call for data-informed decision-making and teaching the underprepared students entering higher education. The 1970s were directed with how-to books to provide road maps for enhancing developmental education plans, becoming better leaders, and creating more effective institutions. The 1980s and beyond began a pattern of showcasing exemplary schools that were providing best practices to model what other schools should be doing.

JER's Insights on Best Practices

"Why was it important to identify best practices in your books?"

Dr. Roueche maintained,

> Because it doesn't do a lot of good to identify problems, issues, or challenges unless you can point people to resolutions or solutions. What we were trying to do with all our books was point out schools that are doing good things. Even though this is a major challenge, a major issue, here is what Miami-Dade is doing, here is what the Community College of Denver is doing, here is what Greenville Tech is doing, and here's what Guilford Tech is doing. We were trying to point out that this is not *Mission Impossible*, that, while this is a tough assignment, many colleges are doing quite well with it now. Today, they are even more so but nowhere near enough. (Roueche, August 31, 2018)

Coauthors' Insights on Best Practices

"Did the book you coauthored with John Roueche provide best practices for community college issues? Please provide examples."

All coauthors agreed that their books were full of best practices and were quick to provide examples. One coauthor confirmed, "*Strangers in Their Own Land* provided good examples of how you effectively recruit faculty members, how you orient faculty, provide staff development, evaluate, and offer cultural integration" (Coauthor 1, 2018). This same author commented, "*Practical Magic* was an overview of how instructors worked their magic" (Coauthor 1, 2018).

Another coauthor responded,

> Certainly, the whole concept of best practice would be the idea of creating a culture of responsible risk-taking and the idea of friend raising. One of the important lessons from the book is that you just don't go and ask for money— that you've got to develop relationships, and from those valued relationships, these people who give you money become your partners. One best practice is that concept of friend raising—that you never know who you're going to come in contact with and the way in which they're going to be able to help you. You have to let people know that you're interested. You've got to develop that

relationship. You've got to not be afraid to ask people to be part of the college and to contribute to the college. (Coauthor 2, 2018)

Another coauthor responded, "Best practices included mentoring, going to conferences, and working steadfastly toward greater achievement in terms of taking responsibility for jobs and roles in the colleges that you're in now. You have to be able to take risks. You have to say I'm willing to do X, Y, or Z. You have to do it with a greater goal in mind—that is advancement of self towards leadership" (Coauthor 3, 2018).

Still another coauthor said,

> Yes, there are all kinds of best practices in the book, from a college in Iowa building dorms and engaging the community to build more of a campus life to Kentucky Community Technical College System utilizing predictive analytics. There are a multitude of practices that were ahead of their time in some ways and then some were tried and true by others. It was just one more example of how that practice was highly effective. (Coauthor 4, 2018)

Another coauthor verified,

> It is incredibly important to be transparent about our own work and our own questions. For the seasoned practitioners to put it on the page, open up about it, and be transparent in front of any reader was very brave and very forthcoming. This book recognized the climate that leaders were in, recognized good ideas, and fostered a creativity to test the idea to develop it into a product that can be used. To have those leaders do that for us is very meaningful. (Coauthor 5, 2018)

The pattern that all coauthors reported included researching literature, and if there was none, they would conduct the research and find out what community colleges were doing. They would identify top community colleges who were having success in the area they were researching. Then, through their writings, they would report out to other community colleges what was being done, what the successes and failures were, and how they could implement the models at their colleges.

Selecting Colleges or Leaders for Best Practices

I followed the discussion of providing best practices with this question to the coauthors: "How did you select colleges/leaders to provide best practices?" While each seemed to have a unique experience, they all were quick to provide a very methodological process to identify top providers in their field of knowledge. One coauthor explained,

> We used a referential snowball sample by going out to programs that were notable in the literature and then ask[ing] them who else we should talk to and who were their models. We expanded that; we ended up doing just round after round of referential sampling. You end up coming back to a family of colleges that gets referenced a lot, so you know you have to talk to them. You also end up coming across some gems that nobody knew about because, in the community college world, just because someone's in the national press doesn't mean they're great—it just means that they have a great press shot. The referential snowball sample strategy was really important for us and did help uncover some really interesting programs—sometimes at some colleges that weren't necessarily the nationally noticeable ones. The faculty book was actually a combination of a population census of faculty members who had been recognized by NISOD. Then, for the focus groups, we did an outreach and invitation for the faculty members who were coming in to be recognized that year; we encouraged them to be a part of the study. There were five focus groups of 50 faculty members each, which was just a great, deep, rich sample of folks—current winners and past winners of the award. (Coauthor 1, 2018)

Another coauthor remembered,

> John and I actually spent a lot of time working on this process as preliminary work for writing the book; we agreed upon a list of criteria, including the overall success rate of an institution, their reputation, and longevity of employees, and we had to find an example where they had done something out of the ordinary that generated additional revenue. This was the criteria we used that makes up an entrepreneurial college. We found colleges that fit all the criteria, and then we did the research and compiled the book. (Coauthor 2, 2018)

One final coauthor did not hesitate to identify Dr. Roueche as being able to identify the cutting-edge leaders. He said,

> John has always had insight into who is doing new, creative, and meaningful work. He has a vast network of leaders, a vast network of learners, and a network of organizations that are influencing the educational climate based upon just the knowledge that he has and the friends and community that he's built. He did suggest several of the leaders in the book. At the same time, there were a couple that I know we had met through the community college leadership program that had been invited by Dr. Roueche and the program to come speak to us, that had been meaningful to us, and that we wanted to include in

the book. It was a shared contribution, but certainly John's connections and knowledge had the most impact. (Coauthor 4, 2018)

Lessons to Be Learned

To round out the information on why the books were important, I asked the coauthors, "What important lessons can aspiring leaders learn from reading about seasoned professionals who have knowledge of processes that can help them be successful?"

One coauthor was quick to affirm,

> I will just be blunt. I think the world of higher education operates very often on a CASE method; CASE method stands for "Copy and Steal Everything." If somebody does something well, you try to pull it in and figure out how you can integrate it. I think one of the things John has been great at is articulating the issues and researching them thoroughly, then identifying people who are engaging in practices or adopting policies that are measurably improving things for the students and the communities that they're serving. He's trying to offer models that you could implement if you're a new leader. One of the things he's trying to do is invite you into that adoption through a combination of (1) research that tells you how credible it is and (2) the practice that shows you how practical it is and how you would take the steps to make it work. (Coauthor 1, 2018)

Another coauthor shared an important lesson: "You have to find someone who will mentor you into these new positions, especially if you are a minority. Women are not a minority, but unless they are able to step on the shoulders of people who already have had positions, it's not that easy for them to get new positions" (Coauthor 3, 2018).

Another coauthor took a different approach and reported,

> Leadership is how you work with people, how you motivate others, how you build buy-in, how you're supportive of their efforts, how you reinforce the things you want to see continue, and how you communicate. It's really the people factor, in my opinion. And that was one of the most heartwarming things that I took from this book. Some leaders talked about having to encourage people to have a family life outside the job because sometimes the job can swallow you up. That's the side of leadership that you don't get in textbooks. (Coauthor 4, 2018)

Another coauthor commented,

There are seasoned leaders that help to influence, shape, teach, and inspire new and upcoming leaders. In doing this, they have been able to leave their legacy for future leaders to be able to continue, even if they are not in that position and capacity anymore. So by actually writing it down and capturing their process (what they were challenged by, what their decision-making was, what their resources were, how they influenced), it helps to create a playbook of sorts for new leaders to be able to face their own challenges. (Coauthor 5, 2018)

WORD ANALYSIS

I conducted a separate word analysis on the transcripts of the interviews and the written book analysis. The analysis of the books began with a comparison of the data recorded in the data analysis worksheets. The data analysis of the transcripts of the interviews began by sending the transcribed interviews to Dr. Roueche and his coauthors for approval. Once two weeks had lapsed, I began the process of comparing words and ideas that emerged from the sessions.

I used ATLAS.ti to generate a list of words that emerged from the transcripts of the interviews and the written book analysis. Through the open-coding process, words associated with the themes of the document analysis began to emerge. After all the interviews were conducted and the open-coding process was applied, a saturation level had been reached. This same process was conducted on the document analysis, and the same words and themes emerged.

Table 14.1 shows the number of times each word was used in an interview and book analysis. The number of interviewees reflects the number of coauthors who mentioned the word during the interview. The number of books represents the numbers of books written on the subject.

The word analysis of the transcripts of the interviews revealed *leadership* was used 59 times, *teaching excellence* was used 33 times, *developmental education* was used 21 times, *diversity* was used 8 times, *partnership* was used 6 times, and *accountability* was used 2 times. Of the six coauthors who were interviewed, at least one author was associated with each major theme.

For words used in the written book analysis, *leadership* was used 72 times, *developmental education* was used 47 times, *accountability* was used 16 times, *teaching excellence* was used 12 times, *diversity* was used 6 times, and *partnership* was used 4 times.

Theme	Times Used in Interviews	Number of Interviewees	Times Used in Book Analysis	Number of Books Written
Developmental education	21	4	47	12
Teaching excellence	33	4	12	11
Leadership	59	5	72	7
Accountability	2	2	16	4
Partnership	6	4	4	2
Diversity	8	1	6	1

In completing the word analysis of the books and interviews, there were seven books written about leadership; however, the word *leadership* appeared 72 times in the book analysis and 59 times in the interview word analysis. Through this analysis, I deduced that leadership is a key factor to effective developmental education, accountability, diversity, collaboration and partnerships, and teaching excellence.

From the written analysis of the books, it is interesting to see that the books in the 1960s were written by Dr. Roueche himself or himself and one colleague. The 1970s followed this pattern, as well, with John and one to two colleagues writing the books. The 1980s, 1990s, and 2000s brought about a change in the coauthors, as Dr. Roueche opened up the opportunity for his community college leadership program doctoral students to write with him; several of them took up the challenge and wrote about emerging issues. During the 2010s, Dr. Roueche primarily wrote with his wife, Suanne. While interviewing Dr. Roueche on how he was able to persuade other writers into writing with him, his comment was that all he did was ask.

CONCLUSION

It is evident by the analysis of the books and the interviews with Dr. Roueche and his coauthors that the purpose of these 37 books was to address topics that the community college movement was facing. The books were timely and evidently touched the community college movement, changing policies and practices at local levels. The books are important because they highlight promising practices from across the country. It is important for the community college leadership to learn from the best practices of other community college leadership. One major contribution of the books is the impact on today's higher education policy and the people who have gone on to key leadership positions.

Dr. Roueche believes that it does nothing toward improvement if the only purpose for writing is to identify problems, issues, or challenges unless you can point people to resolutions or solutions. His books are full of best practices and are quick to provide solutions for leaders to help better their institutions.

One coauthor expressed,

> Dr. Roueche is a special player in the community college scene for a host of reasons, but one of his superpowers is this ambidexterity between research and practice. It's one thing to be able to research an issue and identify it, but then to be able to communicate in both writing and speaking has made him a game-changer in the community college space. I think those translators, the people who translate research into practice and practice into research, genuinely serve the field. Working with John is one of those combinations of serendipity and rocket fuel. You get the serendipity working with a great person with a great mind, and you learn a ton about the entire process. That leads to the rocket fuel, which means you're suddenly in conversations you have not been in before, and you have to learn pretty quick because you're going really fast. For anybody who does those kinds of books with John, you have that combination of serendipity and rocket fuel that come together. You've got to soak up the serendipity, and when the rocket fuel strikes, you've got to hold on tight. (Coauthor 1, 2018)

Dr. Roueche was able to identify cutting-edge leaders who were accomplishing new, creative, and meaningful work. He had a vast network of leaders, a vast network of learners, and a network of organizations that were influencing the educational climate, which reiterates the need to develop partnerships and relationships. As a coauthor stated,

> First off, I miss them both. And of course, Suanne is no longer with us, but they were both so near and dear to everybody who goes through the program; I don't know of one person who probably wouldn't say the same thing about them. They are the most gracious people, down-to-earth, caring individuals. You find those people in life that you want to emulate—whether professionally or personally—and, in this case, both. Everybody has their own characteristics that they want to aspire to have in their own personalities and the way they treat others. I think John and Suanne exemplified many of those characteristics that I would like to have somebody say that I have, whether it be as a profes-

sional, a colleague, a father, a husband, or a community member. They are just
wonderful people, and I think great leaders start by being great people first. I
think they exemplified that on every level that you can possibly imagine. I
always learned from them, whether I knew I was learning or not. John was
always willing to put his arm around you and say, "We work hard in this
program, and we are going to go above and beyond what anybody could
imagine, but we are here for each other." That always stayed with me and that
is why I will do anything I can to help him in the future. (Coauthor 4, 2018)

Through his writings Dr. Roueche delivered the research, data, and best
practices that were being used by productive leaders in progressive community colleges nationwide. Through his writings and leadership, he offered
some sage words of advice on what future leaders should expect as they enter
leadership roles. In his writings, Dr. Roueche set himself apart from other
authors because of his ability to identify and research an issue and then be
able to communicate about it, both in writing and speaking. This made him a
game-changer in the community college field.

Dr. Roueche and his coauthors gathered data and provided necessary
research in order to challenge community college leadership to change habits
and processes that were unsuccessful. Each book focuses on an issue that was
taking place in the nation but was often ignored by community colleges at the
time the book was written. These issues were identified by AACC, community college presidents, foundation donors, doctoral students who were administrators in community colleges, and John himself.

All of the books were written specifically for higher education administration, board of regents, instructors, advisors, and teachers. The purpose of
the books was to provide guides or examples of how higher education could
improve teaching, developmental programs, access for students, diversity,
and collaboration and better prepare leaders for the future. For these solutions, John and his coauthors championed the ideas that worked, and they
brought to light those that did not—all for the sole purpose of inspiring
community college leaders to learn, plan, and take the necessary steps to be
successful.

Part IV

A New Direction

Chapter Fifteen

Retirement from UT Austin

Celebration and Controversy

Martha M. Ellis

Occasionally announcements are released that rock the foundation of a profession. In 2012 two such announcements were made in a matter of a few short months that were seismic for the community college world. Both communications brought reasons to celebrate, and both were laced with controversy.

RETIREMENT ANNOUNCED

John retired from the University of Texas at Austin (UT) in 2012. Colleagues from all segments of higher education bestowed upon him accolades, awards, and tributes. Events were held in Austin and across the county to celebrate his momentous career accomplishments at UT. Articles were written in the higher education press that highlight his body of work (Bradley, 2012; Lorenzo, 2012; Pluviose, 2012; Smith, 2012; Ullman, 2012).

During the Presidents Academy Hail and Farewell Luncheon at the 2012 AACC conference, a moving tribute video honoring Roueche was shown. Former AACC presidents and CEOs reflected on John's influence and contributions to US community colleges across the decades. (A transcript of this video is provided in the next chapter of this book.) Following the video presentation, Walter Bumphus, current president of the AACC, presented Roueche with an award recognizing him for his many years of service. This luncheon was among several events at the AACC annual convention devoted exclusively or partially to hailing Roueche's extraordinary contributions to the community college movement. Indeed, it was a time of great celebration and well-deserved recognition.

A NEW ADVENTURE ANNOUNCED THAT SAME SPRING

As retirement celebrations were continuing, a press release hit the newswire. On May 29, 2012, National American University Holdings, Inc. announced John Roueche would become president of the newly developed Roueche Graduate Center to design an innovative community college leadership doctoral program.

When this news hit the airwaves, it was referred to as a "bombshell" for community college leaders and was the "buzz" at the 2012 annual conference of the National Institute for Staff and Professional Development (Fain, 2012). The bombshell was positive, in that John would continue to provide preparation for community college leaders, albiet at a proprietary institution. The bombshell was troubling, as many believed this news provided confirmation that UT was moving away from supporting a CCLP.

CONTROVERSY ARISES WITH JOHN RETIRING

As documented throughout this book, UT's CCLP had established a reputation as one of the country's premier graduate programs for community college leaders. Data on student outcomes validated the CCLP was the leading program in the nation for preparing community college leaders. Roueche was widely praised for his research, writing, prowess as a fund-raiser, and mentoring of students and alumni, which provided the foundation for the CCLP. With John retiring, some feared the university's commitment to community colleges was on shaky ground (Fain, 2012; Hamilton, 2012). There were justifiable reasons for their fear. From 2010 to 2012, a number of actions by the leadership of the College of Education foreshadowed the changes coming to the CCLP. With John's retirement, the changes moved rapidly.

Merger

Roueche was able to take advantage of a retirement incentive package offered by the university in 2012. He said money was not the primary reason for his departure at that point in time: "I really didn't want to be part of a move I thought was a bad move strategically at a time when community colleges are growing like crazy" (Hamilton, 2012).

The bad move he was referencing was the merger of the CCLP into the university's other programs of higher education, under the new name of the Higher Education Leadership Program. A redesign of the doctoral program was proposed, moving away from the primary purpose of preparing future community college leaders in a CCLP format.

Reduced student enrollment added to the concerns that the CCLP was being dismantled. In 2011, only 4 students were admitted to the CCLP, down from an average of 12 students in previous years. The other concern was unfilled senior faculty positions. The smaller program in students and faculty justifiably fueled worries that UT was relinquishing its long-held dominance in preparing leaders for community colleges.

What would happen to the Center for Community College Student Engagement (CCCSE) and the National Institute for Staff and Organizational Development (NISOD) with the merger of the CCLP into a redesigned Higher Education Leadership Program? What about the Student Success Initiatives? What about the 50 employees of these organizations that were under the aegis of the CCLP?

Imposing Fees

Buttressed by the stalwart leadership of JER, NISOD and CCCSE had seen explosive membership and participation growth. Both entities were programmatically and financially set for a strong and viable future.

In 2010, Manuel Justiz, then dean of the College of Education at UT, proposed charging a 25% administrative fee on the revenue of programs contained within the CCLP that sustained themselves through membership subscriptions and external grants: NISOD and CCCSE (Hamilton, 2012). Academic leaders and attorneys from the University of Texas system met with Roueche, McClenney, and others to discuss the policy and legal implications of the dean's action. The UT System leadership deferred the final decision to UT Austin.

Many community college leaders voiced their concerns, leading the Texas Association of Community Colleges (TACC) president Rey Garcia to send a complaint to Attorney General Greg Abbott requesting that he look into whether it was acceptable for the university to appropriate private funds to divergent purposes when the funds were given to these programs for specific

objectives. The attorney general was not required to and did not respond to
Dr. Garcia.

Ultimately, a 15% administrative fee on the programs' total expenses was
put into place, in part to cover the costs of the department's support services,
though some still thought that was too high. The crowning blow was impos-
ing the fee not only for 2010 but also retroactively, going back five years
(Hamilton, 2012).

The last few years prior to John's retirement were indeed a time of change
at UT. It is often said that timing is everything. The winds of directional
change at the College of Education and new opportunities arising outside of
UT made 2012 the year for JER to retire from the 40 acres and begin his next
venture.

SINCE JOHN'S RETIREMENT FROM UT

Over the next few years, the College of Education Higher Education Leadership Program at UT evolved into its new direction. CCCSE and NISOD
continue to provide research and professional development for community
colleges across the country.

And what about John? He did become president of the Roueche Graduate
Center at National American University.

Chapter Sixteen

AACC Tribute to John E. Roueche

American Association of Community Colleges (AACC)

The AACC prepared a video tribute to John Roueche upon his retirement from the University of Texas at Austin in 2012. The video featured the four then-living former AACC presidents and CEOs and was shown at the AACC convention retirement celebration in April 2012. The transcript remarks by each CEO for this tribute are provided here.

DR. EDMUND J. GLEAZER JR. (CEO, 1958–1981)

John went to the University of Texas, and he developed, without question, the leading center for the development of community college leadership, CCLP. These junior college leadership programs not only developed presidents for our institutions, but they actually became research and development centers, as well.

John was very good at raising money. He did a wonderful job on that, and since I did a little bit of that myself, I developed a high appreciation for his skill, and he got enough money so that he endowed the first chair for community colleges that was established at Austin. He developed, without question, what the contemporary public community college was going to be.

Hey John, you know, I'm awfully sorry that I can't be here for this occasion. We've had a wonderful experience and companionship together through the years. You kept me learning after I had got out of my learning experiences with the association. It's been a wonderful voyage together, and

195

you told me that you were going to be leaving your post soon. And I wish you the best as you start on this new journey.

DR. DALE P. PARNELL (CEO, 1981–1991)

I can't think of any individual that I've encountered in the community college movement that's done more for the community colleges than John Roueche. John Roueche is the one and single individual that I look to, to say that's the way it ought to run—training leaders and educating leaders for the new century of the community college.

Probably no other individual in the community college rank has done more to impact the literature about community colleges than John Roueche. Well, John was persistent. When he started something, he didn't stop, but also very likable. John was very encouraging to students that were involved in his program.

John, I want to say a tip of the hat to you. I've admired your leadership, and I'll welcome you to the community of retirement, but I don't think you'll probably be retired. Your leadership and your work will go on for a long, long time.

DR. DAVID R. PIERCE (CEO, 1991–2000)

In 40 years, I have no idea how many leaders he has produced or led the production of, but it is enormous, and they have impacted in a very meaningful and positive way community colleges all across the country and around the world. And we are just tremendously better off because of that.

John has a passion for practices. Every time he hears of a practice, a good practice going on someplace, he pursues it aggressively and grabs it and brings it back into his program, his classes, and writes it up and makes everybody aware of it. And that way has made another enormous impact.

It's impossible to truly describe the impact that he's had. It is unprecedented and unparalleled and probably will never be matched again, but his service has been great. And we are all so much better off because he was around during the time that he was. I would just like to wish him nothing but the very best.

DR. GEORGE R. BOGGS (CEO, 2000–2010)

Dr. Roueche has been one of the most significant leaders in shaping the American community college movement over the last four decades. He's been recognized repeatedly for his scholarship, his influence on leadership development.

His publications have focused on the most critical issues facing community colleges at any particular time, whether they be adjunct faculty, relationships with the community, improving college success rates. You name it, whatever the issue of the day is, Dr. Roueche has contributed to understanding of that particular issue through his scholarly activity.

Well, of course, I'm one of Dr. Roueche's former students, and I consider him a mentor and a friend. I remember the first time I met Dr. Roueche many years ago when he was speaking at an administrator's conference in California, and I was so inspired by what he said that I wanted to bring him to my college. I was at Butte College as an associate dean at the time, and I invited him to kick off our orientation day with a keynote speech, and he accepted. In a matter of less than a minute after I introduced Dr. Roueche, he had us all in the palm of his hand—all focused on what was really important for our college, beyond the crisis of the day: the importance of effective teaching and student learning.

His lasting impact is in many ways hard to zero in on one particular aspect because he has had an influence on so many areas in community colleges. Anything that was important, Dr. Roueche was studying and speaking about and writing about. So, his contribution to the community college movement has been a significant one and across just about every area that's important to us.

Well, Dr. Roueche, I want to congratulate you and to thank you personally for all you've done for me; for the many graduates of the Texas program; and, of course, for the community college movement in general. So, thank you and congratulations on your retirement.

Chapter Seventeen

A New Doctoral Model

Martha M. Ellis

May 29, 2012 04:20 PM Eastern Daylight Time

RAPID CITY, S.D.—(BUSINESS WIRE)—National American University Holdings, Inc. (the "Company") (NASDAQ: NAUH), which through its wholly owned subsidiary operates National American University ("NAU"), a regionally accredited, proprietary, multi-campus institution of higher learning, today announced the development of the Roueche Graduate Center.

The Roueche Graduate Center will be led by Dr. John E. Roueche, who will retire from his position as Director of the Community College Leadership Program (CCLP) and Sid W. Richardson Regents Chair at The University of Texas at Austin to join National American University (NAU). He will begin his role as President of the Roueche Graduate Center effective July 1, 2012. Dr. Roueche currently chairs NAU's Community College Advisory Board, which serves as an advisory and decision-making group on matters related to the university's academic programs, services and initiatives related to community and technical colleges.

"NAU remains committed to offering quality academic programming at the graduate level, and the development of the Roueche Graduate Center will allow us to continue to do so as well as pursue additional graduate opportunities," said Dr. Ronald Shape, Chief Executive Officer of the Company. "To have Dr. Roueche, who is well known in graduate education, lead our efforts is an excellent opportunity for the university. I look forward to seeing more students graduate and succeed under his leadership in our existing master's programs as well as in our future developing graduate programs." (National American University Holdings, 2012)

And thus began the next chapter on the influence of John Roueche on community colleges.

DESIGNING A NEW DOCTORAL MODEL

"NAU had been tracking the withdrawal of support from some of the major universities to continue strong preparation programs for community college leaders," John said. "If you look at universities around the country that 20 to 30 years ago were turning out some of the best leaders for our community colleges, many of their community college leadership programs are now defunct" (Roueche, March 2, 2018).

In 2011, Bob Paxton and other NAU leaders visited with John about his interest in starting a doctoral program for NAU. After multiple conversations and completing due diligence about NAU, John began looking at the curriculums of four or five universities, including Walden and Corinthian. The curriculums of these programs were "very good" (Roueche, March 2, 2018). However, something was missing. Dr. Terry O'Banion stated he was embarrassed to tears with students calling him and saying, "Dr. O'Banion, do you think I will ever get to meet my mentor? Do you think there might be a program that I will get to meet some other students?" (Roueche, March 2, 2018) These programs were good ones, but what John thought was missing was students interacting with each other and with faculty members. The NAU program needed to be a hybrid model of online and face-to-face delivery modalities.

The second aspect that was crucial to this new doctoral program was that every course in the curriculum focus on community college issues and be taught by a successful community college leader. This was revolutionary because, even at UT, there were courses taught by people in higher education who knew nothing about community colleges; they did not know how they were governed, how the finances were pulled together, or what the legislation was for community colleges (Roueche, March 2, 2018).

The third aspect Roueche felt was crucial for accreditation by the HLC was having NAU support a national advisory board made up of people with absolutely sterling reputations in the world of higher education. John originally chaired the advisory board that began in 2012. The other members included

- Dr. George Baker III, faculty emeritus at North Carolina State University;

- Dr. George Boggs, president emeritus of the AACC;
- Dr. Donald Cameron, president emeritus of Guilford Technical Community College;
- Dr. Gerardo de los Santos, president and chief executive officer of the League for Innovation in the Community College;
- Dr. Terry O'Banion, president emeritus and senior league fellow of the League for Innovation in the Community College and senior advisor of higher education programs at Walden University;
- Dr. Christine Johnson-McPhail, Morgan State University; and
- Dr. Margaretta Brédé Mathis.

NAU provost Samuel D. Kerr and online learning president Robert Paxton served as ex-officio members and as internal resources for the advisory board.

The group met a couple of times that first year. The first meeting of the advisory board was for two and a half days! The board members made an investment of time in that first year as together they developed a community college curriculum based on the competencies needed by future leaders to lead in the 21st century. Without a national advisory board and a world-class faculty, a new doctoral program would never happen; "This ain't gonna happen if you don't have the horses" (Roueche, March 2, 2018).

In spring 2013, the accrediting team from the HLC made a visit to the Roueche Graduate Center in Austin. The team walked in and said, "Well, why do you think you should be accredited? Because we are most interested in your research base." Roueche replied, "Well, so am I. In fact, you will want to take a look at everything that has been written about community colleges, research studies, and grant funding in the last 50 years. I would say that 75% has been conducted and written by our advisory board and faculty. The documentation is in the boxes around the room." They were absolutely blown away (Roueche, March 2, 2018).

The accrediting team met with students from the first cohort who began that spring semester at Johnson County Community College in Overland Park, Kansas. The NAU CCLP was accredited in less than a year.

DESCRIPTION OF THE NEW DOCTORAL MODEL

The new doctoral model was a hybrid, cohort, EdD program delivered at community colleges across the United States. Key elements of the UT program were replicated in this new model. The cohort model was a signature component at UT and hence was part of the new doctoral strategy. The cohort model allows students to be admitted together and work together throughout the program with team projects, travel, and taking the same classes every semester.

A Two-Pronged Approach

A significant difference between previous doctoral models and this new model was the evolution of the cohort design for the program. Dr. Terry Calaway, then president of Johnson County Community College, hosted the first cohort for the NAU CCLP. The 10 students in the first cohort were from a variety of institutions in Kansas and Colorado.

The second cohort was at Cuyahoga Community College in Cleveland. Dr. Alex Johnson was coming in as the new president, following the recent retirement of Dr. Jerry Sue Thornton. Dr. Johnson wanted the doctoral program to be an investment in the growth and development of leaders throughout the college and increase the competency of the work at the college. The board of trustees agreed to provide 40% tuition assistance for 20 people, under the agreement that it was for Cuyahoga Community College employees and that the program curriculum would use data and issues facing the college for projects and research. The cohort ended up with 27 people, and the board funded all of them.

Then Kaye Walter, president at Bergen Community College (BCC) in Paramus, New Jersey, designed a similar leadership development strategy with the CCLP for BCC employees. The BCC board approved 100% tuition assistance for 24 employees.

About the same time, a cohort began at Lone Star College in the Woodlands, Texas, made up of students from institutions all over Texas. No college provided a financial commitment beyond the traditional tuition assistance protocols from each individual institution.

The two-pronged approach to providing doctoral programs at community colleges across the country had emerged. One approach featured a cohort of employees from a single college, with the college providing some level of tuition assistance and incorporating projects and data that were institution specific. The second approach was a cohort comprised of students from various institutions across a state or several states. A college agreed to host the cohort, and faculty and students brought data and issues from their respective institutions for projects and coursework.

Considerable effort was required to get these cohorts started. Multiple trips to campuses were made by John and his team to visit with the college presidents and chancellors, leadership teams, sometimes board members, and prospective students. Information sessions were held, with usually 40 to 50 potential students attending. The process from initial conversation to starting the first class usually took 9 to 12 months—a slow process, especially for a proprietary higher education institution.

Faculty

Delivering courses at community colleges across the country was based on the model from NOVA University, where both Roueche and O'Banion had taught. Taking renowned faculty to the students rather than the students coming to the faculty was central to the new program.

More than 60 successful community college leaders became part-time faculty in the new CCLP. Each faculty member brought specific expertise and experience to the program. There were three full-time administrators who also taught classes for the cohorts. The purpose for having a cadre of robust professors who were highly successful leaders with years of practical and proven experience was to expose students to national, state, and local leaders throughout their doctoral experiences.

Each cohort had an on-site cohort coordinator. This coordinator was the "faculty member down the hall" who students could go to when they needed to talk about issues, guidance on projects, and assistance in completing the doctoral program. The cohort coordinator was a person employed and recommended by the president of the host college. Qualifications included a vice presidential–level position at the college with doctoral credentials and leadership experience.

The cohort coordinator attended face-to-face sessions, assisted the faculty with logistics and local guest speakers, and acted as a liaison between the students and the faculty. The coordinator did not teach or grade papers. Each course was taught by a different faculty member, but the cohort coordinator was with the students from the first class through the last class. The cohort coordinator was the glue, consistency, and mentor for the students.

Hybrid Component

Each course in the program (excluding the six semester credit hours of practicum and six semester credit hours of dissertation) was taught in a hybrid format. All learning materials were provided to students online. Textbooks were kept to a minimum, allowing the learning materials to be revised annually to incorporate the latest research, case studies, and data. Most courses were eight weeks in length, with students meeting in face-to-face sessions on Friday afternoons and all day on Saturdays two to three times during the eight-week course. Zoom technology was used extensively to engage the students in small groups and with guest speakers between the face-to-face sessions.

This hybrid approach addressed the concern expressed by John and the advisory committee that online-only programs do not allow for students to intensely engage with faculty and other students.

Results After Five Years

As of fall 2018, five cohorts in the new CCLP had completed the doctoral program coursework, and five additional cohorts were in process. More than 60 students had completed the EdD, with more than 20 being promoted to higher administrative leadership positions at community colleges.

IN THE BLINK OF AN EYE

In October 2018, word came from NAU leadership that no new cohorts would be starting and that the university was sunsetting the CCLP program. The HLC was notified, and a teach-out for the currently enrolled doctoral students was put in place. And then, in early December, NAU leaders informed John that he and the CCLP administrative team had three weeks until the offices would be closed and they would no longer be employed by the university. Students were assured they could finish the doctoral program, and faculty were assured they would be paid to teach out the remaining classes.

The CCLP faculty received the following e-mail from Ron Shape on December 11, 2018, at 8:32 a.m.:

> Dear CCLP Doctoral Faculty:
>   During its meeting on October 29, 2018, the Board of Governors of National American University endorsed a strategic plan that increases investment in the university's new distinctive programs, expands upon its core programs, and suspends new enrollment in programs that serve a limited number of students.

Doctoral students currently enrolled in NAU's Community College Leadership Program (CCLP) are not affected by the Board action and will have the opportunity to complete the program as originally planned. However, new students will no longer be accepted into the program. It is anticipated that all current CCLP students will complete the program and earn an EdD degree in Community College Leadership by 2023.

Inactive CCLP students who are not currently enrolled in the program may re-enter the program if they meet re-admission requirements, remain continuously enrolled, and are able to complete the program by June 1, 2023.

Dr. Lynn Moore, Dean of Doctoral Academic Operations, will lead the transition and teach out of the Community College Leadership Program. Dr. Moore and the program's faculty remain committed to preparing CCLP students to become our nation's future community college leaders. If you have questions or suggestions, please do not hesitate to contact Dr. Moore.

You are a valued member of the Community College Leadership Program. Thank you for your efforts in building strong community colleges across our country.

In the blink of an eye, a highly successful EdD program for community college leaders was shuttered.

A NEW HOME

Within a couple of months of John leaving NAU, opportunities emerged for the continuation of the highly successful doctoral model. Dr. Blake Flanders, president and CEO of the Kansas Board of Regents, was a good friend of Bob Paxton—yes, the same Bob Paxton from the NAU connection. (Bob had left NAU a number of months before the dismantling of the CCLP.) Paxton told Dr. Flanders about the ending of the CCLP.

Dr. Flanders, an alumnus of Kansas State University (KSU) with professional experience with community colleges in Kansas, had an idea. He knew of the incredible need for preparing future community college leaders in Kansas and around the country. He also knew that the KSU College of Education had the only adult learning and leadership program in the state and a global campus that served graduate students across the county. Dr. Flanders connected Duane Dunn, who oversees the KSU global campus and is a former community college president, and Dr. Debbie Mercer, dean of the College of Education, with John (Mercer, 2019; Roueche, 2019).

By April 2019, the John E. Roueche Community College Leadership Center and doctoral program became part of the KSU Department of Educational Leadership. An EdD in adult learning and leadership was put into place and began in summer 2019. The offices for the CCLP remained in Austin.

The Department of Educational Leadership at KSU is an umbrella for master's and doctoral degrees in school leadership. The creation of the CCLP added a new dimension to the department by moving into community college leadership preparation. According to Dean Mercer, the community college program is a mutually beneficial partnership. She stated, "Our current programs have significant impact on K–12 education. John's programs have a long history of incredible impact on community colleges. So, let's have impact together" (Mercer, 2019).

The KSU College of Education has two academies for K–12 principals and superintendents. The school districts identify students who are current teachers. The courses are taught on-site at the school districts. Case studies and data from that district are used in the curriculum, and students are in a cohort throughout the graduate program. The master of arts in teaching is offered in 23 states using technology through the KSU global campus. Sound familiar? Indeed, there is philosophical and structural alignment with John's philosophy and design for preparing future community college leaders.

KSU has strong processes in place for qualifications for dissertation committee members and faculty, curriculum design, new course approvals, and new degree approvals. Internally, within the College of Education, there were no issues for the community college program because it followed the model used for the K–12 leadership program. At the time of the interviews for this chapter, not all the details were finalized for the program. For example, the university had not established key metrics for the success of the program, nor had all the details been established on how the dissertation committee chair and member appointments would be crafted.

Dr. Mercer did emphasize that this would be a high-quality program that aligns with John's philosophy to create a pipeline for future leaders to obtain the skill set and thinking perspective to take on the challenges that community colleges face. KSU is committed to long-term sustainability (Mercer, 2019).

THE TRANSITION

KSU was generous in providing options for students who were well into the EdD program at the Roueche Graduate Center at NAU. As is often the case, the transition for students and faculty who were part of the CCLP at NAU was a bit confusing. Students received multiple messages in one day.

Dr. Margaretta Mathis sent out an e-mail on April 23, 2019, at 11:26 a.m. to all students who were enrolled in the NAU CCLP, announcing the new affiliation with KSU:

> We are writing to share the exciting news that the John E. Roueche Community College Leadership Center and program for doctoral preparation of community college leaders has been established in the Department of Educational Leadership at Kansas State University, with offices in Austin, TX. K-State welcomes doctoral students to this distinguished national program and commits to the successful transfer and completion of current and new doctoral candidates.
>
> Attached are materials that provide information regarding doctoral transfer credits. . . . Zoom sessions are scheduled for Wednesday, April 24 and Friday, April 26 at noon Central.
>
> Please let your colleagues know that plans are in place to welcome doctoral students and candidates starting this summer to complete their studies and dissertations under the leadership of Drs. John E. Roueche, Margaretta B. Mathis, Terry O'Banion, and other national-renowned faculty.

Dr. Mathis did not notify the faculty members at NAU of this new affiliation at KSU.

Later that afternoon, at 3:43 p.m., Dr. Lynn Moore, vice president and dean at NAU, sent out the following e-mail to NAU faculty that included her e-mail to students:

> Colleagues;
>
> Below is the email which was just sent to our NAU CCLP doctoral students via their CCLP Cohort Coordinators. As one of our valued NAU CCLP faculty members, I wanted to share this email with you as well, to keep you up to date and since you may receive questions from your students. Please let me know if you have questions.
>
> Tuesday, April 23, 2019 2:36 PM
>
> Dear NAU CCLP Students and Cohort Coordinators;
>
> It has come to our attention that Margaretta Mathis has emailed some of you this morning introducing the new association between John E. Roueche, Margaretta Mathis, and Terry O'Banion with Kansas State University. I want to let you know that NAU has had no discussion with KSU regarding their existing or developing doctoral programs. The NAU Community College Leadership Program has not changed and continues to be dedicated to the

successful completion of your Ed. D., just as planned and scheduled. We are
happy to answer any questions you may have.

While students talked with Dr. Mathis and Dr. Moore, they had close ties
with the faculty members, including their dissertation chairs and committee
members. Students immediately began contacting these faculty members to
garner advice on their next steps.

John once again provided stability and strong leadership to assist in the
transition process. He quickly responded to questions from faculty so they
could have the most up-to-date answers for students. Because of his commitment to students, each student got the assistance needed to make a good
decision in selecting the appropriate university for completing the doctoral
degree.

There is little doubt about the future success of the John E. Roueche
CCLP at KSU. John and the CCLP have found a home. As Dean Mercer said,
"Why this program will work is because of who John is. He has a good heart
and he is a good thinker. The collaboration is a personal, professional pleasure to get to know him and work with him. Impact drives him, and that is
important to KSU and the future of community colleges" (Mercer, 2019).

POST–UT AUSTIN DECISIONS

Why did John choose to go with NAU? John said,

> They asked. NAU had the idea and they made the commitments. The thing I
> think that most people do not get is that everything we have done to date is
> about relationships. These relationships are developed over years and years
> and years of work together. Alex Johnson and I have been friends for years. I
> went to Delgado when he was there. He and Jerry Sue and Walter (Bumphus)
> are friends. You (Martha Ellis) had the relationship with Kaye (Walter). Terry
> (O'Banion) was consulting with Joel Kinnamon at the College of the Desert
> where we are starting a cohort. (Roueche, March 2, 2018)

Why did John choose KSU? "They asked and were willing to work with the
current doctoral students," he said (Roueche, 2019).

A new doctoral model was developed, implemented, and is proving to be
successful. With JER's vision, a cadre of highly experienced community
college leaders worked with him to identify and develop the optimal method
for how future community college leaders will acquire doctoral studies. John

reimagined and led the creation of an EdD program to prepare knowledge-able, incisive, and collaborative senior leaders for the nation's community colleges.

John fosters relationships, and this continues to underpin his immense success and profound influence. His wisdom, knowledge, and astute envi-sioning skills continue to be the intellectual foundation for this immense success and profound influence—a confluence of heart and mind.

Chapter Eighteen

A Final Word

Margaretta B. Mathis

From the perch of being a University of Texas at Austin (UT) distinguished graduate, colleague, and friend, I have watched John navigate tough terrain and elevate those around him in an unparalleled journey that puts purpose above self in developing leaders to guide our nation's community colleges. An innate and award-winning scholar of leadership and culture, John instills the values of access, success, equity, and completion and also reinforces the expected norms of persistence, discipline, quality, and rigor in his graduates.

The multiplying effect of such culture and leader development is incomparable: "[C]ulture has the power to shape our identity. Over time and under the right circumstances, the norms and values of the group to which we belong become our own. We internalize them. We carry them with us. *The way we do things around here and why* eventually becomes *the way I do things and why*" (Duckworth, 2016).

Thinking about the past 15 years of working with John at UT at the Roueche Graduate Center (RGC) and now at Kansas State University (KSU), several common elements come to mind.

SHARED VISION

Many times over the years, John has spoken about "sticking to your knitting" and those things one does well. He has been complimented for bringing together a cadre of strong professionals as faculty and guest lecturers with shared values and norms. Together, a shared vision was shaped for serving and elevating the country's community college students through initiatives focused on improving access, equity, success, and completion—a common mantra among those who served as an extended part of the UT Community College Leadership Program (CCLP) family. This shared vision was used to inform decisions about national initiatives and educational endeavors with which the UT team was involved.

Fast-forward to the CCLP at the RGC, which was accredited in August 2013; colleagues and friends familiar with the UT CCLP vision, values, and norms gathered to perpetuate the requisite knowledge, skills, and abilities of a quality leadership program for the future. More than 60 highly successful faculty members, leaders with decades of practical experience in community colleges, were among the cadre of RGC CCLP colleagues guiding the next generation of leaders. Gatherings of UT and RGC alumni and friends provide opportunities for like-spirited individuals to share effective practices and glean from real-time challenges and solutions.

Drawing on the leadership competencies from the UT CCLP, the American Association of Community Colleges, Achieving the Dream, and the Aspen Institute, the EdD program develops and hones leadership skills in how to address daunting issues and involve stakeholders to develop a desired future.

In *Rising to the Challenge: Lessons Learned from Guilford Technical Community College*, the authors conclude that we are "living in the futures we create." They state that the institution's reputation has been achieved through the

> unique collection of robust, well-thought-of practices being implemented— practices in leadership, stewardship, partnership, and teaching and learning. These practices thrive in a culture that consistently raises the bar for high performance and achievement standards. . . . College leaders should decide to live in the future that the college envisions and creates, not the future it would otherwise inherit. (Roueche and Roueche, 2012)

RESEARCH AND RELATIONSHIPS

Founded on similar leadership competencies, the UT, RGC, and KSU CCLPs are all grounded on scholarly research. John has received extensive national recognition for his research, teaching, service, and overall leadership as discussed throughout this book. A full listing of books, articles, awards, research, grants, and professional responsibilities are found in the appendixes. This impressive history of research and awards, coupled with John's firm belief and active support of relationships, carried forward to the doctoral program at KSU.

John's fundamental outlook in life is based on the importance of relationships, which he fosters through continuous communication, collaboration, and support of alumni and friends. In a recent communique with a colleague pursuing a community college presidency, John both inspired and reminded the candidate,

> What a wonderful opportunity for you and the college. Do your homework before the next visit. Make sure you know everyone with whom you will be meeting or interviewing—where they have worked and in what capacities, where they attended grad school, etc. etc. You are an excellent "listener"—a terrific quality at this point in time. Also let them see your good self-deprecating humor. Don't hesitate to call or email whenever I can be of assistance to you.

Always taking time to follow up with a note, a good joke, an invitation to lunch, or practical reinforcement during challenging times, John kindles relationships and the nucleus of collaboration, which has been an underpinning of his extensive network and success.

Not one to be taken lightly yet not taking himself too seriously, John's fast wit, humor, and stories often are designed to engage friends and new acquaintances in work to be done to accomplish goals that many would not have the vision to foresee. As he is apt to remind, it is often not the *what* that is important but the *how* and *respect* for others that can make a difference in achieving desired outcomes.

PERSISTENCE, PASSION, AND PURPOSE

Dedicated to a life and career in the development of community college leaders and the improvement of student outcomes and equity, John stays laser-focused on the game ahead. I reflected on John and his extended circle of long-term friends and colleagues; they tend to rekindle a renewed dedication to a life of passion and purpose. Several coauthors in this book reference the following T. E. Lawrence quote when describing JER: "All people dream, but not equally. Those who dream by night in the dusty recesses of their minds wake in the day to find it was vanity. But the dreamers of the day are dangerous people, for they may act their dream with open eyes and make it possible" (Lawrence, n.d.).

John has placed an indelible mark on the community college movement, setting in place the research, relationships, and vision for a better tomorrow—founded on a knowledge of what it takes and how—to lead in an ever-shifting terrain.

Notes

INTRODUCTION

1. See Appendix B for a full listing of John's awards and recognition.

1. SHAPING A LEGACY

1. The quotes shared in this chapter are from a face-to-face interview with John Roueche on April 24, 2018, in his office in Austin, Texas.
2. The references to the CCLP Block Guide come from the Fall 1999 edition.

5. TEAMING WITH JOHN EDWARD ROUECHE

1. Captain Robb and Lynda were married December 9, 1967. They honeymooned privately at Camp David, just before Captain Robb was deployed to Vietnam.
2. Wolfe was an American novelist of the early 20th century. His autobiographical *Look Homeward Angel* about Asheville, North Carolina, angered his family and friends. Such readings would give us clues concerning the difficulty of making progress in increasing student learning and success in the assigned regions of the Carolinas and Virginia. King's life and assassination April 4, 1968, inflamed America and certainly had both positive and negative effects on desegregation in higher education and especially where we were working in the Carolinas and Virginia.
3. Salinger's early boyhood was as complex as JER's. Roueche's great energy and influence of others in his life propelled him forward, where he was required to make his own way. Steinbeck is another writer whose work is similar to that of JER, in that both were transformational leaders. They combined sympatric humor and keen social perception of how to influence change in individuals, groups, and organizations.

4. Rockwell's influence in the Second World War was tremendous on morale. His illustrations for the *Saturday Evening Post* emphasized the Four Freedoms: from want, from fear, of speech, and of worship. These also align with what JER learned at home and school, from mentors and his students. These were part of the engine that drove this man to push for a worldwide community college movement.

5. Our democracy looks different today than where JER and I grew up, scarcely 100 miles from each other. JER can take credit for the progressive education within the community college system for African Americans and Latinx.

6. Mitchell Junior College is now a comprehensive community college that serves Iredell County in central North Carolina.

7. The RELCV was part of John F. Kennedy's vision that was continued in LBJ's Great Society. The idea was to close the 20-year gap between research and practice in public organizations, including community colleges. JER's team was to design an intervention to influence and support decision-making by administrators and ultimately the teaching faculty, especially those who led and taught developmental education.

8. Kittrell College was one of the 20 RELCV colleges. This was an African American–serving college of the Methodist Episcopal Church. JER provided funds and help for the college to get a federal Title III grant that literally saved the college from closing.

9. Hurlburt was the father of the North Carolina Community College System of more than 50 colleges. Doc Hurlburt had adopted JER as his son, and their relationship and partnership at Duke University for a period of time changed the conservative nature of departmental leadership to one more progressive. Dr. Hurlburt died on July 1, 1983.

10. Instructional systems development model. One of the programs was a 2½-day workshop for community college instructors. Later we developed two modules, one for instructors and one at the program level for the management of training in the Department of Defense. This model is still saving billions of dollars in the training of DOD offices and enlisted across all technical programs for the DOD.

11. Brownell was my officemate at NLHE. During the years at the lab, the concept of accountability was being discussed. JER, Dick, and I developed and wrote an accountability model for America's community colleges that portrayed the CEO as the organizational leader accountable for the success of students in their colleges. Some presidents in the NLHE consortium supported this model, while other national leaders were not ready to accept the ideas of being held accountable. As more reinforcements from AACC and, at that time, Dale Parnell (president of AACJC) came forward, the idea began to spread and over the years has blossomed into many innovations across the higher education landscape.

7. LESSONS IN LEADERSHIP IN TWO ACTS

1. Over its 100-year history, the American Association of Community Colleges (AACC) has modified its name to reflect the evolving nature of its member colleges. The American Association of Junior Colleges (AAJC) and the American Association of Community and Junior Colleges (AACJC) refer to the same national organization, which became the AACC in 1992 by a majority vote of its membership.

13. AHEAD OF THE CURVE

1. Substantial content in this chapter is drawn from an interview I conducted with John E. Roueche on April 6, 2018. References to Roueche (2018) refer to that interview, follow-up conversations for clarification, and fact checking.

14. THE BOOKS OF JOHN ROUECHE

1. Two books are not included in the analysis due to the inability to obtain copies of these publications: John E. Roueche and Donald T. Rippey (eds.) (1981, Spring), "Teaching and Learning in the 1980s," *Community College Frontiers*, special issue; and John E. Roueche, William H. McFarlane, and Barton R. Herrscher (1971), *The Private Junior College: Prospects for the '70s* (Durham, NC: National Laboratory for Higher Education).

Appendix A

Education and Career Résumé

EDUCATIONAL RECORD

AA	Mitchell Community College, 1958
BA	Lenoir-Rhyne University, 1960
MA	Appalachian State University, 1961
PhD	Florida State University, 1964
DH Letters	

POSITIONS HELD

2019–current	Teaching professor, John E. Roueche Center for Community College Leadership, Kansas State University, Manhattan, Kansas
2012–2018	President, Roueche Graduate Center, Austin, Texas, National American University, Rapid City, South Dakota
1971–2012	Sid W. Richardson Regents Chair, professor, and director, Community College Leadership Program, the University of Texas at Austin
1969–1971	Director and associate professor of education, Institute on Junior College Administration, Duke University, and director, Community College Division, National Laboratory for Higher Education, Durham, North Carolina

1967–1969   Associate director, ERIC Clearinghouse for Junior Colleges, and associate research educator, University of California at Los Angeles

1964–1967   Assistant to the president, dean of students, Gaston Community College, Gastonia, North Carolina

1962–1964   Kellogg fellow, the Florida State University, Tallahassee

1960–1961   History and English instructor, Appalachian State University, Boone, North Carolina

1959–1960   History and English teacher, Wilkes Central School, North Wilkesboro, North Carolina

Appendix B

Awards and Recognition

RESEARCH, TEACHING, AND ACHIEVEMENT AWARDS

- Career Leadership Achievement Award, American Association of Community Colleges (AACC), 2012
- Diverse Champion Award, *Diverse: Issues in Higher Education*, lifetime achievement in developing minority and female leaders, 2012
- Distinguished Service Award, Council for the Study of Community Colleges, 2012
- O'Banion Award for Leadership in Teaching and Learning (with Suanne D. Roueche), Educational Testing Service (ETS), 2011
- Distinguished Graduate Award, Mitchell Community College, 2009
- President's National Leadership Award, National Council of Marketing and Public Relations, 2006
- Mirabeau B. Lamar Leadership Award, Texas Association of Universities and Colleges, for outstanding contributions to leadership development in Texas and nationally, 2005
- Distinguished Leadership and Service Award, Texas Association of Community Colleges, 2003–2004
- Distinguished Research Award, National Council for Advancement of Standards, 2002
- Outstanding Service to Community Colleges Award, National Council of Instructional Administrators, 2001
- Distinguished National Fellow, National Council for Advancement of Standards, 2001

- Excellence Award for Research and Development in Community College and Colleges of Further Education, third conference of the International Collaboration and Community and Further Education Colleges, Cape Town, South Africa, 2000
- Distinguished Graduate Award, Lenoir-Rhyne University, 2000
- University of Texas Career Research Excellence Award, the highest research prize awarded at the University of Texas, 1998
- Distinguished Senior Scholar Award, Council of Universities and Colleges, 1996
- Inter-Association Award for Distinguished Scholarship, National Council for Student Development, 1996
- Dean's Distinguished Faculty Award, College of Education, the University of Texas at Austin, 1994
- Distinguished Senior Scholar Award, Council of Universities and Colleges, 1994
- Frances Crain Cook Distinguished Lecture, the University of Texas at Austin, 1994
- Earl V. Pullias Distinguished Lecture, University of Southern California, 1993
- International Hall of Fame Award, Nova University, Florida, 1992
- Distinguished National Service Award, National Council for Student Development, 1990
- Distinguished Research Publication Award, Council of Universities and Colleges, 1990
- B. Lamar Johnson Distinguished National Leadership Award, League for Innovation in the Community College, 1988
- Distinguished Research Award, National Council for Student Development, 1987–1988
- Distinguished Research Publication Award, National Council for Staff, Program, and Organizational Development, 1987–1988
- Distinguished Research Publications Award, National Association of Developmental Education, 1986
- National Distinguished Leadership Award, American Association of Community and Junior Colleges, 1986
- Distinguished Research Award, National Council for Staff, Program, and Organizational Development, 1985
- Distinguished Research Publication Award, Council of Universities and Colleges, 1985

- University of Texas Outstanding Researcher Award, Golden Key National Honor Society, 1985
- Award for Outstanding Research Contributions, National Association of Developmental Education, 1984
- Distinguished Achievement Award, Miami-Dade Community College, 1984
- Distinguished Service Award, Council of Universities and Colleges, 1984
- Outstanding Learned Article Award, United States Education Press Association, 1983
- Teaching Excellence Award, the University of Texas at Austin, 1982
- Distinguished Graduate Award, the Florida State University, 1981
- The Legion of Honor Medal, International Order of DeMolay for Outstanding Contributions to American Youth, 1981
- Distinguished Alumnus Award, Appalachian State University, 1978
- Outstanding Research Award, Council of Universities and Colleges, 1978
- Distinguished Service Award, African Methodist Episcopal Church, 1971

RECOGNITION

- Contemporary Authors
- Dictionary of International Biography
- International Authors and Writers Who's Who
- Men and Women of Achievement
- Phi Beta Kappa, Phi Delta Kappa
- Who's Who in American Education
- Who's Who in the World, 1986–2011
- Who's Who in America, 1986–2011
- Commissioned an Admiral, Texas Navy, by Governor Mark White, 1983
- Named Arkansas Traveler by Governor Frank White for Contributions to Arkansas Higher Education, 1981
- Who's Who in the South and Southwest, 1980–2011
- Named Kentucky Colonel by Governor Julian B. Carroll and the Kentucky General Assembly, 1979
- Ambassador for North Carolina, by Governor James Hunt, 1978
- Inducted into the Order of Long-Leaf Pine, Lifetime

Appendix C

Books

John E. Roueche and Suanne D. Roueche, with Martha M. Ellis and Melinda Valdez-Ellis. 2012. *Rising to the Challenge: Lessons Learned from Guilford Technical Community College.* Washington, DC: Community College Press.

John E. Roueche, M. Melissa Richardson, Phillip W. Neal, and Suanne D. Roueche. 2008. *The Creative Community College: Leading Change through Innovation*, with contributed chapters. Washington, DC: Community College Press.

John E. Roueche and Barbara R. Jones. 2005. *The Entrepreneurial Community College*, with contributed chapters. Washington, DC: Community College Press.

John E. Roueche, Mark D. Milliron, and Suanne D. Roueche. 2003. *Practical Magic: On the Front Lines of Teaching Excellence.* Washington, DC: Community College Press.

John E. Roueche, Eileen E. Ely, and Suanne D. Roueche. 2001. *In Pursuit of Excellence: The Community College of Denver.* Washington, DC: Community College Press.

John E. Roueche and Suanne D. Roueche. 1999. *High Stakes, High Performance: Making Remedial Education Work.* Washington, DC: Community College Press.

John E. Roueche, Laurence F. Johnson, and Suanne D. Roueche. 1997. *Embracing the Tiger: The Effectiveness Debate and the Community College.* Washington, DC: Community College Press.

John E. Roueche, Suanne D. Roueche, and Mark D. Milliron. 1995. *Strangers in Their Own Land: Part-Time Faculty in American Community Colleges.* Washington, DC: Community College Press.

John E. Roueche, Lynn S. Taber, and Suanne D. Roueche. 1995. *The Company We Keep: Collaboration in the Community College.* Washington, DC: Community College Press.

John E. Roueche, Dale Parnell, and Carl Kuttler Jr. 1994. *1,001 Exemplary Practices in America's Two-Year Colleges.* New York: McGraw-Hill.

John E. Roueche and Suanne D. Roueche. 1993. *Between a Rock and a Hard Place: The At-Risk Student in the Open-Door College.* Washington, DC: Community College Press.

John E. Roueche, with Rosemary Gillett-Karam and Suanne D. Roueche. 1991. *Underrepresentation and the Question of Diversity: Women and Minorities in Community Colleges.* Washington, DC: Community College Press.

John E. Roueche, with George A. Baker III and Rosemary Gillett-Karam. 1990. *Teaching as Leading: Profiles of Excellence in the Open-Door College.* Washington, DC: Community College Press.

John E. Roueche, George A. Baker III, and Robert Rose. 1989. *Shared Vision: Transformational Leadership in American Community Colleges.* Washington, DC: Community College Press.

John E. Roueche and George A. Baker III. 1987. *Access and Excellence: The Open-Door College.* Washington, DC: Community College Press.

John E. Roueche and George A. Baker III. 1986. *Profiling Excellence in America's Schools.* Arlington, VA: American Association of School Administrators.

John E. Roueche and George A. Baker III, eds. 1984. *Community College Leadership in the Eighties.* Washington, DC: Community College Press.

John E. Roueche, George A. Baker III, and Suanne D. Roueche. 1984. *College Responses to Low-Achieving Students: A National Study.* Orlando, FL: HBJ Media Systems.

John E. Roueche, ed. 1983. *A New Look at Successful Programs for Low-Achieving Students.* San Francisco: Jossey-Bass.

John E. Roueche and George A. Baker III. 1983. *Beacons for Change.* Iowa City: American College Testing Service.

John E. Roueche and Donald T. Rippey, eds. 1981, Spring. *Teaching and Learning in the 1980s.* Special Issue. *Community College Frontiers.*

John E. Roueche. 1980. *Holistic Literacy in College Teaching.* New York: Harcourt Brace Jovanovich, Media Systems.

John E. Roueche and Oscar G. Mink. 1979. *Improving Student Motivation.* New York: HBJ Media Systems.

John E. Roueche, Barbara P. Mink, and Oscar G. Mink. 1979. *Assessing Student Opinions of the Learning Experience.* New York: HBJ Media Systems.

John E. Roueche, Barbara P. Mink, and Oscar G. Mink. 1979. *Confronting Student Attitudes.* New York: HBJ Media Systems.

John E. Roueche and Jerry J. Snow. 1977. *Overcoming Learning Problems.* San Francisco: Jossey-Bass.

John E. Roueche and Suanne D. Roueche. 1977. *Developmental Education: A Primer for Program Development and Evaluation.* Atlanta, GA: Southern Regional Education Board.

John E. Roueche, ed. 1977. *Increasing Basic Skills by Developmental Studies.* New Directions for Higher Education. San Francisco: Jossey-Bass.

John E. Roueche, Barton R. Herrscher, and George A. Baker III. 1976. *Time as the Variable, Achievement as the Constant: Competency-Based Instruction in the Community College.* Washington, DC: American Association of Community and Junior Colleges.

John E. Roueche and R. Wade Kirk. 1973. *Catching Up: Remedial Education.* San Francisco: Jossey-Bass.

John E. Roueche and Barton R. Herrscher. 1973. *Toward Instructional Accountability: A Guide to Educational Change.* Palo Alto, CA: Westinghouse Learning Press.

John E. Roueche, with John C. Pitman. 1972. *A Modest Proposal: Students Can Learn.* San Francisco: Jossey-Bass.

John E. Roueche, George A. Baker III, and Richard L. Brownell. 1971. *Accountability and the Community College: Directions for the '70s.* Washington, DC: American Association of Junior Colleges.

John E. Roueche, William H. McFarlane, and Barton R. Herrscher. 1971. *The Private Junior College: Prospects for the '70s.* Durham, NC: National Laboratory for Higher Education.

John E. Roueche and Barton R. Herrscher, eds. 1970. *The Junior College.* New York: Selected Academic Readings.

John E. Roueche and Barton R. Herrscher. 1970. *Junior College Instruction.* New York: Selected Academic Readings.

John E. Roueche and Arthur M. Cohen. 1969. *Institutional Administrator or Educational Leader? The Junior College President.* Washington, DC: American Association of Junior Colleges.

John E. Roueche. 1968. *Salvage, Redirection, or Custody? Remedial Education in the Junior College.* Washington, DC: American Association of Junior Colleges.

John E. Roueche and John R. Boggs. 1968. *Junior College Institutional Research: The State of the Art.* Washington, DC: American Association of Junior Colleges.

Appendix D

Chapters and Journal Articles

Margaretta B. Mathis and John E. Roueche. 2019. "Transformative Leadership Wanted: Making Good on the Promise of the Open Door." In Terry O'Banion, ed., *13 Ideas That Are Changing the Community College World.* Lanham, MD: Rowman & Littlefield.

John E. Roueche and Barbara Jones-Kavalier. 2010, April–May. "Reimagining the Community College." *Community College Journal.*

John E. Roueche and Evelyn Waiwaiole. 2009, September. "Developmental Education: An Investment We Cannot Afford Not to Make." *Diverse: Issues in Higher Education.*

John E. Roueche and Suanne D. Roueche. 2008, August. "The Creative Community College: Leading Change through Innovation." *Great Leadership*, Wayne County Community College, Detroit, pp. 1–2, 8.

John E. Roueche and Kathleen Ciez-Voz. 2007. "Teaching and Learning with Heart: The Affective Domain in the Community College." *Celebrations*, NISOD, the University of Texas at Austin.

John E. Roueche and Suanne D. Roueche. 2007. "The Art of Visionary Leadership: Painting a Face on the Future." *Celebrations*, NISOD, the University of Texas at Austin.

Walter G. Bumphus and John E. Roueche. 2007, July 12. "Community Colleges Often Lead the Way in Diversity Efforts." *Diverse*, p. 82.

John E. Roueche, Cathy S. Kemper, and Suanne Davis Roueche. 2007, December–January. "Learning Colleges: Looking for Revolution—But Embracing Revolution." *Community College Journal*, pp. 29–33.

John E. Roueche and Barbara R. Jones. 2005, June–July. "Profits in a Non-Profit World: Celebrating Entrepreneurship in the Community College." *Community College Journal*, pp. 26–30.

John E. Roueche and Barbara R. Jones. 2005, Spring. "Leadership Lessons from Babe." *Celebrations*, NISOD, the University of Texas at Austin.

John E. Roueche and Barbara R. Jones. 2005, January. "Leadership and the Way of the Pig." *Community College Journal*, pp. 6–7.

John E. Roueche and Suanne Davis Roueche. 2004, November. "Affairs of the Heart: Dealing with Long-Distance Colleagues." *Community College Week*, Fall Supplement, p. 4.

John E. Roueche. "More Students, Less Money." 2004, October 29. *Chronicle of Higher Education*, p. B12.

John E. Roueche. 2004, July. "Extraordinary Challenges, Unique Opportunities." *Community College Week*, pp. 4–5.

John E. Roueche, Mark David Milliron, and Suanne Davis Roueche. 2004, January. "Practical Magic: Perspectives from Teaching Excellence Award Recipients." *Celebrations*, NISOD, the University of Texas at Austin.

John E. Roueche and Suanne Davis Roueche. 2003, Fall. "More Than Arm's Length: Distance Makes a Difference." *Community College Week*, Technology Special Edition, pp. 3, 10.

John E. Roueche, Mark David Milliron, and Suanne Davis Roueche. 2003, September. "The Power of Practical Magic." *Community College Journal*, pp. 34–39.

John E. Roueche and Suanne Davis Roueche. 2003, March 17. "From Cell Phones to Collaboration." *Community College Week*, pp. 4–6.

John E. Roueche and Suanne Davis Roueche. 2002, November 11. "Online Learning Can Be Seductive." *Community College Week*, pp. 2–9.

John E. Roueche and Suanne Davis Roueche. 2001, February 19. "From 'Wow' to 'How' Possibilities to Practice." *Community College Week*, Supplement, pp. 11–21.

John E. Roueche, Eileen Ely, and Suanne Davis Roueche. 2001, December–January. "Challenges of the Heart: Pursuing Excellence at the Community College of Denver." *Community College Journal*, pp. 30–34.

John E. Roueche and Suanne Davis Roueche. 2000, October 16. "Touched by Technology." *Community College Week*, pp. 3–27.

John E. Roueche and Suanne D. Roueche. 2000, April–May. "Facing the New Millennium: Making Friends with the Future." *Community College Journal*, pp. 16–22.

John E. Roueche and Suanne D. Roueche. 2000, February. "Remedial Education Efforts That Work." *American Association of Higher Education Bulletin*, pp. 7–9.

John E. Roueche. 1998, Spring. "Two Sides of the Same Coin: Part-Time Faculty: Isolation or Integration." *Michigan Community College Journal*, pp. 9–18.

John E. Roueche and Suanne Davis Roueche. 1998, Spring. "Colleges Must Stay the Course to Secure a Place in the Techno-Driven Future." *Community College Week*, pp. 3–7.

John E. Roueche and Suanne Davis Roueche. 1998, April. "Dancing as Fast as They Can: Community Colleges Facing Tomorrow's Challenges Today." *Community College Journal*, pp. 30–36.

John E. Roueche, Suanne Davis Roueche, and Laurence F. Johnson. 1997. "Embracing the Tiger: The Institutional Effectiveness Challenge." *Leadership Abstracts*, vol. 10, no. 8.

John E. Roueche, Laurence F. Johnson, and Suanne Davis Roueche. 1997, September. "Writing the Tale of the Institutional Effectiveness Tiger." *Occasional Paper of the Southern Association of Community, Junior and Technical Colleges*, vol. 15, no. 1, September 1997.

John E. Roueche, Laurence F. Johnson, and Suanne Davis Roueche. 1997, September 9. "Embracing the Tiger from the Authors' Perspectives." *Community College Times*.

John E. Roueche, Laurence F. Johnson, and Suanne D. Roueche. 1997, April–May. "Embracing the Institutional Effectiveness Tiger." *Community College Journal*, pp. 34–40.

John E. Roueche and Suanne D. Roueche. 1996. "Those Who Tempt Fate and Those Who Advise Them: Designing Strategies for Serving Underprepared Students." In Joseph N. Hankin, ed., *The Community College: Opportunity and Access for America's First-Year Student*. Columbia: University of South Carolina Press.

John E. Roueche and Suanne D. Roueche. 1996, Fall. "Making Good on the Promises of the Open-Door." In Patricia Williamson and Andrew Matonak, eds., *The 21st Century: Investing in Our Students*. Washington, DC: National Council on Student Development.

John E. Roueche, Suanne D. Roueche, and Mark D. Milliron. 1996, October. "A Part-Time Faculty Support System That Makes Sense." *Academic Leadership*, pp. 3–7.

John E. Roueche, Suanne D. Roueche, and Mark D. Milliron. 1996, Spring. "Identifying the Strangers: Exploring Part-Time Faculty Integration in American Community Colleges." *Community College Review*, pp. 33–48.

John E. Roueche. 1996, April–May. "Leadership Challenges for 2000." *Community College Journal*, pp. 12–13.

John E. Roueche, Suanne D. Roueche, and Mark D. Milliron. 1996, March–April. "In the Company of Strangers: Addressing the Utilization and Integration of Part-Time Faculty in American Community Colleges." *Community College Journal of Research and Practice*, vol. 20, no. 2, pp. 105–18.

John E. Roueche, Lynn S. Taber, and Suanne D. Roueche. 1995, February. "Choosing the Company We Keep: Collaboration in American Community Colleges." *Community College Journal*, pp. 36–40.

John E. Roueche and George A. Baker III. 1994. "Case Study of an Exemplary Developmental Education Program." In Martha Maxwell, ed., *From Access to Success*. St. Petersburg, FL: H and H.

John E. Roueche and Suanne D. Roueche. 1994. "Creating the Climate for Teaching and Learning." In Terry U. O'Banion, ed., *Teaching and Learning*. Washington, DC: Community College Press.

John E. Roueche and Suanne D. Roueche. 1994, April. "Building Better Mouse Traps and Tooting Horns: A Modest Proposal for Disseminating Teaching/Learning Innovation in the '90s." *Community College Journal*, pp. 36–43.

John E. Roueche and Suanne D. Roueche. 1994, March. "Climbing Out from Between a Rock and a Hard Place: Responding to the Needs of the At-Risk Student." *Leadership Abstracts*.

John E. Roueche and Suanne D. Roueche. 1994, February. "Responding to the Challenge of the At-Risk Student." *Community College Journal of Research and Practice*, pp. 1–11.

John E. Roueche and Larry Johnson. 1994, January. "A New View of the Mission of American Higher Education." *Leadership Abstracts*.

John E. Roueche. 1993, December. "What America Requires of Higher Education." Invited chapter in *An American Imperative: Higher Expectations for Higher Education*. Racine, WI: Wingspread Group on Higher Education.

John E. Roueche and Suanne D. Roueche. 1993, Summer. "Has Friendship Cooled, and Has the Love Affair Ended? Responding to the Realities of the At-Risk Student." *College Board Review*.

John E. Roueche and Suanne D. Roueche. 1993, April–May. "Making Good on the Promise: The View from Between a Rock and a Hard Place." *Community College Journal*.

John E. Roueche. 1992. *High Tech for High Touch*. Research brief. Boston: Digital Equipment.

John E. Roueche. 1992. *Leadership for Teaching Effectiveness*. 14th Earl V. Pullias lecture. Los Angeles: University of Southern California Press.

John E. Roueche. 1992, Summer. "Establishing College Priorities." *Trustee Quarterly*, Washington, DC: Association of Community College Trustees.

John E. Roueche. 1991. "The Role of the Chairperson in Assuring Faculty and Teaching Excellence." In William E. Cashin, ed., *Academic Chairpersons: Developing Faculty, Students, and Programs*. Manhattan: Kansas State University Press.

John E. Roueche, with Don Doucette. 1991, October. "Arguments with Which to Combat Elitism and Ignorance About Community Colleges." *Leadership Abstracts*, vol. 4, no. 13.

John E. Roueche. 1991, Spring. "Is Quality Job One?" *Trustee Quarterly*. Washington, DC: Association of Community College Trustees.

Rosemary Gillett-Karam, Suanne D. Roueche, and John E. Roueche. 1991, December–January. "Underrepresentation and the Question of Diversity." *Community and Junior College Journal.*

John E. Roueche. 1990. "Assessing Leadership." In *Association of Boards of Trustees Proceedings.* Albany, NY: Association of School Boards.

John E. Roueche. 1990. *Leadership for 2000.* Research brief. Sacramento: Association of California Community College Administrators.

John E. Roueche. 1990, June. "Insuring Excellence in Community College Teaching." *Leadership Abstracts.*

George A. Baker III, John E. Roueche, and Rosemary Gillett-Karam. 1990, April–May. "Teaching as Leading: A Theme for a New Decade." *Community and Junior College Journal.*

John E. Roueche. 1990, Winter. "Leading Is Teaching." *ACCT Trustee Quarterly.*

John E. Roueche. 1989. "The University Perspective." In David B. Wolf and Mary Lou Zoglin, eds., *External Influences on the Curriculum.* San Francisco: Jossey-Bass.

John E. Roueche and Suanne D. Roueche. 1989. "Innovations in Teaching: The Past as Prologue." In Terry U. O'Banion, *A Renaissance of Innovation.* Washington, DC: Macmillan, American Council on Education.

John E. Roueche. 1989, September 12. "Excellence and the Community College Mission." *Community College Times.*

John E. Roueche. 1989, Winter. "Leadership and Shared Vision." *ACCT Trustee Quarterly.*

John E. Roueche. 1989, January. "Shared Vision and Staff Selection." *Leadership Abstracts.*

John E. Roueche, George A. Baker III, and Robert R. Rose. 1988, June–July. "Transformational Leaders in the Community College: The Best of the Best." *Community, Technical, and Junior College Journal.*

John E. Roueche and Terry U. O'Banion. 1988, June–July. "Transformational Leaders: An Emerging National Response." *Community, Technical, and Junior College Journal.*

John E. Roueche, George A. Baker III, and Robert R. Rose. 1988, April–May. "The Community College President as Transformational Leader: A National Study." *Community, Technical, and Junior College Journal.*

John E. Roueche and Terry O'Banion. 1988, January. "Revitalizing Leadership for Community Colleges." *Leadership Abstracts.*

John E. Roueche, Suanne D. Roueche, and George A. Baker III. 1987. "A Silver Anniversary Special: The Anatomy of Excellence in the Community College." In John Keyser and Deborah L. Floyd, eds., *Toward Mastery Leadership.* Iowa City: American College Testing Program.

John E. Roueche, George A. Baker III, and Suanne D. Roueche. 1987, April–May. "Open Door or Revolving Door?" *Community, Technical, and Junior College Journal.*

John E. Roueche. 1986. "Teaching Excellence: Old Wine in New Bottles." In Suanne D. Roueche, ed., *Celebrating Teaching Excellence.* Austin: University of Texas, National Institute for Staff and Organizational Development.

John E. Roueche, George A. Baker III, and Suanne D. Roueche. 1986. "Access with Excellence." In George Voegel, ed., *Advances in Instructional Technology.* San Francisco: Jossey-Bass.

John E. Roueche and Suanne D. Roueche. 1986. "Teaching and Learning." In Lee Noel et al., eds., *Increasing Student Retention.* San Francisco: Jossey-Bass.

John E. Roueche and George A. Baker III. 1986, April. "The Success Connection: Examining the Fruits of Excellence." *Community, Technical, and Junior College Journal.*

John E. Roueche and George A. Baker III. 1986, February. "Take Your Leadership Role Seriously." *School Administrator.*

John E. Roueche. 1985. "President as Educational Leader." In Dale F. Campbell, ed., *Leadership Strategies for Community College Effectiveness.* Washington, DC: American Association of Community, Technical, and Junior Colleges.

John E. Roueche and George A. Baker III. 1985, September. "The Success Connection: Creating a Culture of Excellence." *Community and Junior College Journal.*

John E. Roueche, George A. Baker III, and Suanne D. Roueche. 1985, Spring. "Access with Excellence." *Community College Review.*

John E. Roueche and George A. Baker III. 1985, April. "The Success Connection: Toward Equality with Excellence." *Community and Junior College Journal.*

John E. Roueche, George A. Baker III, and Suanne D. Roueche. 1984, Summer. "College Responses to Low-Achieving Students." *American Education.*

John E. Roueche and Lynn B. Burnham. 1984, Spring. "Models of Excellence for Professional Educators." *Journal of Staff, Program, and Organizational Development.*

John E. Roueche. 1984, April. "Between a Rock and a Hard Place: Meeting Adult Literacy Needs." *Community and Junior College Journal,* pp. 21–24.

John E. Roueche and Nancy Armes. 1983, September. "Structure Is the Linchpin of Teaching." *Community and Junior College Journal.*

John E. Roueche. 1983, Spring. "WANTED: Teaching Excellence in the Community College." *Community College Review.*

John E. Roueche and Suanne D. Roueche. 1982. "Literacy Development: Foundation for General Education." in B. L. Johnson, ed., *General Education in Two-Year Colleges.* San Francisco: Jossey-Bass.

John E. Roueche and Karen Watkins. 1982, September. "A Commitment to Great Teaching." *Community and Junior College Journal,* pp. 22–25.

John E. Roueche and Oscar G. Mink. 1982, Spring. "Overcoming Learned Helplessness in Community College Students." *Journal of Developmental and Remedial Education,* pp. 2–5, 20.

John E. Roueche, George A. Baker III, and Nancy R. Armes. 1982, March. "Staff Development: Nipping at the Heels of the Master." *Community and Junior College Journal,* pp. 28–32.

John E. Roueche. 1982, Winter. "Community Colleges: Realizing Potential in the '80s." *Community Services Catalyst,* pp. 17–22.

John E. Roueche. 1982, January. "Don't Close the Door." *Community and Junior College Journal,* pp. 17–23.

John E. Roueche. 1981. "Egalitarianism in College." In *Serving Ethnic Minorities.* Los Angeles: ERIC Clearinghouse for Junior Colleges.

John E. Roueche and Nancy R. Armes. 1981, Fall. "Building Communities for Change in Higher Education." *California Journal of Teacher Education,* pp. 1–10.

John E. Roueche. 1981, Spring. "Affective Development in the Classroom." *Community College Review,* pp. 38–43.

John E. Roueche, Oscar G. Mink, and Nancy R. Armes. 1981, May. "Coaching Against Helplessness." *Community and Junior College Journal,* pp. 36–39.

John E. Roueche and Donald L. Clarke. 1981, Winter. "Compensatory Education: Toward a Holistic Approach." *Community College Frontiers,* pp. 35–40.

John E. Roueche. 1980, Fall. "Meeting Critical Community Needs." *Community Services Catalyst,* pp. 7–8.

John E. Roueche and Carolyn Thompson. 1980, Spring. "Good Teaching Promotes Student Success," *Journal of Developmental and Remedial Education*, pp. 12–17.

John E. Roueche and Nancy R. Armes. 1980, March. "Basic Skills Education: Point-Counterpoint." *Community and Junior College Journal*, pp. 21–26.

John E. Roueche and Karen Watkins. 1980, Winter. "Increasing Teaching Effectiveness." *Community College Frontiers*, pp. 14–18.

John E. Roueche and Patricia F. Archer. 1979, Spring. "Entry Level Assessment in College." *Community College Review*, pp. 15–28.

John E. Roueche, et al. 1979, Spring. "Impact of Administrative Climate, Instruction, and Counseling on Completion Rate of Postsecondary Educationally Disadvantaged Vocational/ Technical Students." *Journal of Vocational Education Research*, vol. 6, no. 2, pp. 1–13.

John E. Roueche. 1978. "College Teaching: Putting the Pieces Together." In George Del Grosso, ed., *College Perspective: Confrontation or Collegiality*. Sarnia, ON: Canadian Community College Association.

John E. Roueche. 1978, September. "Let's Get Serious About the High-Risk Student." *Community and Junior College Journal*, pp. 28–32.

John E. Roueche and Jerry J. Snow. 1978, September. "The Teacher and College Remedial Programs." *Today's Education*, pp. 69–72.

John E. Roueche. 1978, Spring. "What's Happening in Developmental Education." *Journal of Developmental and Remedial Education*, pp. 5–8.

John E. Roueche, Oscar G. Mink, and Michael L. Abbott. 1978, January. "Effects of Individualized Instruction on Control Expectancy: A Field Test." *Community/Junior College Research Quarterly*, pp. 111–18.

John E. Roueche and Donald T. Rippey. 1977, Fall. "Implications of Reduced Funding Upon the Open-Door Commitment." *Community College Review*, pp. 55–58.

John E. Roueche. 1976. "Compensatory Education." In *Will Higher Education Be Ready for the Eighties*? Atlanta: Southern Regional Education Board.

John E. Roueche. 1976. "Creative Learning Environments." In Maxwell C. King and Robert L. Breuder, eds., *Contemporary Issues on Post-Secondary Education*. Cocoa, FL: Brevard Community College.

John E. Roueche. 1976. "New Learning Principles." In N. Entwistle and Dai Hounsel, *How Students Learn*. Lancaster, UK: University of Lancaster, Institute for Research in Postsecondary Education.

John E. Roueche. 1976. "A Place to Begin: A Systems Approach to Instruction." In Charles W. Ford and Margaret K. Morgan, eds., *Teaching in the Health Professions*. St. Louis, MO: C. V. Mosby.

John E. Roueche and Oscar G. Mink. 1976, Spring. "Helping the Unmotivated Student: Toward Personhood Development." *Community College Review*, pp. 40–50.

John E. Roueche. 1976, March. "Creating an Environment for Learning." *Community and Junior College Journal*, pp. 48–51.

John E. Roueche. 1976, Winter. "Feeling Good About Yourself: What Is Good Remedial Education?" *Community College Frontiers*, pp. 10–12.

John E. Roueche. 1975, June. "Can Mastery Learning Be Human? The Case for Performance-Based Instruction." *Community College Review*, pp. 14–21.

John E. Roueche. 1974. *Developmental Education: Toward a Model*. Princeton, NJ: Educational Testing Service.

John E. Roueche. 1974, Spring. "Causing Learning in the Community College: The Recipe." *Community College Review*, pp. 42–52.

John E. Roueche. 1973. "Assumptions Underlying Individualized Instruction." In George del Grosso, ed., *Pragmatics of Accountability*, 3rd annual Institute on the Community College, Canadian Junior College Association.

John E. Roueche. 1973. "Community Colleges and the University of Texas." In F. R. Kintzer, ed., *Community Junior Colleges and Universities*. Los Angeles: University of California Press.

John E. Roueche. 1973. "Two-Year College Accountability." In R. W. Hostrop, ed., *Accountability for Educational Results*. Hamden, CT: Linnet Press.

John E. Roueche and George A. Baker III. 1973, October. "Accountability in Community Colleges Must Come from Within." *College and University Business*, pp. 9–14.

John E. Roueche, with Charles L. Wheeler. 1973, Summer. "Instructional Procedures for the Disadvantaged." *Improving College and University Teaching*, pp. 222–25.

John E. Roueche. 1973, July–August. "Accommodating Individual Differences." *Community College Review*, pp. 24–30.

John E. Roueche. 1972. "Accountability in the Two-Year College." Chap. 24 in Frank J. Sciara and Richard K. Jantz, *Accountability in American Education*. Boston: Allyn and Bacon.

John E. Roueche. 1972. "The Educational Development Officer: A Focus for Leadership." In B. Lamar Johnson, ed., *Educational Development in the Junior College*. Los Angeles: University of California Press.

John E. Roueche. 1972, November. "Accountability for Student Learning." *Interamerican Revista/Review*, pp. 6–14.

John E. Roueche. 1971. "Accountability for Student Learning: A Board Responsibility." In B. Lamar Johnson, ed., *The Community College Trustee*. Los Angeles: University of California Press.

John E. Roueche, George A. Baker III, and Richard L. Brownell. 1971. "Accountability in the Two-Year College." In *Instruction and Curriculum*. Durham, NC: National Laboratory for Higher Education.

John E. Roueche. 1971, February. "Accountability and the Community College." *Educational Technology Magazine*.

John E. Roueche. 1970. "Instruction: Causing Learning." In Bonnie E. Cone and Ben H. Hackney Jr., eds., *The Community College in an Era of Change*. Charlotte: University of North Carolina Press.

John E. Roueche and William H. McFarlane. 1970, December. "The Junior College and Instructional Systems: The Key to Equal Opportunity." *Journal of Higher Education*, vol. 14.

John E. Roueche and Barton R. Herrscher. 1970, October. "A Learning Oriented System of Instruction." *Junior College Journal*, vol. 41.

John E. Roueche. 1969. "Gaps and Overlaps in Institutional Research." In Selden Menefee and Jack Orcutt, eds., *Focus on Action*. Washington, DC: American Association of Junior Colleges.

John E. Roueche. 1969. "The Junior College President and Institutional Research." In B. Lamar Johnson, ed., *The Junior College President*. Los Angeles: University of California Press.

John E. Roueche. 1969. "New Models for Community College Systems." In *Junior College Systems*. Boulder, CO: Western Interstate Commission for Higher Education.

John E. Roueche. 1969. "Open-Door College or Open-Door Curriculums." In Selden Menefee and Jack Orcutt, eds., *Focus on Action*. Washington, DC: American Association of Junior Colleges.

John E. Roueche. 1969, Spring. "Needed: Remedial Teachers for Community Colleges." *Improving College and University Teaching*.

John E. Roueche and John R. Boggs. 1969, May. "A Survey of Institutional Research in American Junior Colleges." *California Journal of Educational Research.*

John E. Roueche and Dale Gaddy. 1969, March. "Nursing Education in the Junior College." *Junior College Research Review*, vol. 3, no. 7.

John E. Roueche and Arthur M. Cohen. 1969, February. "Memo to a Junior College Trustee." *College and University Business.*

John E. Roueche and Natalie Rumanzeff. 1968. *The College President.* Los Angeles: ERIC Clearinghouse for Junior College Information, 13 pp.

John E. Roueche and Natalie Rumanzeff. 1968. *Guidance in the Junior College.* Los Angeles: ERIC Clearinghouse for Junior College Information, 12 pp.

John E. Roueche and Natalie Rumanzeff. 1968. *The Junior and Community College Faculty: A Bibliography.* Washington, DC: National Faculty Association of Community and Junior Colleges, 20 pp.

John E. Roueche. 1968, November. "Adult Education in the Junior College." *Junior College Research Review*, vol. 3, no. 3.

John E. Roueche and Allan S. Hurlburt. 1968, November. "The Open-Door College: Problems of the Low Achiever." *Journal of Higher Education.*

John E. Roueche. 1968, September. "Junior College Guidance and Counseling." *Junior College Research Review*, vol. 3, no. 1.

John E. Roueche. 1968, June. "The Junior College President." *Junior College Research Review*, vol. 2, no. 10.

John E. Roueche. 1968, March. "Needed Research in the Junior College." *Junior College Research Review*, vol. 2, no. 7.

John E. Roueche and Allan S. Hurlburt. 1968, March. "Research on Junior College Teachers." *Junior College Research Review*, vol. 2, no. 7.

John E. Roueche. 1968, Winter. "Superior Teaching in Junior Colleges: Research Needed." *Improving College and University Teaching.*

John E. Roueche and David M. Sims. 1968, February. "Open-Door College or Open-Door Curriculums?" *Junior College Journal*, vol. 38.

John E. Roueche. 1968, January. "Junior College Researchers Have a Friend Named ERIC." *College and University Business*, vol. 44.

John E. Roueche and John R. Boggs. 1968, January. "Placement Testing in Junior Colleges." *Junior College Research Review*, vol. 2, no. 5.

John E. Roueche. 1967. *The Community and Junior College: A Bibliography of Doctoral Dissertations.* Washington, DC: American Association of Junior Colleges, 18 pp.

John E. Roueche. 1967. "Student Personnel Records." In *Manual for Student Personnel Records in Area Vocational-Technical Schools.* Atlanta: Georgia State Department of Education.

John E. Roueche. 1967, November. "Gaps and Overlaps in Institutional Research." *Junior College Journal*, vol. 38.

John E. Roueche. 1967, November. "The Junior College Remedial Program." *Junior College Research Review*, vol. 2, no. 3.

John E. Roueche. 1967, October. "The Junior College Dropout." *Junior College Research neview*, vol. 2, no. 2.

John E. Roueche. 1967, June. "Experimentation in Junior Colleges." *Junior College Research Review*, vol. 1, no. 5.

John E. Roueche and David M. Sims. 1967, April. "Curriculum Studies in Junior Colleges." *Junior College Research Review*, vol. 1, no. 3.

John E. Roueche. 1967, March. "Characteristics of Junior College Students." *Junior College Research Review*, vol. 1, no. 2.

John E. Roueche. 1967, February. "Follow-Up Studies of Junior College Students." *Junior College Research Review*, vol. 1, no. 1.

John E. Roueche. 1966, September. "Which Door While in College?" *North Carolina Education Association Journal.*

John E. Roueche. 1966, Spring. "Which Door for Me?" *Open Door.*

John E. Roueche and Raymond E. Schultz. 1966, February. "All That Glitters Is Not Gold." *Journal of Higher Education.*

Appendix E

Research and Development

SELECTED RESEARCH AND DEVELOPMENT ACTIVITIES

- Principal Investigator: Houston Endowment, Inc., Achieving the Dream Project, 2006–2011, $4.5 million
- Principal Investigator: Lumina Foundation, Achieving the Dream Project, 2004–2009, $4.6 million
- Principal Investigator: Lumina Foundation, Keeping America's Promise, 2004–2005, $17,000
- Principal Investigator: Lumina Foundation, CCSSE Validation Research, 2004–2005, $250,000
- Principal Investigator: Ford Foundation, Community College Bridges to Opportunity Initiative, 2003–2007, $2.495 million
- Principal Investigator: Houston Endowment, Texas Small Colleges Consortium, 2003–2005, $182,000
- Principal Investigator: MetLife Foundation Initiative on Student Success, 2002–2006, $550,000
- Principal Investigator: League for Innovation, College and Careers Transition Initiative (CCTI), 2002–2005, $305,000
- Principal Investigator: Lumina Foundation for Education Project to establish CCSSE, 2001–2004, $1.47 million
- Principal Investigator: The Pew Charitable Trusts Grant to establish CCSSE, 2001–2004, $1.5 million
- Principal Investigator: MetLife Foundation Project for Benchmarking Community College Programs, 2001–2003, $300,000

- Co–Principal Investigator and Project Director (with Terry O'Banion): W. K. Kellogg Leadership Project, 1996–1999, $800,000
- Co–Principal Investigator and Project Director (with Terry O'Banion): W. K. Kellogg National Community College Leadership 2000 Project, 1993–1995, $675,000
- Co–Principal Investigator and Project Director (with Terry O'Banion): W. K. Kellogg National Diversity Mentor Project, 1990–1995, $1 million
- Co–Principal Investigator and Project Director (with Terry O'Banion): W. K. Kellogg National Community College Leadership 2000 Project, 1987–1992, $1.8 million
- Principal Investigator and Project Director: W. K. Kellogg Foundation Project to Assist Community Colleges with Excellence in Teaching, 1984–1988, $505,000
- Co–Principal Investigator: *In Pursuit of Teaching Excellence: A National Study*, Sid W. Richardson Foundation, 1983–1984, $65,000
- Principal Investigator: Diffusing Exxon Foundation Innovations to Community Colleges, Exxon Education Foundation, 1983–1984, $28,000
- Principal Investigator: *College Responses to Low-Achieving Students: A National Study*, HBJ Media Systems Corporation, 1982–1983, $18,750
- Principal Investigator and Project Director: Building Information and Networking Capabilities for Diffusing Innovations to Community Colleges and Other Post-Secondary Institutions, Fund for the Improvement of Post-Secondary Education, 1981–1982, $50,000
- Principal Investigator and Project Director: W. K. Kellogg Project to Improve Community College Teaching and Learning, W. K. Kellogg Foundation Grant, 1978–1983, $1.171 million
- Principal Investigator and Project Director: Continuing Professional Education of Community College Staff through Utilization of Learning Modules Toward Increasing Student Achievement, Fund for the Improvement of Post-Secondary Education, 1978–1981, $250,000
- Principal Investigator: A Multidisciplinary Field Investigation Aimed at Permeating the Reality of the Culturally Different Student's Acquisition of Literacy in the Community College, National Institute of Education Grant, 1978–1981, $512,000
- Principal Investigator: Installation and Assimilation of Educational Innovations in Vocational/Technical Programs within Post-Secondary Institutions, US Office of Education (Vocational Education) Grant, 1976–1977, $157,616

- Principal Investigator: Study of the Impact of Administrative Climate, Instruction, and Counseling on Control Expectancy, Anxiety, and Completion Rate of Postsecondary Educationally Disadvantaged and Minority Vocational-Technical Students, US Office of Education Vocational Education Grant, 1975–1976, $118,560
- Principal Investigator: Impact of Instruction and Counseling on Disadvantaged Youth, National Institute of Mental Health Grant, 1973–1976, $239,527
- Principal Investigator: Study of Innovative Community College Remedial Programs, US Office of Education, Bureau of Research Grant, 1972–1973, $10,000
- Principal Investigator: Study of Educational Development Officers in Selected North Carolina Community Colleges, Office of Economic Opportunity Grant, 1970–1971, $76,500
- Director: Study of Community College Remedial Programs, ERIC Clearinghouse for Junior Colleges, 1968, UCLA, $6,000

SELECTED TRAINING GRANTS

- Director: Houston Endowment, Inc., Jesse H. Jones Endowed Fellowships in Community College Leadership, 2001, $1 million
- Director: Sid W. Richardson Foundation Fellowship Award to Community College Leadership Program, 1984–1987, $330,000
- Director: Sid W. Richardson Foundation Fellowship Award to Community College Leadership Program, 1981–1983, $270,000
- Director: Sid W. Richardson Foundation Fellowship Award to Community College Leadership Program, 1976–1980, $205,000
- Director: US Office of Education, Education Professions Development Act, Fellowship Award to Community College Leadership Program, 1975–1976, $27,000
- Director: US Office of Education, Education Professions Development Act, Fellowship Award to Community College Leadership Program, 1974–1975, $118,500
- Director: US Office of Education, Education Professions Development Act, Fellowship Award to Community College Leadership Program, 1973–1974, $133,500

- Director: US Office of Education, Education Professions Development Act, Fellowship Award to Community College Leadership Program, 1972–1973, $124,600
- Director: US Office of Education, Education Professions Development Act, Fellowship Award to Community College Leadership Program, 1971–1972, $72,141

Appendix F

Selected Professional Responsibilities and Community Activities

PROFESSIONAL RESPONSIBILITIES

- National Community College Advisory Board, 3D/International-Parsons, Inc., Houston, Texas, 2001–2011, chairman of the board for five years
- Member, International Advisory Committee, Ontario Institute on the Study of Education, the University of Toronto, March 1998–2005
- Board member, Publications Commission, American Association of Community Colleges, 1994–2000
- Member, Editorial Board, *Community College Research Quarterly*, 1992–2000
- Member, Board of Directors, American Association of Community and Junior Colleges, 1989–1994
- Member, Editorial Advisory Board, *Community and Junior College Journal*, 1989–1994
- Member, Editorial Board, *Community College Times*, 1989–1994
- National Advisory Committee on the Future of the Community College, Kellogg Foundation, 1982–1997
- Member, Editorial Board, *Journal for Staff and Organizational Development*, 1982–1993
- National Advisory Board for Community Colleges, SUNY, Albany, 1980–1989
- Member, Editorial Board, *Community College Review*, 1980–1986

- Member, Editorial Board, *Journal of Competency-Based Education*, 1979–1991
- National Advisory Board, Media Systems Corporation, New York, 1979–1986
- National Advisory Board, Center for Educational Development, Appalachian State University, North Carolina, 1977–2005
- National Advisory Committee for Lifelong Learning, American Association of Community and Junior Colleges, 1977–1983
- Member, Editorial Board, *Community College Frontiers*, 1976–1985
- President, Council of Universities and Colleges, 1976–1977
- National Advisory Board, ERIC Clearinghouse for Higher Education, 1975–1977
- National Advisory Board for Community Colleges, Educational Testing Service and College Entrance Examination Board, 1975–1976
- Consulting editor, *Journal of Higher Education*, 1974–1980
- Board of Directors, Council of Universities and Colleges, 1974–1978
- Member, Editorial Board, *Research in Higher Education Journal*, 1971–1992
- National Advisory Board for Community Colleges, American College Testing Service, 1971–1976

COMMUNITY ACTIVITIES

- Past president, Doss Elementary School PTA, Austin, Texas
- Past chairman, Administrative Board, Northwest Hills United Methodist Church, Austin, Texas
- Past chairman, Council of Ministries, Northwest Hills United Methodist Church, Austin, Texas

References

American Association of Community Colleges. 2012. *John E. Roueche, PhD, A Tribute*. Video presentation at AACC 2012 Annual Convention.

———. 2012. *Reclaiming the American Dream: Community Colleges and the Nation's Future*. Washington, DC: American Association of Community Colleges. http://www.aacc21stcenturycenter.org/wp-content/uploads/2014/03/21stCenturyReport.pdf

———. 2017. *AACC Competencies for Community College Leaders*, 2nd ed. Washington, DC: American Association of Community Colleges. https://www.aacc.nche.edu/wp-content/uploads/2017/09/AACC_Core_Competencies_web.pdf

———. 2018. *AACC Competencies for Community College Leaders*, 3rd ed. Washington, DC: American Association of Community Colleges. https://www.aacc.nche.edu/wp-content/uploads/2018/11/AACC2018Competencies_111618_FINAL.pdf

———. 2019a. *Leadership Award*. Washington, DC: American Assocation of Community Colleges. https://www.aacc.nche.edu/about-us/awards/leadership.award/

———. 2019b. *Truman Award*. Washington, DC: American Associaton of Community Colleges. https://www.aacc.nche.edu/about-us/awards/

American Association of Community Colleges and Association of Community College Trustees. 2016. "Joint Statement of Commitment to Equity, Diversity, and Excellence in Student Success and Leadership Development." Washington, DC. https://www.aacc.nche.edu/wp-content/uploads/2017/09/JOINT_STATEMENT_OF_COMMITMENT_TO_EQUITY-1.pdf

American Association of Junior Colleges. 1970. *American Association of Junior Colleges 1970 Annual Report*. Washington, DC: American Association of Community Colleges.

Bailey, Thomas. 2009. "Challenge and Opportunity: Rethinking the Role and Function of Developmental Education in Community College." CCRC Working Paper, no. 14. New York: Teachers College, Columbia University.

American Council on Education. 1996. *Educational Record 1995–1996, v. 76*. Washington, DC: American Council on Education.

Baker, George A., III. 1995. *Team Building for Quality*. Washington, DC: Community College Press, American Association of Community Colleges.

———. 2012. *The Making of a Marine-Scholar: Leading and Learning in the Bear Pit*. Bloomington, IN: iUniverse.

Boggs, George. 2018, October 15. Personal interview with Thornton.

Biggerstaff, Charlotte. 2018, October 29. Personal communication with Waiwaiole.

Bradley, Paul. 2012. "End of an ERA." *Community College Week*. http://ccweek.com/article-2966-cover-story:-end-of-an-era.html

Bumphus, Walter G. 2018, September 12. Personal interview with Thornton.

Brinkley, David. 2019. David Brinkley Quotes. BrainyQuotes.com. BrainyMedia Inc, 2019. https://www.brainyquote.com/quotes/david_brinkley_130590

Calaway, Terry. 2018, August 23. Personal interview with Thornton.

Bumphus, Walter G. 2018, November 5. Written communication with Ellis.

CCLP Alumni Directory. 1960–2012. Community College Leadership Program, the University of Texas at Austin, Department of Educational Administration, College of Education.

Center for Analysis of Postsecondary Readiness. 2018. https://postsecondaryreadiness.org/

Coauthor 1. 2018, August 15. Personal communication with Adams.

Coauthor 2. 2018, August 30. Personal communication with Adams.

Coauthor 3. 2018, August 30. Personal communication with Adams.

Coauthor 4. 2018, August 24. Personal communication with Adams.

Coauthor 5. 2018, August 22. Personal communication with Adams.

Coauthor 6. 2018, August 17. Personal communication with Adams.

Commission on Colleges, Southern Association of Colleges and Schools. 1987. *Resource Manual on Institutional Effectiveness.* Atlanta, GA: SACS.

Core Principles for Transforming Remediation within the Context of a Comprehensive Student Success Strategy: A Joint Statement. 2015, November. N.p. https://strongstart.org/sites/default/files/core_principles_nov9.pdf

Daily Staff. 2017, December 29. "The 'First Voice' for At-Risk Students." *Community College Daily.* http://www.ccdaily.com/2017/12/the-first-voice-for-at-risk-students/

Davis, Daniel. 2017, January 19. "Southwest Airlines: Flying High with Employee Enablement." *IBM Collaboration Solutions.* https://www.ibm.com/blogs/collaborationsolutions/2017/01/19/southwest-airlines-flying-high-employee-enablement/

Dembicki, Matthew. 2016. "Losing the Architect of the Modern Community College Movement." *Community College Journal*, vol. 87, no. 2, p. 4.

Duckworth, A. 2016. *Grit: The Power of Passion and Perseverance.* New York: Scribner.

Eliot, T. S. 1915, June. "The Love Song of J. Alfred Prufrock." In *Poetry: A Magazine of Verse*, edited by Harriet Monroe.

Ellis, Martha M. and Linda L. Garcia. 2017. *Generation X President's Leading Community Colleges.* Lanham, MD: Rowman & Littlefield.

Ewell, Peter. 2018, October 18. Personal communication with Waiwaiole.

Fain, Paul. 2012, May 30. "Texas Shake Up." *Inside Higher Education.* https://www.insidehighered.com/news/2012/05/30/u-texas-community-college-leadership-programs-founder-moves-profit

Flores, Michael. 2018, August 2. Personal communication with Byron McClenney.

Gardner, John W. 1990. *On Leadership.* New York: Free Press.

Gleazer, Edmund J. 1970. "The Community College: Issues of the 1970s." *Educational Record*, vol. 51, no. 1, pp. 47–52.

Grainger, George. 2018, October 16. Personal communication with Waiwaiole.

Hamilton, Reeve. 2012, June 13. "Director's Exit Fuels Fears About Community College Leadership Program." *Texas Tribune.* https://www.texastribune.org/2012/06/13/uts-relationship-community-colleges-spotlight

Johnson, Steve. 2018, November 1. Personal communication with Waiwaiole.

Kanter, Rosabeth Moss. 1989. *When Giants Learn to Dance.* New York: Simon and Schuster.

Knight, Brent. 2018, October 11. Written personal communication with Thornton.

Knowledge@Wharton. 2018, November 15. "Good 'Food Citizens': Why Collaboration Is Key to Feeding the World."

Ku, Peter. 2003. Written communication with Baker.

Lasher, William E. 2018, April 17. Written personal communication with Boggs.

Lawrence, Thomas Edward. 1991. *Seven Pillars of Wisdom: A Triumph.* New York: Anchor Press.

Lewis, Ted. 2018, May 18. Personal communication with O'Banion.

Lorenzo, George. 2012, May 5. "On John Roueche, Community College Leadership Programs and the Real World of Retirement." *Source.* https://edpath.typepad.com/source_scholars/2012/05/on-john-roueche-community-college-leadership-programs-and-the-real-world-of-retirement.html

Manzo, K. K. 1996, September 23. "Developing Strong Leadership for Community Colleges." *Community College Week.*

———. 2007, June 23. "Building Leaders: Leadership Development Program Important Step for Community College Presidents." *Diverse: Issues in Higher Education.*

Mathis, Margaretta B. 2019, April 23. E-mail communication.

McClenney, B. N., and R. M. Flores. 1998. "Community College of Denver Developmental Education." In *Developmental Education: A Twenty-First Century Social and Economic Imperative,* edited by R. H. McCabe and P. R. Day. Mission Viejo, CA: League for Innovation and the College Board.

McClenney, Byron. 2018, October 30. Personal communication with WaiWaiole.

McClenney, Byron, and Margaretta Mathis. 2011. *Making Good on the Promise of the Open Door.* Washington, DC: Association of Community College Trustees.

McClenney, Kay. 2018, August 21. Written personal communication with Bumphus.

———. 2018, September 21. Personal communication with Thornton.

———. 2018, October 11. Personal communication with Waiwaiole.

McCrohan, Betty. 2018, October 18. Personal communication with Waiwaiole.

McKnight, Michael, and Deborah Irvine. 2014. "United Way and Success by 6: Growing Up with Collective Impact." *Philanthropist,* vol. 26, no. 1, pp. 91–94.

McLaughlin, Keith. 2018, April 27. Personal communication with O'Banion.

Meacham, John. 2018. https://www.brainyquote.com/authors/jon-meacham-quotes

Mercer, Debbie. 2019, June 21. Personal communication with Ellis.

Miles, Cindy. 2018, June 11. Personal communication with B. McClenney.

Mitchell Community College. 2019. "Mitchell Endowment Receives $100,000 Donation." https://mitchellcc.edu/news/mitchell-endowment-receives-100000-donation

Moore, F. Lynn. 2019, April 23. E-mail communication.

Myers, Verna. 2015, December 10. *Diversity is being invited to the party: Inclusion is being asked to dance.* Women's Leadership Conference. https://www.youtube.com/watch?v=9gS2VPUkB3M

National American University Holdings. 2012, May 29. "National American University Holdings, Inc. Announces Development of Roueche Graduate Center." *Business Wire.* https://www.businesswire.com/news/home/20120529006559/en/National-American-University-Holdings-Announces-Development-Roueche

National Commission on Excellence in Education. 1983. *A Nation at Risk: The Imperative for Educational Reform.* Washington, DC: US Department of Education.

National Commission on Higher Education Issues. 1982. *To Strengthen Quality in Higher Education.* Washington, DC: American Council on Education.

National Institute for Organizational Development (NISOD). 2018. "History of NISOD." https://www.nisod.org/history-of-nisod/

O'Banion, Terry. 2016, May. "Leadership Development Is All About Collaboration." *Leadership Abstracts*, vol. 29, no. 5.

———. 2018, November 15. Personal communication with Thornton.

O'Banion, Terry, and John E. Roueche. 1988, January. Revitalizing Leadership for Community Colleges. *Leadership Abstracts*, vol. 1, no. 1.

Pluviose, David. 2012, April 24. "Retiring CCLP Director John Roueche Celebrated at AACC Conference." *Diverse: Issues in Higher Education*. http://diverseeducation.com/article/17022/

———. 2012, May 12. "Editor's Note: An Ode to John Roueche." *Diverse: Issues in Higher Education.* http://diverseeducation.com/article/17100/

Rhodes, Richar. 2018, October 23. Personal communication with Waiwaiole.

Roueche, John E. 1968. *Salvage, Redirection, or Custody? Remedial Education in the Junior College.* Washington, DC: American Association of Junior Colleges.

———. 1977. *New Directions for Higher Education: Increasing Basic Skills by Developmental Studies.* San Francisco: Jossey-Bass.

———. 1980. *Holistic Literacy in College Teaching.* New York: Harcourt Brace Jovanovich, Media Systems.

———. 1983. *A New Look at Successful Programs for Low-Achieving Students.* San Francisco: Jossey-Bass.

———. 2018, March 2. Personal communication with Ellis.

———. 2018, April 6. Personal communication with McClenney.

———. 2018, April 29. Personal communication with Boggs.

———. 2018, July 18. Personal communication with Waiwaiole.

———. 2018, August 13–September 14. Oral and written personal communications with Bumphus.

———. 2018. August 31. Personal communication with Adams.

———. 2018, October 22. Personal communication with Thornton.

———. 2019, May 23. Personal communication with Ellis.

Roueche, John E., and George A. Baker III. 1983. *Beacons for Change.* Iowa City: American College Testing Service.

———, eds. 1984. *Community College Leadership in the Eighties.* Washington, DC: Community College Press.

———. 1986. *Profiling Excellence in America's Schools.* Arlington, VA: American Association of School Administrators.

———. 1987. *Access and Excellence: The Open-Door College.* Washington, DC: Community College Press.

Roueche, John E., George A. Baker III, and Richard A. Brownell. 1971. *Accountability and the Community College: Directions for the '70s.* Washington, DC: American Association of Junior Colleges.

Roueche, John E., George A. Baker III, and Rosemary Gillett-Karam. 1990. *Teaching as Leading: Profiles of Excellence in the Open-Door College.* Washington, DC: Community College Press.

Roueche, John E., with George A. Baker III and Robert Rose. 1989. *Shared Vision: Transformational Leadership in American Community Colleges.* Washington, DC: Community College Press.

Roueche, John E., George A. Baker III, and Suanne D. Roueche. 1984. *College Responses to Low-Achieving Students: A National Study.* Orlando, FL: HBJ Media Systems.

Roueche, John E., and John R. Boggs. 1968. *Junior College Institutional Research: The State of the Art.* Washington, DC: American Association of Junior Colleges.

Roueche, John E., and Arthur M. Cohen. 1969. *Institutional Administrator or Educational Leader? The Junior College President.* Washington, DC: American Association of Junior Colleges.

Roueche, John E., Eileen E. Ely, and Suanne D. Roueche. 2001. *In Pursuit of Excellence: The Community College of Denver.* Washington, DC: Community College Press.

Roueche, John E., with Rosemary Gillett-Karam and Suanne D. Roueche. 1991. *Underrepresentation and the Question of Diversity: Women and Minorities in the Community College.* Washington, DC: Community College Press.

Roueche, John E., and Barton R. Herrscher. 1970, October. "Of Instruction." *Junior College Journal,* vol. 41, no. 2, pp. 22–26.

———. 1973. *Toward Instructional Accountability: A Guide to Educational Change.* Palo Alto, CA: Westinghouse Learning Press.

Roueche, John E., Barton R. Herrscher, and George A. Baker III. 1976. *Time as the Variable, Achievement as the Constant: Competency-Based Instruction in the Community College.* Washington, DC: American Association of Community and Junior Colleges.

Roueche, John E., Laurence F. Johnson, and Suanne D. Roueche. 1997. *Embracing the Tiger: The Effectiveness Debate and the Community College.* Washington, DC: Community College Press.

Roueche, John E., and Barbara R. Jones. 2005. *The Entrepreneurial Community College.* Washington, DC: Community College Press.

Roueche, John E., and R. Wade Kirk. 1973. *Catching Up: Remedial Education.* San Francisco: Jossey-Bass.

Roueche, John E., William H. McFarlane, and Barton R. Herrscher. 1971. *The Private Junior College: Prospects for the '70s.* Durham, NC: National Laboratory for Higher Education.

Roueche, John E., Mark D. Milliron, and Suanne D. Roueche. 2003. *Practical Magic: On the Front Lines of Teaching Excellence.* Washington, DC: Community College Press.

Roueche, John E., Barbara P. Mink, and Oscar G. Mink. 1979a. *Assessing Student Opinions of the Learning Experience.* New York: HBJ Media Systems.

———. 1979b. *Confronting Student Attitudes.* New York: HBJ Media Systems.

Roueche, John E., and Oscar G. Mink. 1979. *Improving Student Motivation.* New York: HBJ Media Systems.

Roueche, John E., Dale Parnell, and Carl Kuttler Jr. 1994. *1,001 Exemplary Practices in America's Two-Year Colleges.* New York: McGraw-Hill.

Roueche, John E., with John C. Pitman. 1972. *A Modest Proposal: Students Can Learn.* San Francisco: Jossey-Bass.

Roueche, John E., Melissa M. Richardson, Phillip W. Neal, and Suanne. D. Roueche. 2008. *The Creative Community College: Leading Change through Innovation.* Washington, DC: Community College Press.

Roueche, John E., and Donald T. Rippey, eds. 1981, Spring. *Teaching and Learning in the 1980s. Community College Frontiers,* Special Issue.

Roueche, John E., and Suanne D. Roueche. 1977. *Developmental Education: A Primer for Program Development and Evaluation.* Atlanta, GA: Southern Regional Education Board.

———. 1993. *Between a Rock and a Hard Place: The At-Risk Student in the Open-Door College.* Washington, DC: Community College Press.

———. 1999. *High Stakes, High Performance: Making Remedial Education Work.* Washington, DC: Community College Press.

Roueche, John E., and Suanne D. Roueche, with Martha M. Ellis and Melinda Valdez-Ellis. 2012. *Rising to the Challenge: Lessons Learned from Guilford Technical Community College.* Washington, DC: Community College Press.

Roueche, John E., Suanne D. Roueche, and Mark D. Milliron. 1995. *Strangers in Their Own Land: Part-Time Faculty in American Community Colleges.* Washington, DC: Community College Press.

Roueche, John E. and Jerry J. Snow. 1977. *Overcoming Learning Problems.* San Francisco Jossey-Bass.

Roueche, John E., Lynn S. Taber, and Suanne D. Roueche. 1995. *The Company We Keep: Collaboration in the Community College.* Washington, DC: Community College Press.

Roueche, John E., and Evelyn N. Waiwaiole. 2009, September 17. "Developmental Education: An Investment We Cannot Afford NOT to Make." *Diverse: Issues in Higher Education*, vol. 26, no. 16, p. 16.

Shape, Ronald. 2018, December 11. E-mail communication.

Shakespeare, William. Translation 2014. *Macbeth, Act 1 Scene 4.* https://www.litcharts.com/shakescleare/shakespeare-translations/macbeth/act-1-scene-4

Smith, Susan. 2012, May. "A Man for All Seasons: As He Readies for Retirement, the Lasting Legacy of John E. Roueche Is Secure." *Community College Week*, vol. 24, no. 21.

———. 2012, May 22. "John Roueche: Community College Renaissance Man." *Diverse: Issues in Higher Education.* ⸜

———. 2012, May 30. "John Roueche Awarded Inaugural Diverse Champions Award." *Diverse: Issues in Higher Education.* http://diverseeducation.com/article/17104/

Southwest Airlines. 2017. *One Report 2017.* https://southwestonereport.com/about-the-one-report/

Southwest Airlines. 2017, November 28. "Southwest Airlines Breathes New Life into Nearly 675,000 Pounds of Seat Covers and Other Discarded Materials in 2017."

Srivastva, Suresh, David Cooperrider, and Associates. 1990. *Appreciative Management and Leadership: The Power of Positive Thought and Action in Organization.* San Francisco: Jossey-Bass.

Study Group on the Conditions of Excellence in American Higher Education. 1984. *Involvement in Learning: Realizing the Potential of American Higher Education.* Washington, DC: US Department of Education.

Thelin, John R. 2004. *A History of American Higher Education.* Baltimore, MD: Johns Hopkins University Press.

Ullman, Ellen. 2012, April 2. "Community Reflects on Leadership Guru Roueche as He Retires." *Community College Times.* http://www.communitycollegetimes.com/Pages/Academic-Programs/College-community-reflects-on-leadership-guru-Roueche-as-he-retires.aspx

United Way. N.d. "Our Mission." https://www.unitedway.org/our-impact/mission

The University of Texas at Austin. 2009. *Block Guide: Community College Leadership Program.* Austin: University of Texas.

Valdes-Dapena, Carlos. 2018, September 11. "Stop Wasting Money on Team Building." *Harvard Business Review.* https://hbr.org/2018/09/stop-wasting-money-on-team-building

Valverde, Leonard. 2018, April 25. Written communication with Boggs.

Waiwaiole, Evelyn. 2018. *Celebrations.* Austin: University of Texas at Austin.

Warren, Rick. 2019. "Rick Warren Quotes." https://www.goodreads.com/author/quotes/711. Rick_Warren

Wheelan, Belle. 2018, February 18. Personal written communication with Boggs.

———. 2018, May 24. Personal communication with B. McClenney.

———. 2018, August 9. Personal interview with Thornton.

Wingspread Group on Higher Education. 1993. *An American Imperative: Higher Expectations for Higher Education.* Racine, WI: Johnson Foundation.

Wright, Cathy. 2013, August 8. "Collaboration Is Key to Success, Says Southwest's Randy Babbitt." Southwest Airlines Community. https://www.southwestaircommunity.com/t5/Southwest-Stories/Collaboration-is-Key-to-Success-Says-Southwest-s-Randy-Babbitt/ba-p/41333

Zusman, Ami. 2005. "Challenges Facing Higher Education in the Twenty-first Century." In R. O. Altbach and P. G. Berdahl, eds., *American Higher Education in the 21st Century: Social, Political, and Economic Challenges*, 2nd ed. Baltimore, MD: Johns Hopkins Press.

Zylka, Sherry. 2018, August 21. Written personal communication with Bumphus.

About the Editor

Martha M. Ellis, PhD, is director of higher education strategy, policy, and services for the Charles A. Dana Center and professor of practice at the University of Texas at Austin. Ellis is a leadership coach for Achieving the Dream and Texas Pathways. She is a consultant for community colleges and universities throughout the United States working with executive leaders and boards of trustees.

Prior to joining the Dana Center, Ellis was associate vice chancellor of academic affairs at the University of Texas System and adjunct professor at UT Austin. Martha has 35 years of experience in community colleges, including two presidencies, provost, chief information officer, dean, and faculty member. Martha has continued to teach throughout her career at both the undergraduate and graduate levels. She was a facilitator and coach for the Future Leaders Institute, High Impact Teams, and the President's Academy for the American Association of Community Colleges.

Ellis was recognized by the Texas House of Representatives and US Congress for her outstanding contributions to community college leadership. She has won numerous teaching awards; is coeditor of the popular book *Generation X Presidents Leading Community Colleges: New Challenges, New Leaders*; and is an invited presenter at national conferences on leadership development, strategic partnerships, math/guided pathways, and change leadership.

Dr. Ellis is a member of the New York Academy of Sciences and the American Psychological Association. She served on the Appeals Committee for the Commission on Colleges and the Board of the American Association of Community Colleges. She was a member of the Commission on Women in Higher Education for the American Council of Education and was a commissioner for the Commission on Colleges for the Southern Association of Colleges and Schools. She was president of the Association of Texas Colleges and Universities. Martha has volunteered on various chamber, economic development, and hospital boards.

In addition to her PhD from the University of North Texas, Ellis completed postgraduate work at Columbia University in New York, an internship at the Albert Ellis Institute at State University of New York, and the President's Institute at Harvard University. Martha lives in Austin with her husband, Steve.

About the Contributors

Dr. Tammy Adams has worked in leadership roles in higher education for 35 years. She is the leading researcher on the books of John E. Roueche. Tammy received her doctoral degree from the CCLP at the Roueche Graduate Center, National American University. Her favorite pastime is spending time with her family, husband, Bubba, and two children, Lauren and Tyler—all of whom have completed graduate degrees.

Dr. George A. Baker III is distinguished emeritus professor at North Carolina State University and director of College Planning Systems, a private consulting organization. Baker was named the Joseph D. Moore Endowed Chair in Community College Leadership at NCSU in August 1992 and remained in that position until his retirement in June 2001. Previous to these assignments, he had served as professor of higher and community college education at the University of Texas at Austin. Baker is a community college graduate from Warren Wilson College; he received his bachelor degree from Presbyterian College, master's from Shippensburg State University, a PhD in educational administration from Duke University under Dr. John E. Roueche, and a master's of public administration as a dual instructor and student at the Naval War College. Baker was a professor of organizational behavior and leadership at five different colleges and universities, before joining the faculty at the University of Texas in 1978. He served in the US Marine Corps for 20 years, including 2 years in combat and 3 years on the staff of the 36th president of the United States, Lyndon B. Johnson. Besides the President Service Medal, he earned 10 awards for distinguished service and heroism in Vietnam. Among his most treasured awards are the Teaching Excellence Award at UT Austin in 1983, the Distinguished Scholarly Award at North Carolina State University in 1992, the Order of the Long Leaf Pine in 1991 for service to North Carolina's 50 community colleges, and Distinguished Alumni Awards from all three attended institutions of higher learning.

Dr. George R. Boggs is president and CEO emeritus of the American Association of Community Colleges and superintendent/president emeritus of Palomar College in California. He continues to be an active consultant, author, speaker, and professor, teaching in community college leadership doctoral programs. He has served on many higher education and government boards and serves as chair of the Phi Theta Kappa International Student Honor Society Board. He is a prolific writer of books and articles on community college leadership and governance.

Dr. Walter G. Bumphus is president and CEO of the American Association of Community Colleges. He previously served as a professor in the Community College Leadership Program and as chair of the Department of Educational Administration at the University of Texas at Austin, holding the A. M. Aikin Regents Endowed Chair in Junior and Community College Education Leadership. From 2001 to 2007, Dr. Bumphus served as president of the Louisiana Community and Technical College System (LCTCS). Prior to 2001, he was chancellor of Baton Rouge Community College (BRCC). Before joining BRCC, Dr. Bumphus worked in the corporate world, serving as president of the Higher Education Division of Voyager Expanded Learning. Six years earlier, he served as president of Brookhaven College in the Dallas County Community College District. Dr. Bumphus was recognized as a distinguished graduate from both Murray State University and the University of Texas at Austin. Dr. Bumphus holds the distinction of being one of the few leaders in the field of education to chair the AACC Board of Directors and to receive the ACCT Marie Y. Martin CEO of the Year Award, the John Roueche and Terry O'Banion International Leadership Award, and the AACC Leadership Award. He was appointed to the Department of Homeland Security's Academic Advisory Council, the 100,000 Strong Initiative, and the White House Initiative on Educational Excellence for African Americans under President Obama. He was selected as 1 of 20 commissioners to serve on the Task Force on Apprenticeship Expansion under President

Trump. Currently, he serves as 1 of 25 members of the American Workforce Policy Advisory Board. He serves on the Board of Visitors of Marine Corp University and Air University.

Dr. Linda L. García is the executive director of the Center for Community College Student Engagement (the Center) at the University of Texas at Austin (UT). Prior to this role, she served as the assistant director of college relations at the Center. Also, Linda was vice president of community college relations at the Roueche Graduate Center at National American University, and she has worked at Lone Star College, Maricopa Community Colleges, and the University of Texas at Brownsville and Texas Southmost College. Linda's experience includes student development, instructional support, grant writing, and teaching. She serves as a coach for the American Association of Community Colleges Pathways 2.0 and Texas Pathways Project. Linda earned a bachelor of journalism with a concentration in broadcast and a doctorate in higher education administration with a specialization in community college leadership from the University of Texas at Austin. Her master of arts in interdisciplinary studies is from the University of Texas at Brownsville.

Dr. Margaretta B. Mathis serves as senior director, Educational Leadership Department, College of Education, and professor of practice at Kansas State University. Prior to joining KSU, she was senior vice president, Roueche Graduate Center, and senior lecturer, the University of Texas at Austin, working on Achieving the Dream, Board of Trustees Institute, College and Career Transitions Initiative, Governance Institute for Student Success, Developmental Education Initiative, and Center for Community College Student Engagement's Survey of Entering Student Engagement. She is coauthor, with Byron McClenney, of *Making Good on the Promise of the Open Door: Effective Governance and Leadership to Improve Student Equity, Success, and Completion*; and is coeditor, with John Roueche, of columns in *Community College Week* and *Diverse: Issues in Higher Education*. Before joining the community college field, Dr. Mathis served for 25 years in national association management and in federal and state government relations and policy development, including professional positions with the Institute of Supply Management; Committee on Ways and Means, US House of Representatives; and, the Arizona Governor's Community Policy Office. Mathis holds a BA from Ohio Wesleyan University; an executive MBA in international management from the Thunderbird School of Global Management; and a PhD in higher education administration from the University of Texas at Austin, where she was a distinguished graduate and senior Roueche fellow.

Dr. Byron N. McClenney has completed 58 years as an educator, including almost 33 years as a community college CEO and 50 years as an active consultant in 47 states and internationally. He served for 10 years as director of Student Success Initiatives at the University of Texas at Austin, which included the role of national director of leadership coaching for Achieving the Dream. McClenney received the 2011 AACC Leadership Award, the 2002 PBS O'Banion Prize, the 2000 TIAA-CREF Hesburgh Award for the Community College of Denver, and the 1996 NISOD International Leadership Award, among many recognitions over the years. McClenney's numerous publications and speaking engagements have focused on student success, institutional effectiveness, leadership, strategic planning, and organizational transformation. He led a UT partnership with ACCT to develop the Governance Institute for Student Success, which continues in 2019. He serves as chair of the Colorado State Board for Community Colleges and Occupational Education and is a member on the board of the Colorado Opportunity Scholarship Initiative. His three degrees were awarded by the University of Texas at Austin, from which he received the College of Education Distinguished Graduate Award in 1983.

Dr. Kay M. McClenney is a partner in Mc2 Consultants and serves as senior advisor to the president and CEO of the American Association of Community Colleges. She was founding director of the Center for Community College Student Engagement at the University of Texas at Austin, also serving as a faculty member in the UT program in higher education leadership, where she also earned her PhD. McClenney has led an array of foundation-funded national projects focused on student success and equity; authored numerous publications on student success, leadership, engaged learning, and institutional change; and received a number of national awards, including the national leadership award from the American Association of Community Colleges (2011), the Diverse Champions Award (2017), and the PBS O'Banion Prize (2002) for contributions to teaching and learning in America. She was cochair of AACC's 21st-Century Commission on the Future of Community Colleges. In 2014, Phi Theta Kappa honored Dr. McClenney with the Alliance for Educational Excellence Award, presented in recognition of the body of work undertaken to improve student success in community colleges.

Dr. Coral M. Noonan-Terry is the program manager of special projects at the Community College Center for Student Engagement. Prior to joining the Center, she was the vice president and dean of the Roueche Graduate Center at National American University (NAU), overseeing NAU's master's programs. She also served as the interim director, associate director, and conference and partnership coordinator at the National Institute for Staff and Organizational Development (NISOD). She directed the Technology Leadership Academy, a Preparing Tomorrow's Teachers to Use Technology Catalyst grant. Dr. Noonan-Terry is a teacher at heart and has taught bilingual special education through graduate levels, and her expertise is in working with limited-English-proficient students with disabilities. She started her teaching career as a developmental communications (ESL) instructor at Austin Community College. Dr. Noonan-Terry earned her bachelor of science in elementary bilingual special education, master of arts in multicultural special education, and a doctorate of philosophy in educational administration in the Community College Leadership Program (CCLP) at the University of Texas at Austin. She was named a distinguished graduate of the CCLP and is a graduate of the Executive Leadership Institute hosted by the League for Innovation in the Community College.

Dr. Terry O'Banion is president emeritus of the League for Innovation in the Community College and senior professor of practice at Kansas State University. Terry has worked in the field of community colleges for 59 years. He has consulted in more than 1,000 community colleges and authored 16 books and more than 200 articles. Five national awards have been established in his name, including the Microsoft Student Champion Award and the Educational Testing Service O'Banion Prize for Teaching and Learning. He has been a dean in two Florida community colleges; a professor of higher education at Illinois, Berkeley, Texas, Toronto, Hawaii, and NOVA; and president of the League for Innovation for 23 years.

Dr. Jerry Sue Thornton is the president of DreamCatcher Education Consulting, which provides professional development and coaching for newly appointed college and university presidents. She retired in July 2013 as president of Cuyahoga Community College (Cleveland, Ohio), the largest and oldest community college in the state. A native Kentuckian, she earned her bachelor's and master's degrees from Murray State University (Kentucky) and doctorate from the University of Texas (Austin). She has also served as president of Lakewood Community College (now Century College) in Minnesota. She began her higher education career at Triton College (River Grove, Illinois) as a faculty member, where she rose through the ranks to become the dean of arts and sciences. She has served on numerous corporate boards, such as American Greetings; American Family Insurance; Office Max; Barnes and Noble Education; FirstEnergy, Inc.; and National City Corporation (now PNC Bank), among others. She is a sought-after speaker on high-performance leadership and leading from the middle.

Dr. Evelyn N. Waiwaiole is the senior advisor to the executive director of the Center for Community College Student Engagement (the Center) at the University of Texas at Austin (UT). Prior to this role, she served as the executive director at the Center for five years. She has spent the majority of her career at the University of Texas, serving as the Suanne Davis Roueche NISOD director and lecturer in the College of Education at UT and leading grant-funded initiatives, including the Bridges to Opportunity Initiative and the MetLife Foundation Initiative on Student Success. She has also served as associate director of NISOD, college relations coordinator for the Center, and policy analyst for the Center for Community College Policy at the Education Commission of the States (ECS). Evelyn earned a doctorate in higher education administration from UT, with a specialization in community college leadership; a master's in economics from the University of Oklahoma; and a bachelor's in psychology from Texas A&M University.

Dr. Belle S. Wheelan serves as president of the Southern Association of Colleges and Schools Commission on Colleges and is the first African American and the first woman to serve in this capacity. Her career spans more than 40 years and includes the roles of faculty member, chief student services officer, campus provost, college president, and secretary of education. She has received numerous awards and recognition, including *Washingtonian Magazine*'s 100 Most Powerful Women in Washington, DC (2001); the AAUW Woman of Distinction Award (2002); the Suanne Davis Roueche National Institute for Staff and Organizational Development's Distinguished Lecturer Award (2007); the John E. Roueche National Institute for Staff and Organizational Development's International Leadership Award (2010); the

AACC Leadership Award (2011); the John Hope Franklin Award from *Diverse: Issues in Higher Education* for outstanding leadership in higher education; and the Educational Testing Service (ETS) Terry O'Banion Prize in Education from the League for Innovation in Community Colleges. In 2017, Central Virginia Community College named her president emerita. She holds and has held membership in numerous local, state, and national organizations. Dr. Wheelan received her bachelor's degree from Trinity University in Texas, with a double major in psychology and sociology; her master's from Louisiana State University in developmental educational psychology; and her doctorate from the University of Texas at Austin in educational administration.